Cash Tracks

Compose, Produce, and Sell

Your Original Soundtrack Music

and Jingles

by Jeffrey P. Fisher

THOMSON

COURSE TECHNOLOGY ™

Professional ■ Technical ■ Reference

Publisher and General Manager, Thomson Course Technology PTR: Stacy L. Hiquet

Associate Director of Marketing: Sarah O'Donnell

Manager of Editorial Services: Heather Talbot

Marketing Managers: Heather Hurley and Cathleen Snyder

Executive Editor: Mike Lawson

Marketing Coordinator: Jordan Casey

Project and Copy Editor: Marta Justak

Thomson Course Technology PTR Editorial Services Coordinator: Elizabeth Furbish

Cover Designer & Interior Layout Tech: Stephen Ramirez

Indexer: Sharon Shock

Proofreader: Gene Redding

Thomson Course Technology PTR, a division of Thomson Course Technology
25 Thomson Place
Boston, MA 02210
www.courseptr.com

Dedication

This book is for my wife, Lisa—friend, cheerleader, and love of my life. Without her kindness, understanding, encouragement, tolerance, and love, my life could never be so wonderful.

Acknowledgments

"The only sensible ends of literature are, first, the pleasurable toil of writing; second, the gratification of one's family and friends; and, lastly, the solid cash."—Nathaniel Hawthorne

The people I've met either directly or through their work have had—and continue to have—a profound effect on my life. These are some I wish to recognize. The Beatles, Roddy Frame, Mel Brooks, Sir George Martin, Mark Isham, Bernard Herrmann, Leon Russell, Gustav Mahler, Ray Harryhausen, Jeffrey Lant, David Lynch, Herman Holtz, Patrick O'Hearn, Marsha Sinetar, Robert Gunning, Robert Rich, Bruce Bendinger, Brian Holmsten, Jan Hammer, Willie Nelson, Len Kuzmicki, Craig Anderton, Dennis Muren, Jim Shorts, Ken Tobias, Andy Summers, Miro Ledajaks, Rob Kole, Jane Talisman, Mary Cosola, Bill Forsyth, Patricia Pribyl, Sting, Ed Brunke, Steve Armstrong, Marshall Cook, Harlan Hogan, Alfred Hitchcock, John Gardner, David Carradine, Peter McWilliams, David Torn, Ben Burtt, Gary Rydstrom, Douglas Spotted Eagle, Mannie Francis, Tony Santona, my students, past and present, those clients who hired me (and those tire-kickers who didn't), Sears, Ensoniq, all the fine folks at Sony Media Software, iZotope, MXL, and *Electronic Musician*. Mom and Pops, my brother Charlie and my other brother Charlie, Peggy, Sandy, a man called Tuna, all those nieces and nephews, the President and CEO of Skoober Enterprises, my delightful son Adam, and mostly that little voice inside my head that simply said: DO IT!

A few people specifically contributed to this book—to them I am most grateful.

▶ Brian Holmsten for his initial technical edit of the manuscript, which allowed me to meet a killer deadline by knowing my words were in very capable hands. Couldn't have done it without you!

▶ Marta Justak for her marvelous edit of the manuscript. Editors do far more than dot i's and cross t's, and I'm fortunate to have had her on my side working to make the book stronger.

▶ Mike Lawson for buying my first book– and then buying it again. I want to publicly thank him for his support of my written work all these years.

▶ And special thanks with great appreciation to those who graciously gave up their precious time to complete my interviews for the book: Eric Beheim, David Jaedyn Conley, Douglas Spotted Eagle, Keith Kehrer, Ronen Landa, Lori Rae Martin, John Seguin, Winifred Phillips, Wes Talbot, Brian Tarquin, and David Was.

About the Author

Jeffrey P. Fisher works from his project studio providing music, sound, writing, video, training, and media production services for corporate, cable, and commercial clients. He writes about music, sound, and video for print and the Web, including nine books:

Cash Tracks: Compose, Produce, and Sell Your Original Soundtrack Music and Jingles (ArtistPro, 2005)

The Voice Actor's Guide to Home Recording (with Harlan Hogan, ArtistPro, 2005)

Instant Surround Sound (CMPBooks, 2005)

Instant Vegas 5 (with Douglas Spotted Eagle, CMPBooks, 2004)

Instant Sound Forge (CMPBooks, 2004)

Moneymaking Music (ArtistPro, 2003)

Profiting From Your Music and Sound Project Studio (Allworth Press, 2001)

Ruthless Self-Promotion in the Music Industry (MixBooks, 1999)

How to Make Money Scoring Soundtracks and Jingles (MixBooks, 1997)

Jeffrey's library music CD, *Dark New Age* (Fresh Music 2004) along with his *Atmospherics* CD and two-volume, buy-out music library, *Melomania*, showcase his musical vision. He also teaches audio and video production and post-production at the College of DuPage Motion Picture/Television department in Glen Ellyn, IL. And he co-hosts the ACID, Sound Forge, and Vegas forums on Digital Media Net (www.dmnforums.com). For more information visit his Web site at www.jeffreypfisher.com or contact him at jpf@jeffreypfisher.com.

Contents

CHAPTER 1

Introduction

"As a general rule, the most successful people in life are those who have the best information."
—Benjamin Disraeli

You Can Do This!

Do your peers say your music sounds like movie music? Do you find yourself hearing radio and TV commercials and saying to yourself, "I could write a better song than that"? Have you ever wanted to compose music for games? The Web? If you answered *yes* to any of those questions, perhaps you have a future in the commercial music industry composing, producing, and selling your original soundtrack music and jingles.

While the traditional music industry flounders at times, the opportunities to write music for other avenues continue to grow. Movies, radio, TV, cable, games, video, multimedia, the Web, and other audiovisual presentations really need your original music scores and jingles. Traditional music users, such as advertisers, episodic television, theatrical motion pictures, and their ilk, are not the only outlets starving for original music content. Corporate presentations, countless cable TV channels (and the production companies that produce all that content), the Internet, the ever-expanding games market, and so many more companies that make and deliver multimedia content all need original music. Working from a well-equipped home project studio, the opportunities to make a decent full- or part-time career in the commercial music industry abound.

All it takes is a smattering of talent, the right tools, and a generous helping of tenacity. Once you understand how this business works and then develop the right plan to make your way in it, then you will enjoy a successful career making money from your music. However, there is one critical piece to this puzzle that you must fully recognize and understand. Promotion is *the key* to making it. Therefore, this book's primary focus will center on finding people who will buy your music and making sure they do buy it. While there will be a smattering of creative and technical advice, this is a business guide, first and foremost.

Please don't think of this resource as a get-rich-quick scheme. This book is for people who truly want success for their music and their life. True success doesn't come overnight, and if it does, it rarely endures. Success making and selling commercial music requires hard work, dedication, and a carefully considered strategy that you work every single day. Always. Follow the procedures detailed in this resource, and you will, slowly and steadily, build and maintain your career at the level of success you desire. It's you, your talent, and your unwavering commitment that will make this happen. Use this book wisely, and you will have a successful and profitable commercial music business and an equally enriching life.

The tools we composers have at our fingertips are nothing short of amazing, and they are getting better, faster, and cheaper every single day. One person, working from a home project studio, can be successful and earn a decent living composing music to be used for a variety of clients, companies, and multimedia presentations. I'm evidence that these principles work. These techniques also worked for the other successful composers interviewed for this book. And this approach will work for you, too. Success in this field is within your reach.

I know you can do this. So, let's get started!

Why I Wrote This Book

Thankfully, the elusive record contract, playing in bars, and other so-called traditional music careers are not the only way for you to earn your living from your music. Unfortunately, most industry guides rarely mention alternative careers, and when they do, there's only a scant paragraph or two—hardly enough information to get you started, let alone succeed. This book fills that void by showing you exactly how to make money as you compose, produce, and sell your original soundtrack music and jingles for movies, games, radio/TV, the Web, and more.

Sadly, many how-to books—including those that address music business issues—contain more "what to do" information than specific "how to" do it. My goal with this book, indeed all my writing (books, magazines, and more), is to give you the step-by-step details you need in an honest, no-nonsense way. You may not always agree with my candor, but I guarantee that this highly opinionated book is practical and loaded with proven advice you can use right away. There's little theory, no statistics, and, in short—no BS. My pledge to you is simple: I wrote this book for you, to help *you* succeed.

Please give careful scrutiny to the peer interviews that are in many of the chapters. These are not some added fluff tacked on as an afterthought. I was adamant that this book should include other opinions from which I knew you could benefit. Some of these interviews are with successful composers, while others profile people who may have experienced only moderate success. Study and learn from the viewpoints, tips, techniques, and cautionary notes they tell.

What's in This Resource

Right from the start, "What You Need to Begin Today" explains precisely what you need to know and do to turn your music tracks into cash. You will learn the crucial steps to success, including the most important secret to making it in today's commercial music business.

"How This Business Works" explains the vagaries of today's commercial music business—how it works and the steps you need to take to make it work with clients. It has the insider information you must possess to effectively compose, produce, and sell your original soundtrack music and jingles. This is an intense chapter, so study its contents carefully.

"Building Your Project Studio" is where you'll learn how to organize your talents and equipment so you are ready to produce the kind of music that people want to buy. Next, "Demo Success Secrets" gives you the essentials of preparing and presenting your music demo so that you'll sell more of your commercial music services.

If you don't understand the promotional aspects of this business, you are doomed to failure. That's why this book devotes page after page toward helping you master these skills. First, "Finding the People Who Buy Original Music" tells you how and where to find the people who will buy your scores and jingles. Next, "Turning Prospects into Paying Music Clients" delivers the step-by-step promotional details that bring you to the attention of music buyers. Follow these precise details, and you're on your way. The "Inside Secrets to Moneymaking Promotions" teaches you to craft profit-producing promotions that convince people to purchase your music. And finally, in "Promotional Potpourri," you'll discover more ways to get additional clients by using specific promotional methods, including the Web.

Both "Taking Care of Business" and "Money Matters" show you all the vital information that helps you run your music business right. You'll discover how to get, report, keep, and leverage your money into more cash and swell your bank account accordingly.

The rights issue is all too often misunderstood, so "Rights Right" sets the record straight about what you must do to protect your work *and* get the money you deserve. Next, follow the steps in "Set and Get Your Fee" to learn how to price and quote your music services.

Pay close attention to the final chapter. The keys to making a decent living today are found in "Diversify and Thrive." You will be more successful if you exploit all your musical talent.

Your Journey Begins

I am a music composer and producer specializing in soundtracks and jingles. After several years struggling and learning how to make my commercial music business a success, I decided to share this information and knowledge with *you*! I felt and continue to feel that you shouldn't have to learn the hard way as I did.

As you devour this book and realize all that you must do to succeed, you may want some additional attention, though. Perhaps, you just need a point clarified, some further, more detailed explanations, a push in the proper direction, or even the chance to work directly with me. Consider my role in your life as adviser, coach, and friend when you read through this manual. Let me help you improve your music business career, increase your sales, and be a success. You can rest assured that I will give you the following information:

▶ Tell you what has worked and show you how to duplicate those results.

▶ Point out important points you may be missing and help you find practical solutions to the problems you and your business may face.

▶ Be the sympathetic ear, confidant, and sounding board for both your problems and your inevitable triumphs.

Please note that I do provide personal assistance in the areas of music, recording, and business matters. If you'd like me to help you with your music and business activities, you just need to email me at jpf@jeffreypfisher.com or call me at **(630) 378-4109**. I'm usually available to start immediately helping you achieve your goals.

There are very few authors who would give you their email address and telephone number so readily. Unlike them, I'm eager to help you in any way that I can. Your buying this book is not the end of our relationship—on the contrary, this is just the beginning. You and I shall cover much ground in the next few hundred pages. Make sure you take advantage of all the opportunities that can and will make your music endeavors and your life rewarding, satisfying, and complete.

Additionally, I'm always uncovering new information about the commercial music industry—and how to get your slice of it—and I share this information regularly in my free email newsletter *Moneymaking Music Tip of the Week* and on my Web site. Subscribe to my free weekly newsletter by sending an email message to:
mmmtow-subscribe@yahoogroups.com

And/or visit my Web site at:
www.jeffreypfisher.com

Why not do it right now?

With those thoughts, let's begin your journey getting *cash* for your music *tracks* as you compose, produce, and sell your original soundtrack music and jingles for movies, games, radio/ TV, and the Web.

CHAPTER 2

What You Need to Begin Today

"It does not matter how slowly you go so long as you do not stop."—Confucius

The time is now for all your music and recording equipment to stop costing you money and start making you money. No matter what your current standing in the music business is—band, solo artist, project studio owner, or serious hobbyist—you *can* make money composing, producing, and, of course, selling your original soundtrack music and jingles for movies, games, radio/TV, the Web, and more. You can have a *reel* music career that puts cash in your pocket while you do something you love—make music!

The Soundtracks and Jingles 411

Hollywood, network television, and the big-name advertisers are not the only places for your music, though. The markets for your music keep expanding every day. And most of the business is right outside your door. Corporations make videos, CD-ROMs, Web-based, and other multimedia presentations for sales, training, contests, and other communications. Local broadcast and cable TV need themes and underscoring for the shows they produce. There is an ever-growing pool of independent narrative, documentary, and other special interest films/videos that need music. The gaming industry brings in more money than Hollywood, and game producers know the power that original music compositions bring to the player's experience. The Web, including Flash-based projects, adds more possible outlets. Don't forget that local commercials on radio and TV always need jingles and catchy music scores. All these markets—and so many more—can benefit from your music. In short, it is an ideal time to be a soundtrack music and jingle composer.

Getting into the media music industry is far easier than it was in the past, too. This revolution of sorts owes its roots to three primary reasons:

1. The proliferation of inexpensive, high-quality digital music production and recording equipment greatly reduces the costs of creating, recording, and delivering music.

2. The burgeoning media marketplace, driven by cable TV expansion, the Web, gaming, and corporate embracing of richer multimedia presentations, opens up a larger pool of content desperately in need of original music and sound.

3. The trend for musicians is to seek nontraditional outlets for their musical creations and more meaningful work. Part of this is by necessity as the traditional music industry, e.g., recording artist, continues to dwindle. Many of us aren't interested in playing in a bar band or going after the increasingly rare record deal. Today's independent musician has more—and better—opportunities than before.

However, there is a lot of competition out there, but not just from where you might expect. The big music houses in Chicago, New York, and Los Angeles are *not* your only competition. There are many independent composers who are working to maintain their own slice of the industry and grab a bigger slice when they can. Also, you must compete with the ever-present, royalty-free, buyout, and needle-drop production library music. What used to be bland, unimaginative, and generic has emerged as a music force and source to be reckoned with. I've heard some amazing music coming from the libraries, and it just keeps getting better. Gone are the thin-sounding MIDI tracks replaced with the likes of full orchestral scores, rock/pop combos, and world music to name a few. Plus, when producers can still get 60 minutes of music for 60 bucks, it's no wonder they reach for these tracks (instead of hiring you).

Loop-based music puts even more rivals in your way. Software programs, such as Sony Acid and Apple GarageBand/Soundtrack. bring composition tools to the masses. In 2004, I toured the U.S. teaching nonlinear video editors how to use Sony Acid to create the music they need in the video editing suite themselves. That brings competition from a new front entirely.

Don't feel this is all doom and gloom, though. Instead, rise to the challenge and shout: "Bring it on!" Embrace the fact that you'll have to work for your supper; it's part of what makes this industry so vibrant and exciting. Nothing of real value comes easily. And composing music must hold meaning for you, or you wouldn't be reading this. So, understand that there are obstacles that you must overcome.

Also, understand that you have a distinct advantage. You have this book to guide you. I'll show you how to position yourself against library tracks so you come out as the better deal in some circumstances. You'll discover some unique methods to beat other music houses in your area. This will take some hard work and creativity, but you'll love the challenge because the reward is so great:

You get paid for your music! You won't have to share royalties (most of the time), you won't have to go on long tours to promote your record, and you won't have to bend to a record company's or some other corporate tower's whims. It will be your music, and you'll be in charge the whole time. And the best part is you get to keep *all* the profits.

Is the Jingle Dead?

Unfortunately, the trend today is for advertisers and their advertising agencies to license existing music tracks for use in commercials. Instead of commissioning a composer to come up with an original musical statement, advertisers prefer to license what's popular and attach it to their product. Record labels, publishers, and recording artists themselves don't seem to mind. The money's good, and the negative impact on the musical act—which is the greatest fear for the recording artist—seems minimal.

Advertising used to be a powerfully creative force. Today, at least when it comes to music choices, the people who create ads seem to have lost their edge, lost their originality. Instead of looking for the right musical solution or trying to break new ground, advertisers keep settling for using popular music tracks. And that's bad news for jingle writers.

The problem, for me at least, is that popular music comes with baggage. What may be one person's favorite song is another person's unwelcome noise. Therefore, associating products and services with certain tunes carries great risk. And when the *same song* is used by different advertisers, the musical impact is diminished even further. But, advertisers don't seem to care. Personally, I boycott companies who feature licensed popular music in their commercials. So, is the jingle dead? Probably not completely, but it sure appears in ill health.

The other problem facing advertisers, and this is not unique to the jingle *per se*, is the use of recording devices, such as Tivo, by the public. People continue to timeshift their favorite TV shows and watch them later. With fingers poised on the fast-forward button, the commercials whiz past with no soundtrack. Sure, products and logos still cut through the video noise, but there is no music to be heard. There's an even bigger trend that finds the public buying repurposed TV content on DVD (in lieu of watching the original broadcast). These come without commercials entirely. And what about commercial-free satellite radio?

What does the future mean to advertising music? And how do these facts trickle down to jingle composers like you and me? Already the sung lyric, unless it's a licensed song, is virtually nonexistent. Jingles today are mostly about instrumentals and sound design. While that's a wonderful challenge when you do get the work, it doesn't speak to the ultimate ramifications of the demise of traditional advertising and the music contained within. This is one reason why advertisers have had to use other means to present their products, for example, sponsoring shows, blatant product placement during the TV shows themselves, and so forth.

To be strictly in the advertising jingle music world now is increasingly difficult. Competition and shrinking budgets work against you in ways that demand more of your time and attention. I'm not saying you should ignore the jingle market—far from it—what I am suggesting is that you must be prepared for its realities. Keep up with the trends. Keep your name, face, and latest reel in front of the people who matter most. Work hard to land gigs, and work even harder to keep clients happy so they come back to you.

How You Get Started

Starting your soundtrack and jingle music business takes some action on your part, but it's not unreasonable. You'll need some seed money, but not a lot. Instead of money, you'll need time, energy, and resourcefulness. You don't have to give up your day job or take other foolish steps. Here's what you really need to know. Success requires hard work, perseverance, and skill, along with some confidence, faith, and a sincere desire to win. This book will fill in the other details.

But reading this resource is passive. Nothing can happen, or will happen, until you apply these ideas to your life. Take them, shape them, and make them your own. Use them, learn from them, and some initial success will come. You are your only real teacher. Others can guide, can push, but *only you* can teach yourself the ultimate knowledge. It comes from within, and it comes from without. Learn. Grow. Succeed. Whatever your background, means, and talents, you can make it in the commercial music industry. It always puzzles me the way some people say they want success, but never do what is really necessary to be successful. I hope you are not like that. It is your sole responsibility to take charge of your life right now.

I'm assuming you chose this book because you welcome earning your living from music. The first step to success is recognizing that you need a formal structure. You can't pursue this business piecemeal or *ad hoc*. You must immerse yourself fully into the commercial music world and follow a specific system to reach the level of success you desire. Commit today to learning about general business practices, understanding the realities of this business and your role in it, and applying your skills to running your own small business. This is important to success, and until you accept that fact you are doomed to fail.

That's why I suggest you start your own company and keep it all for yourself. There are many advantages to running your own commercial music business. The challenges are stimulating, the prizes worthwhile. Frankly, I just don't understand why more people don't run a simple, humble, small—albeit micro—business on the side. The benefits are tremendous. Plus, by turning your hobby or music skill into a tangible business, you can write off (deduct from your taxes) your current lifestyle. You will be leading the life you want, need, and deserve. And it will be remunerative, too. Isn't that what this is all about?

To get started in this lucrative business requires a 12-step process.

1. Prepare yourself to be in business by developing a plan. Plans start by setting goals, both personal and professional, and then working through the steps it will take and the resources required attaining them. Planning your career isn't something you can take lightly. Obviously, you need to take care of both short-term needs and long-term goals. Along with that, make room for regular or steady gigs that contribute to your progress. Additionally, set aside some time for exploration into unknown areas. You never really know where your career will take you unless you spend some time looking at and experimenting with other options. Those short-term plans make up your to-do list, the long-term plans fill your calendar, your regular/steady work keeps the money flowing in, and the explorations can bring potential future gains or make pipe dreams painfully clear.

2. Save money to build a solid financial cushion, both for your personal life and for the start of your business. Worrying about paying your bills every day will stifle your creativity. Contrarily, for some people, this fact may be a great motivator. Learn to invest, too, and not just conventional investment wisdom. First, invest in yourself and work to become a better, more skilled person. Second, invest in your business and personal relationships because the more people you know, the more doors will open up for you. Third, invest in your business to make it stronger (gear, people, promotion, etc.). Fourth, invest in a few things you can hold in your hands (real estate, gold, etc.). And last, obviously, invest in the economy through traditional means (savings, stocks, bonds, etc.) to grow you music success fortune even bigger.

3. Research the music opportunities in your local area—your market—and especially your competition. Use the information you discover to find people and companies who buy original music. You must first identify these target markets and then discover what they need so you can adapt your music services accordingly. You can learn a great deal of useful information from your competitors, too. What are they doing right? Wrong? Can you adapt their successes to your way of doing business? Can you beat them where they are weak? Don't be shy about visiting the competition (if possible) or checking out what they sell (and how they sell it). Dig out your magnifying glass and start searching for clues. You just may learn some valuable information that you can apply to make your situation better.

4. Talk to others and learn from their experience. Don't reinvent the wheel. There is plenty of information, as well as experienced people readily available to answer your questions and give you insight. To model your success, take a detailed look at what another successful music professional does. Make sure you choose somebody you know is successful and carefully dissect

his or her career and promotional tactics. What products do they have? What services do they provide? How do they use publicity? Advertising? Radio/TV? Internet? Now apply all that you discover to your situation. Try mirroring their specific career techniques as closely as possible. You should be able to emulate their ideas on some level and in your own music market. Knowing how the big guys succeed, and patterning your strategy after their success, can lead to bigger and better things for your music career, too.

5. Learn to promote and sell your commercial music services. You must consider how you will make people aware of both their needs and your ability to meet them. You will use many promotional strategies to get to the level of success you have set for yourself. Commit now to learning *how* to promote and to doing what's necessary to bring your message to buyers. Make a list of projects that you'd like to do. Then go find clients who need that kind of work and pitch your services to them. Alternately, if this is a project that only you can do (or you're doing for yourself), put the wheels in motion and start working on it right away. For example, I'll scribble a line or two about an idea—video, music score, etc.—and then pursue those avenues and clients that can bring the project to fruition. Follow this formula: Ideas + Promotion = Gigs and, of course, Gigs = $$$.

6. Practice your skills, both music and business. Be confident, courageous, and have faith in your abilities and your plan. Trust that you've made the right decisions (and be open minded to changing circumstances and willing to adjust and adapt). When you do what you love, it often doesn't feel like work. You get so absorbed in your music that you forget about the real work going on around you. That's a great place to be—a creative well-spring! You are excited and enthusiastic about what you are doing, and this positive attitude comes across in the music you make. It also rubs off on people, too. They sense how much you enjoy what you do and usually can't help but feel swept up in your good vibes. Enthusiasm is a terrific ally to have. Having a positive attitude and the energy to pursue what can often be an arduous journey can help you better realize your success. Many people comment on the excitement I bring to projects, and I notice it in others with whom I have dealings. When somebody is not happy, I sense it immediately. They drag down everything and everyone. But when an enthusiastic person enters my life, I know this person has a greater chance for success.

7. Organize your project studio, equipment, finances, and resources. Good organizational skills are crucial because wasting time on certain tasks will keep you in a time crunch forever. Work your strengths hard and find other ways to accomplish those items on your to-do list. Hire out subcontractors

to help when the pressure's on. Get help by using specialists to fill in the gaps in your knowledge. Add the right people to your team, and you will be better off in the long run. Also, do only what makes sense to build your music business and let the other stuff go. Try multitasking through technology. For example, I can burn CDs on one computer, print booklets, address labels, and such on another, while working on a music or sound project on still another! And I can do laundry and run the dishwasher at the same time, too. Most of all, set aside some time each day to work on your music. Even if you can only steal five minutes, make an appointment and keep it.

8. Prepare your demo and keep it up-to-date. Always feature your latest, greatest music and present your skills in the best light. You demo is your calling card; it's a primary resource prospective clients turn toward when contemplating hiring you.

9. Produce and record your commercial music projects. Work with passion, no matter what you do. Just because you might consider a current gig a real pain, that doesn't mean you shouldn't work hard. *Always* put your full self into everything you do. Remember that small things can often lead to bigger things and more success. People often test you by giving you a menial task today. If you blow it, the better work will never come.

10. Manage your business carefully and effectively. Take control of your career as a business owner and focus on results. There are six key areas you must monitor: sales, promotion, administration, technology, finances, and planning. Don't rest. Sell! You must always be out there selling to both new and current clients. Promote regularly, and in a variety of ways, to get your message out and generate new sales leads. Take timely care of typical daily business matters; don't let these chores pile up. Stay on top of new gear and make sure you have what you need to deliver what your clients want. Always watch the money, in and out, to make sure your business is fiscally sound. Don't forget to look ahead and see what is the right direction for you to take in the future. Keep these six under control and you will have a better music career (and life).

11. Start right now and do it. What's standing in your way?

12. Persist. Just about the time you get tired of promoting, networking, and the other tasks that comprise an active music career is just about the same time people start noticing. Too many artists give up too soon. They think if they aren't an overnight success, there's no reason to go on. I disagree with this notion wholeheartedly. Instead, make a five-year commitment to this

business and stick to it. If you won't do that, then don't bother starting at all. I'm typing these words 15+ years after I thought I'd already had some modicum of success. And still my business and career continue growing in new directions. If I'd have given up, I shudder to think of oh-so-much that I would have missed. It's a long, difficult journey for many of us, full of challenges and setbacks and, hopefully, a few bright, shining moments, too.

I'm assuming, of course, you already possess the necessary composition and technical skills to write and record music. This is not a book about how to *compose*. This book is about how to *sell* music scores and jingles. One word of caution: If you think your music is art, then making and selling commercial music may not be for you. Your music is your product, and all the traditional business rules about promoting and selling a product apply. If you can't stomach that your music can be packaged and sold like chewing gum, this business is not for you. Also, if you think you'll mind that your music will play a supporting role under dialogue and narration—and that means your incredible guitar solo won't even get noticed—then you better not get into this business, because scoring soundtracks and jingles for corporations, TV, films, games, and commercials *is a business!*

Yes, you need musical ability and originality. But you must have business savvy, too. Dare I say that your business and promotional prowess may be even *more* important than the musical skills you possess? You'll be selling your services and running your music business just like any other business. Besides, it will astonish you how little time you actually spend composing. Don't let this scare you off; just be practical. If you don't have any clients, you can't sell your music. So, which really needs to come first? The music? Or the market?

The Anatomy of Music Success

Those who play sports competitively know the value of getting your head into the game. Along with immense physical preparation comes intense mental concentration. To be a success with your music business, you need to bring the same physical and emotional power to the table. To make your music career the success you envision, you need your head, heart, and stomach at their peak performance.

HEAD = BRAINS

There are two sides to your head: creative and logical. You need your creativity to serve you well in your musical pursuits. But don't ignore the logic either. To make it in the crazy world of music, learn all that you can about how the business works. The more you know, the better off you will be.

HEART = PASSION

Desire comes from your heart. It's the love you have for yourself, others, and your music work. According to authors Ron Rubin and Stuart Avery Gold in their *success@life* book: "Passion provides you the best possible odds to successfully catch and live your dream." That's good advice.

Is there a fire inside of you that won't burn out unless you achieve your dreams? If that's you, channel that passion into everything you do. If you don't have the passion inside of you, ask yourself why. And then take steps to stoke the fire. When you feel passionate about your music, that positive energy works in your favor, creating a good experience for others with whom you associate.

STOMACH = GUTS

You have to take risks—whether you have the stomach for them or not. There are two key issues to address. One, it's OK to make mistakes. That's how you learn and grow as a person and as a professional. Vow not to repeat errors and try to limit the downside to every venture you take on. Elbert Hubbard sums this up best: "The greatest mistake you can make in life is to be continually fearing you will make one." Two, give yourself a challenge. Don't rest on your laurels. Always push yourself to do and be better. It is this constant pursuit of bigger, better, brighter that drives the most successful artistic temperament.

Master Ruthless Self-Promotion

It continues to amaze me how people believe that just because they're in business, clients will automatically come to their door. Nothing could be further from the truth. You want to make music, right? You want to make a living from your music, right? Or, at the very least, some extra cash? Well, you must promote, promote, promote to make your dream come true. Using time, effort, imagination, creativity, and some cash will sell your music. For profit. Big money.

How can you break down barriers and achieve the success you want? There is only one way to ensure your continued success in today's music world: *You must master ruthless self-promotion.* And ruthless self-promotion has only two functions:

▶ To find new customers and convince them to buy what you sell.

▶ To keep your existing buyers and, more importantly, get them to buy again (and again).

What is ruthless self-promotion? It's the constant pursuit of new buyers for your music products and services. You use various techniques to uncover the most motivated buyers and then carefully follow up to close sales. Always be on the lookout for promotional opportunities. Essentially, there are only two ways to promote your music products and services: You either contact someone or you convince someone to contact you.

There are three simple methods you can use to contact people. One, you mail (or email) a letter or other sales package. Two, you place a phone call. And three, you make direct contact. Alternately, you can only use four methods to solicit contact: One, you place an ad. Two, you send publicity. Three, you have a storefront. And four, you run a Web site (which is really just advertising, publicity, and a store rolled into one neat package).

I wish that your career could be only about the music. Unfortunately, commerce and the other vagaries of real life intrude on that Utopian ideal. While your primary focus should always be on your music—i.e., honing your craft, polishing your performance, augmenting your skills, and growing as an artist—don't neglect the other aspects of your career that you need to control. Here are some basic solutions that, when implemented, can give you a distinct advantage. These pointers will greatly impact your career, and once you understand and implement this advice, you'll benefit fast.

PREPARE YOUR MIND FOR SELF-PROMOTION

Wrap your mind around this: The key to successful ruthless self-promotion is to promote before you produce. You need to think first and foremost about how you will promote and sell your music before you actually create it. That's a hard concept for many people to come to terms with, but nevertheless it is the mental paradigm you must recognize and implement. "Promote before produce." Hang that on your wall and live it every single day.

This business is demanding, and you must make sure your mind is ready for the challenge. Cultivate these two crucial characteristics: your solid determination and your interminable will to succeed. You must really be hungry for success and truly desire to do whatever it takes to get there. Recognize that promotion comes when *and only when* you put forth the effort required to earn it. So, put your mind to the task and work hard all the time to promote your commercial music services ruthlessly!

Have a real dream (or two) for your career. I'm not talking about some wild fantasy that puts a smile on your face every time it pops into your head (movie stars are not leaving their spouses for you!). I'm talking about an honest-to-goodness dream for your future, or what you want your career to be in the days ahead. Aim high because it's your life we're talking about. Dream your way to success because establishing a dream creates possibilities and opportunities. This dream must be something that motivates you. It must generate passion in your heart and mind. Holding on to the dream and, more importantly, working toward fulfilling that dream gives your mind direction and focus. If things are not going as expected, the dream offers encouragement to help you stay on track. Your dream should come from deep inside you, and if you can't find it, you're not looking hard enough. For those of you who already have the dream—bravo! Now, what are you doing right now to make your personal dream come true?

MASTER ALL ITS TECHNICAL ASPECTS

Are your skills, image, presence, and other factors showcasing your best work? If not, you need to concentrate on improving your technical skills. Your talent must be as good or better than others offering the same music products and services. How are you different? How are you better? In addition to your music chops, you need writing, oral presentation, and business skills. You must be able to communicate effectively, both in writing and through speech. Writing promotional materials, handling interviews, and delivering sales presentations are crucial to sustaining your promotions. You will be meeting with the media and clients by telephone and in person. You must learn to explain ideas in ways they'll understand. You will sell yourself, your ideas, and your music. You must understand the intricacies of these skills, practice using them, and ultimately master them. Go back to school or take adult education courses at a local college if you need help in these areas.

What about business skills? I'm advocating that you run your musical career as a small business. There are many advantages to this. It's up to you to discover what works for your particular situation and then exploit every possibility. You can't afford to take these important points for granted. Yes, your music matters, but your people and business skills are also vital to your eventual success.

TAKE CARE OF YOUR MONEY, TOO
If you are not an employee and instead manage your music career yourself, you are in business. As a small business owner, there are many legal, financial, and tax regulations that apply. Since finances and taxes interrelate, it's crucial that you establish a specific method for tracking them. If you don't keep track of what you make and spend, how will you know your true financial situation? How can you successfully complete your taxes? Setting up a proper bookkeeping system today will save many headaches later.

Learn basic bookkeeping—cash, not accrual—so you can always monitor your inflows and outflows. I know that keeping the books isn't as exciting as messing with new musical gear, but that doesn't mean knowing about all this is less important. You just need to be conversant in the basics and understand what, how, and why they impact your financial situation. You need to know your fixed costs (rent, loans, etc.) and your variable costs (supplies, payroll) and therefore know your break-even point. You need to be sure your current cash flow will support your costs *and* put bread on your table. The more details you collect, the clearer your financial picture will be. If you track specific income streams, differentiating from scoring gigs, product sales, and royalties, for example, you will see which activities are profitable and which are not. Also, carefully monitoring your expenses in detail reveals where you over- or underspend. Resolve today to get a book, take a class, or hire a bookkeeper to set up and run (or show you how to maintain) your business finances.

Don't forget about taxes, either. It's your signature on the 1040! I was once stung by the bee of a substantial tax bill. It was my own fault for having jumped, young and green, into the waters of my first business without researching key issues. I collected check after check from client after client and failed to notice that nothing was being deducted from those checks. Self-employed individuals pay their own "payroll" taxes (federal and state income taxes, Social Security, and Medicare contributions). Consequently, I faced a substantial tax bill come April the next year, owing for the previous year and making my first estimated payment for that current year.

When all this came down, I made two important decisions. One, to research all the issues that affected my business and, two, to go out of my way to help other people avoid these same mistakes. There are many distinct advantages to having your own business, and there are many pitfalls. Make sure you fully understand all the tax issues as they apply to your unique situation. Knowledge here benefits you greatly, as you'll save money and stay out of trouble. Also, examine any legal issues, especially liability, to protect both your business and personal assets.

IMAGE + CREDENTIALS = REPUTATION

Building your reputation is a crucial part of making your career better. When you combine a meticulous image with specific credentials, you'll earn a reputation that buyers will trust and support. As buyers, we are all skeptical because we've made poor purchasing decisions in the past. We don't want to repeat those mistakes, so many of us are less willing to take a chance. However, a good reputation instills confidence and reduces that fear of buyer's remorse. When people trust that you'll deliver what they want based on your past track record, they are more willing to support you. People buy your "rep" so spend your resources growing and selling it.

You build a reputation through image and credentials. An image establishes what you are about and should appeal to the people you are trying to reach. Look at the music acts popular today and see how image is fundamental. Savvy promoters know it's often easier to sell an image than content (a few *celebritneys* come to mind). You, too, need to take time to craft and portray an image to represent both you and your music business. An image wraps up everything you are about into a tight, neat package that won't need explaining, making it quicker and easier to promote what you do. Examples: Bill Gates as nerdy, whiz-kid; Tom Brokaw as elder statesman; Katie Couric as sympathetic friend; Ty Pennington as quirky, eccentric. The image you choose and manufacture must be credible and appealing to the people to whom you are trying to reach. My image is as an accessible, sincere music business professional. I support this image by answering my phone and email, continuing to share my knowledge, and through my willingness to help others. That positions me as someone outside the typical music industry perception of a person in my position. Take time to craft and portray an image for both you and your business. Package your image through diligent and consistent presentation of your music, attitude, dress, speech, graphics, and other visual material you send to the world.

Credentials show people you are legitimate. Having a track record of past projects is the main way to demonstrate your skills and prove you are for real. Other credentials come from third-party endorsements, such as media reviews and testimonials from satisfied buyers, clients, and peers. This evidence of your success works its magic on the doubtful. Don't believe this works? Look at all the movie ads in your local paper. Two thumbs up goes a long way toward getting people into the theaters. Finally, work to win awards of any kind or, ultimately, a Grammy™. These endorsements are credentials you can take to the bank.

CLARIFY WHAT YOU ARE TRYING TO SAY

You need a message that complements your image. You must be more specific beyond simply saying, "I compose music for media." Strong messages come from benefits—what the people hiring you really get. You will highlight these benefits as you develop and deliver promotional material. Make sure your messages are your strongest benefits. Consider making this central message your slogan, too. For example, this book's real message is to help you parlay your skills into a successful business that provides both a creative outlet and financial rewards. What are *you* trying to say?

Most businesses fail because they don't recognize what business they are in and, what is more important, they don't understand what they are *really* selling. And now that you know this, remember: *You are not in the music business!* Yep, that's right. You don't sell music. You *add value* to all those narrative, documentary, gaming, promotional, training, advertising, and other audiovisual presentations by making them better, more memorable, more exciting, and therefore, far more effective. You help producers deliver *their* message better. You must understand this important distinction: don't sell music; sell what your music *does*.

GATHER INFORMATION ABOUT THE INDUSTRY

Here's the problem: You need to get your music into the hands of those who need and want it and who have the means to pay for it. How do you do that? You can't proceed based on assumptions and perceptions about this industry. You might be wrong, and that would seriously interfere with your progress. Instead, you need concrete information that gives you a competitive edge. Therefore, you must research carefully to find the information that provides useful insight into the commercial music world. Where do you get the info? Usually just a Web site visit or a Google search or two will turn up these data you need. Scrutinize your competition, too, for more helpful information.

Once you discover how the industry works, you can formulate a proper plan of action. The first step is to find music buyers and learn about their music requirements in detail. You need to know who buys music, where they are, and how you can reach them, along with details about the kinds of projects (jingles, video soundtracks, games, etc.), specific types of music they do buy, and how often. Adapt what you discover to your business. Take what you learn and position the music products and services you offer to fit the particular needs of the people—your target market—that your research revealed.

TARGET: THE WORLD IS NOT YOUR MARKET

Would you agree that promoting an industrial band in a country music magazine isn't the smartest idea in the world? Yet, every day there's evidence of scattershot promotion when laser-sharp pinpoint accuracy is what works. Our world is deeply segmented, and the tighter you focus on a narrow market segment, the better your results will be. It's a waste of time and money trying to reach everybody with your message. Instead, find the people who already like what you do and concentrate your promotional efforts on them. Do you really know who buys your music? If not, you'd better roll up your sleeves and find out.

UNDERSTAND AND USE MANY PROMOTIONAL TACTICS

For the most success, your image and your message must be conveyed at every step. Your promotions must expose the problems that people have and then show how you can solve these problems. At this point, think of publicity as something you start and put in motion, but can't control. Conversely, you can get complete control over your other advertising and sales opportunities. This is not a sequence of events, but rather it's a loop. All the promotional parts work in tandem. That's why you must take the time to craft a ruthless self-promotion plan and execute it carefully.

YOUR BUSINESS PLAN, OF SORTS

Most business how-to books will advise you to develop a business plan. I say don't do it. Why? Most business and promotion plans are far too vague and full of platitudes. I mean, do you really need a mission statement? My suggestion is to carefully craft a more specific how-to-do-it plan. Deconstruct your final music products and services and then detail, specifically, how to put them back together. In other words, start first with what you sell already in your buyer's hands. Then figure out every—and I really mean every!—step you must take to get your music there.

Establishing, defining, and refining your goals is an important contributor to your success. Far too many people either don't have a goal or their idea of one is so nebulous that it's impossible to understand, let alone reach. Others try to do too many things at once. It's a plague that affects many creative people. I feel it's the side effect of the creative spirit— helpful when you require the muse and destructive because you never finish anything (or burn out trying).

Divide your creative life into four distinct parts. Make sure you pursue these four paths with confidence and passion. Set specific goals within these paths and update your choices as you accomplish goals or decide to take new directions.

1. Choose a main or core goal for your creative career and devote most of your time, money, and general resources to reaching that goal. This objective should be the dominant work that brings you the most satisfaction. Put simply: go make your art.

2. Choose a secondary ambition that quenches your creative thirst. Make this more of a long-term project that you devote some attention toward finishing. Think of this as your lofty want-to-do or need-to-accomplish life goal. Don't neglect it, but don't let it greatly interfere with your main objectives.

3. Obviously, spend energy toward those tasks that finance your lifestyle (e.g., day job, etc.). Hopefully, your core path will supply most or all of your income. If not, this other activity may be necessary. Sometimes commerce comes before your art.

4. Find a passion outside your work for balance. This can be another creative outlet, but whatever you choose, keep it *totally* unrelated to the other three paths. Exercise, travel, volunteering, school—these are all fine choices for such a passion.

Having trouble deciding the right paths? Try these two exercises. First, write the story of your life. Your past may predict your future. Writing your biography, your life's story, is usually quite revealing. Find some quiet time, grab some paper, a pen, and begin at the beginning. To keep your catharsis on track, focus on key factors that brought you to where you are today.

Second, write about your future dreams.

1. What are your have-tos? These are all the things you must do simply to survive.

2. What are your like-tos? These are your fantasies, something you'd like to do someday, but don't necessarily need to do them.

3. What are your real want-tos? These are those experiences you wish (and desperately need) to bring into your life. Now buckle down and address your real goals. When you complete this exercise, you'll have a clearer picture of where you want to go with your life and music career. Congratulations! You are far ahead of the majority of people who ignore their need to make plans.

Now comes the next hard part. How do you plan to reach all these goals and when? Start with this simple format: Here's where I am. Here's where I wish to go. And here's how I plan to get there. You need a one-year plan, a five-year plan, and a life plan. Use this plan as a road map, but be flexible.

With that plan in place, it's time to *get going* on it. Take steps *every single day* that bring you closer to your goals. Do something. Anything. Finish a song, look for some collaborators, hone your craft, go to a networking event, put together a promotion, and so on and so forth. All these little steps add up to something much more significant down the road.

TAKE YOUR MESSAGE TO THE BUYERS

Plop down some change for an ad to promote your music, and people will rush to your door, cash in hand, ready to buy, right? Wake up! It just doesn't work that way. One ad, no matter how ingenious, will not turn an unknown into a celebrity. Unfortunately, too many people waste their cash on such foolish pipe dreams. If any promotions you use don't immediately move more products or services out the door, rethink your approach.

When it comes to promotion, you can spend money or you can spend time. If funds are short, you need to get more creative with your promotions and devote more time to them. Usually, these get-up-and-go tactics are more effective and substantially more profitable than simply throwing money at the problem anyway. Don't fall into the easy trap of relying on passive promotions, such as advertising, when what you really should be doing is being more active or calling, emailing, and meeting prospects and clients!

The personal touch really works in today's often sterile, anonymous world. No ad, letter, email, or flyer is ever going to take the place of standing face-to-face with someone and making the sale. In person, and to a lesser extent on the phone, you can build solid rapport, address every sales objection, and win people over faster.

USE NETWORKING TO ESTABLISH AND MAINTAIN YOUR EFFORTS

As you work to elevate the status of your business, you will encounter many people who have the power to help you. My suggestion is for you to help them first. Give them something of value—something they can use. At that point you are in a prime position to get something in return, for example, some form of promotion. Go out of your way to help people because the reward is so great. Help yourself by helping others. It is the professional and noble thing to do and the most effective for the success of your business.

Building relationships with people who need what you sell is the single most important thing you can do for your music career.

Every year I attend the overwhelmingly huge National Association of Broadcasters (NAB) convention where people and technology merge into a whirlwind of information. Despite the show's grand scale, I've found the show is really about one-on-one relationship building and networking. For example, I always take a lot of time to meet with people and discuss future projects and so forth. Before I even leave my studio, I formulate a specific plan with desired goals and outcomes, and I work that plan hard. Even with the unrelenting activity that is NAB (or any large convention for that matter), make sure you find mentors (and peers) and then nurture these give-and-take relationships. Surround yourself with success and be a part of the industry where you want to go and be. It works, believe me.

On a similar note, surround yourself with like-minded people, too. Don't wallow in naysayers. Find people who share your values and aspirations. Jettison the moody, broody, "everything sucks" people who bring nothing but negativity to your life. It only takes one doom-and-gloom person to bring down a positive vibe. Don't let them ruin your fun as you pursue your dreams. Instead, find positive people who influence what you do in ways that create success. Have a cheerleader along for the ride to keep the energy up in the long arduous days that go into creating a musical career. Life is not a series of problems; it's a boundless universe of opportunities. Negative people see only the downside, doubt, and failure. Positive people work the upside, exude confidence, and see success. Look around at the people on whom you depend. Are they reinforcing your career or dragging you down? If it's the latter, it might be wise to reconsider their place in your life.

YOU HELP OTHER PEOPLE = OTHER PEOPLE HELP YOU

I often hear from would-be composers wanting to score independent films. Quickly, I discover that they don't hang out with indie filmmakers, don't attend indie film festivals, or have never read an indie film magazine. I guess they feel the indie filmmakers will find them, somehow. It's crucial that you start associating with the people who are either in a position to help your career along or ready to hire you. You can't make it completely on your own.

Join and participate in the music scene where you want to work and start networking with industry people, media, and your peers. Start helping others in whatever ways you can. Help people first and give them something of value they can use. At that point you are in a prime position to get something in return—some form of promotion, even new business. Ask about what they do and what they need. Let them know about your skills and what you are looking for, too. Networking is a form of barter. You want to build long-term, mutually beneficial relationships with people, not just take, take, take. When you approach and give assistance first, people will, out of a sense of obligation, help you in return with referrals, good word of mouth, and occasionally a paying gig.

Building relationships with other people whom you know (and who can help you) is vital to maintaining the longevity of your career. You need two distinct networks.

▶ First, build a support network. Creative people need nurturing and encouragement. Sometimes, you need somebody to hold your hand while you cross the street of uncertainty. Other times you need a cheer-leader to scream D-E-F-E-N-S-E in times of strife and to yell HOORAY when you succeed.

▶ Second, you need a network of people who can help you. This network includes people in the industry, media, and others. The best way to build this network is to join and participate with the right people. When you are at stores, industry events, trade shows, meetings, and more, make sure you have a supply of business cards or other promotional material. Talk with everyone you meet and don't be shy about letting people know what you do. It might help if you practice describing your work in 20 words or less, too.

KNOWLEDGE + ACTION = SUCCESS

Learn all you can about how this business really works. Read, take classes, find a mentor or two, and get real-world, hands-on experience. The more information you gather, the easier it will be to make good decisions that lead to your taking appropriate actions and moving closer to your goals.

Don't sit on your hands waiting for something to happen, either. Be proactive. Building a reputation, cultivating business relationships, and growing your career take time and effort. You need to push hard always. What are you doing today to reach those people who want and need the music products and services you sell? What actions can you take that move you closer to your goals?

Success is somewhat self perpetuating. The more you achieve, the easier it is to sustain. But that doesn't mean you can ever become complacent. Don't take your clients for granted, or you'll risk losing everything you've struggled to earn.

PRODUCE THE PROMOTIONAL MATERIAL YOU NEED

To promote you and your work, develop suitable collateral material: demo(s), biography, picture, sales letters/email, brochures, news releases, Web site, and more. You can't succeed without this necessary material. Either develop this material yourself or find other professionals to help you put this sales material together. If more musicians would put the same time and attention they put into their music into promoting and selling their talents, there would be many more successful artists in the world. You can't exist with just an email address and a few MP3s. The basic, ruthless, self-promotion arsenal consists of dozens of promotional techniques and items that work together to support, promote, and build your image, message, and reputation.

Let me clarify this important point. The people who will buy your music are *not* interested in you. They are only interested in *themselves*. To succeed, you must ensure your promotional material and sales presentations focus totally on your client's or prospect's wants and desires. It's a subtle but critical difference. You can't yell at the top of the mountain, "I'm great, hire me!" and expect people to work with you. You must take this tactic: "You have a problem or need that I understand. By working with me, we can solve that problem (or fulfill that need) together. Here's how."

See the difference? *Feel* the difference? Begin thinking about your clients. What do they want? How can you benefit them? Focus on what *your client* wants, *not* on what you offer. Sell *solutions*. Your music creates moods, enhances images, and helps deliver a message effectively. If you follow this advice, you will save tons of money that you would otherwise waste on promotional gambits and materials that don't work, or that won't sell your music.

COMMIT TO SUCCESS

I believe you can have anything in the world, just not everything. To be the musical success you envision, you need to sacrifice something, give something up. You can't have a full social calendar, and a full-time job, and a family, and be a media composer…and devote your full energy to each. Something's gotta give, and you must decide what it is going to be.

That may seem cold-hearted. Surely, this is America. And the American dream is to "have it all!" Unfortunately, many well-intentioned people have failed miserably or even gone to an early grave while chanting that anthem. You must first decide what it is you want and then concentrate on getting what you want. There is no middle ground. I believe author Holbrook Jackson described it best when he said that "sacrifice is a form of bargaining." Suffice it to say that *you* must determine where it is you want to head and must commit, indeed pledge, that you will do what is necessary, make the appropriate sacrifices, to reach your goal. That is how it must be. You can blame nobody for your failure. All that prevents you from getting there is…uh…you.

DETERMINE HOW TO MEASURE YOUR SUCCESS

When you set your goals and how you plan to achieve them, make sure you also include a measuring device. Is scoring the next David Lynch film a dream? What if you get a documentary for PBS? Did you succeed? These are hard questions, almost philosophical in nature. Set yourself some general goals with the specific outcomes you desire. Take a few minutes to think about how you would measure your success. Write it down to make it real and keep this paper where you can revisit it often.

For example, that paper might read that you want to make money from your music. That's far too vague. Try this instead: I will earn my living entirely from music-related ventures within two years. That kind of prediction is easier to measure. If you are still holding down a part-time job to pay the bills 25 months from now, you know you didn't reach the goal you set for yourself.

REVIEW THESE STEPS REGULARLY

Don't make the mistake of thinking about these areas only once and then filing them all away. Regularly review all of these points and determine what is working, so you can keep on doing it, and what may be failing, so you can fix it *fast*. Take time out from your daily work to reflect on what you did, are doing, and should do next. This very process can at times be a sobering experience. Or a wake-up call. More often, you come away with a good feeling about your music career with a sense of focus and accomplishment. Always review your past, learn from it, and apply what you learn to either changing or staying on course.

What if your music career isn't going where you'd like it to go? When you feel like giving up, *stop*. Take a step back and analyze the situation. If you have no money coming in, then start promoting. Pick up the phone, send a promotion to past buyers/new prospects, and look for new business. In short, get busy! If your profits are down, then cut some costs by either eliminating waste or shopping smarter. If you're just discouraged, then take a vacation, outsource tasks you hate, or consider doing something different for a short time. Hopefully, these techniques will get you back on track fast.

Get Started Now!

At a recent Self Employment in the Arts Conference (www.seaconference.org), they mentioned the keys to success for independent artists. There were only four suggestions:

1. Care more than others think is wise.

2. Risk more than others think is safe.

3. Dream more than others think is practical.

4. Expect more than others think is possible.

While these four points don't contain specific how-to-do-its, they nevertheless are seeds upon which to grow your successful music career.

Working hard on your self-promotion will keep your name alive, build credibility, and ultimately put money in your pocket. Make sure that everything you do adds value to your business. Present a strong, helpful image, solve problems, give others (people, clients, prospects, and the media) in return more than they give or expect, and make sure they come away with a good feeling about you, your business, and your music.

Remember this: Ego has nothing to do with this. Ruthless self-promotion is about making your business stronger by leveraging the success you've achieved into more success. First, you must have an initial success and then go crazy telling the world about it. Recognize that your success comes through careful diligence, growing your business day-in and day-out, slowly and methodically. Keep your eye on the goals you've set for yourself and the prizes your hard work should generate.

By the way, I feel so strongly about the importance of promotion that I've written an entire book about the subject just for you. It's called *Ruthless Self-Promotion in the Music Industry*. You owe it to yourself to discover more about this crucial path to success with your soundtrack and jingle music. A new, updated second edition of this popular and practical book will be available soon after the release of the resource you now hold in your hand.

CHAPTER 3

How This Business Works

"The greatest moments of the human spirit may be deduced from the greatest moments in music."
—Aaron Copland

Somebody needs music for a media project, and you get hired to realize this person's musical vision. Getting the work is half the battle (90% of the battle if you're just starting out). This book devotes greater detail to that topic later. For now, let's assume you have the gig, and it's time for the actual music composition process to begin.

Jingo Lingo

Like many industries, the soundtrack and jingle world has its own jargon. Here's a list of the most common terms you should know and understand.

AC-3 (AKA DOLBY DIGITAL)

The standard format for delivering audio, stereo, and 5.1 surround on DVD. It is a lossy encoding format that uses perceptual masking encoding techniques to reduce file size by only allocating bits to data that the ear perceives as dominant sounds. Go to www.dolby.com for complete info on how this works.

AUDIO POST-PRODUCTION

The part of the post-production cycle that fixes and sweetens dialogue, sound effects, and music to complement the visual presentation.

BED

Typically a melody-less musical sequence composed or mixed to hold under narration and other dialogue, such as on-camera interviews.

BIG AND BOLD
Director-speak for "I want my music to sound *exactly* like every other movie I've ever heard." Translation: Rip-off the greats, such as Bernard Herrmann.

BUDGET
The "thing" that there is never enough of for music. For example, "we've spent a million dollars on the commercial spot. Can you write the music for $500? That's all there is left in the budget."

BUMPER
Short musical sequence used on radio and TV when going to and/or returning from a commercial break. *See also Stinger.*

BUYOUT ROYALTY FREE
Typical of music for commercial spots, this is selling your music outright for one fee with no royalties. You essentially give up your copyright to the music. Also, the "pay once, use it forever" method of selling library or production music. Additionally, many sample libraries, such as ACID loop libraries, license this way. You can use the music (or sample) in your own productions without further payment beyond the initial fee.

COPY
Advertising slang for the words—dialogue and voice-over (VO)—in a commercial spot. Y'know, those pesky voices that always seem to drown out your music?

CUE
Signifies a specific musical sequence in a scene or part thereof. For example, the music used during a love scene would be the "love scene cue."

CUE SHEETS
Detailed written descriptions of on-screen action with timings. These cue sheets or timing notes list every event that happens in a scene and precisely when each event occurs. They are broken out by musical cues and based on the spotting notes. The composer uses these cue sheets/timing notes to create music that synchronizes appropriately with the show. *See spotting notes.*

Also, the mandatory listings of music used for broadcast. These cue sheets are required by ASCAP/BMI/SESAC to determine and pay performance royalties to music publishers/writers.

DAW
Acronym for digital audio workstation used for writing, arranging, recording, mixing, and delivering music and soundtracks.

DIEGETIC/NONDIEGETIC

Sound (including music) that is part of a visual scene, such as dialogue, sound effects, and music coming from an on-screen source (band playing, jukebox, etc.). Nondiegetic is sound from outside the scene, such as an unseen narrator and all dramatic music underscore.

DONUT

A jingle where there is a hole in the middle for the voice-over announcer. The jingle may start with full lyrics, go to instrumental only in the middle, and return with the full lyrics (or slogan or company name) at the end.

DV

This is short for digital video. There are several formats, such as Apple's QuickTime and Windows AVI, and even more codecs for those generic containers. You do not need the highest quality video for scoring, but you do need the right frame rate. Ask for your projects on mini-DV, the consumer format (aka DV-25), which virtually every DAW supports. You may get a file or a tape. The tape player will need to either be locked to your gear via timecode (try to avoid this) or digitized to a file format your software can read (strive for this!).

FULL-SING

The increasingly rare jingle form that contains both music and lyrics for the entire sequence. *See donut.*

HIT (JUMP)

A musical hit point is a moment where a musical event corresponds to a specific screen action, for example, a crescendo when the hero wins. Hits may be subtle or more pronounced. Simply starting or stopping the music at a critical moment is one way to "hit." Through composing and orchestrating, you can achieve a good balance of hits with your scores. *See also mickey-mousing.*

In horror films, using music this way is called a *jump*, such as when the killer appears accompanied by a loud cymbal crash and orchestra hit. Why jump? Because its purpose is to make the audience jump in their seats!

HYBRID (PRE- /POST-SCORE)

With this approach, you provide a basic music track that an editor can use when cutting the picture and then post-score the rest after the picture is locked. For example, you compose an upbeat tune with bass, drums, and piano. You get the edited segment back with your basic track cut in. Now you sync the music to the edited master, flesh out the score adding solos, drums fills, etc., and then replace the basic track with the more complete piece. *See pre-score and post-score.*

INTROS AND OUTROS

Short musical segments used at the very beginning and end respectively of a sequence, commercial spot, TV show, etc.

JINGLE

The music, usually with sung lyrics, used to sell a commercial product in a radio/TV advertisement. The absence of lyrics is usually called a *score*. The absence of music is called *sound design*. Music has a way of sticking in people's minds, so associating products and services with music is good business for advertisers.

KNOCK-OFF (AKA SOUND-ALIKE)

Agency-speak for "write something to sound exactly like fill-in-the-blank, but not too close so we get sued." *See also lawsuit.*

LOCKED (PICTURE)

Denotes that the editing of a media project is complete. Composing to a locked picture means not having to revise your music should the edit change.

MICKEY-MOUSING

Matching the action too closely with the music, like cartoons often do. While this is accepted and encouraged in the animation (and comedy) world, it is frowned upon when used excessively in a dramatic context.

MP3

A digital audio encoding format that reduces file size significantly (simultaneously reducing the quality of your music exponentially). Also, this is an audio format popularized by young people who have never heard what high-quality, real music actually sounds like.

MUSICAL IMAGE CAMPAIGN

This is a dubious euphemism used by those who don't want to associate with the word "jingle" and all the possible negative baggage that comes with it. As the sung jingle slowly fades away, replaced by mostly instrumental music, sound design elements, genre-specific sound-alike music, and licensed songs, you may sometimes hear this "new" label.

NEEDLE DROP

Paying for library music only when you actually use it. The payment amount depends on the intended use.

NLE

Acronym for nonlinear editing (editor), this is mostly applied to software-based video editing programs, such as Avid, Final Cut Pro, and Sony Vegas.

POINTS

The method of paying composers part of the profits (1% = 1 point) from the project they work on. This may be a percentage of sales or some other formula.

PRE-SCORE

To write music before a project is in production. An example would be composing a song that actors/singers would lip sync to when filmed on a set. It also means to supply a finished or nearly finished score before post-production begins. This music is often used when editing, such as building a montage that is specifically cut to the music.

POST-SCORE

The more common practice of composing music to a complete, or locked, picture edit.

ROUGH CUT

An initial draft, or work-in-progress, of a media project. Composers often use this to start the composition process.

ROYALTIES

Getting ongoing income for your music above and beyond the initial fee. There are mechanical, synchronization, and performance royalties available for composers.

SCORE

The noun and verb that describe the music and process of composing it when used for a media presentation. *See soundtrack.*

SHOW

Generic term for a movie or TV program.

SOMETHING SIMPLE

Director- or agency-speak for "we'll make you work your tail off 'cos we have no clue what we want."

SOUND DESIGN

Developing sounds (musical and nonmusical) for media productions to create new textures and to underline events and messages. Also, the process of using these sounds in a mix.

SOUNDTRACK

The entire audio portion of a media presentation. Often used interchangeably to describe only the music portion, i.e., the film soundtrack, meaning the music score only.

SOUNDTRACK ALBUM

Hollywood's attempt to milk money from the viewing public by releasing an album comprised of popular songs heard for mere seconds during the movie. *See Shrek* and *Shrek 2.* Also, the dubious practice of releasing a K-Tel-like compilation album of songs "inspired" by a film or TV show, but actually having nothing to do with it outside of using the vehicle to make money. Rarely, the actual music composed for the film or TV show released on CD.

SPOT
Slang for radio or TV commercial.

STEMS
You rarely deliver music for films, TV, and even commercials as mixed stereo (or surround) files. Instead, you provide a group of component, grouped submixes, called *stems*, which the re-recording mixer uses to balance and remix your music during the final mix. Eight tracks is the standard for delivering music stems, but this varies by project. For example, typical stems may include a stereo drum track, mono bass, stereo rhythm instruments, mono melody, and a stereo "special" track (e.g., strings/orchestra, ethnic instruments, etc.). While you don't give the re-recording mixer complete control over the multitrack, they can use these compiled stems to adjust the main components as needed. For example, it is easy for them to bring the drum volume up or down without affecting the other music elements.

With surround, music stems can get increasingly complex. For *Star Wars: Episode III—Revenge of the Sith*, music stems came to the final mix as 29 tracks: 5.1 stems of orchestra, synths, percussion, and other and a 5.0 stem of choirs.

STINGERS
Short musical statements, often more sound design than musical, used for dramatic effect. Fox Sports and many radio commercials use these for emphasis. *See bumper.*

SOURCE MUSIC
Previously composed or recorded music used to evoke a time period or locale. For example, using Russian folk music as the basis for a score. Also refers to the use of licensed popular songs for a show.

Additionally, the same term applies to music that comes from a diegetic on-screen "source," such as a radio playing in the background.

SPOTTING SESSION
Generally, a meeting or series of meetings between the director, producer, and picture editorial department and the sound and music supervisors, including the composer, to discuss the use of sound and music in a film, TV show, or commercial. The program gets screened and discussed in detail. Unfortunately, it is rare that the music and sound effects spotting sessions happen together. This often causes problems later when music and effects come to the re-recording (final) mix and have to fight for attention. Many composers are shocked by how their much-labored-over music gets buried under a heavy sound effects mix.

SPOTTING NOTES
The formal notes generated from a music spotting session. These notes contain the start and end times for every music cue and indicate whether the music will be underscore, source, or a song. *See also cue sheets.*

SMPTE TIMECODE
The acronym for the Society of Motion Picture and Television Engineers used frequently to reference timecode. Timecode is a method of assigning time values to frame-based media. The format is hours:minutes:seconds: frames. Use these numbers when spotting and composing projects to keep music events synchronized with screen action. The timecode values can also be used to keep equipment synchronized, such as VCR and a digital audio workstation (DAW).

TAG
The final instance of music, sung or instrumental, placed at the end of a commercial spot. This is often the slogan or client name, e.g., McDonald's "I'm lovin' it."

TEMP TRACK
The music that clients often place into projects before hiring a composer. If the client is married to the temp tracks, your composing life will be difficult unless you deliver something very close to the temp. Worse still, they may end up licensing the temp track and not using your music at all.

TIMECODE
See SMPTE timecode.

TIMING NOTES
See cue sheets.

UNDERSCORE
The nondiegetic dramatic music that enhances the drama. *See score.*

WINDOW BURN
The process and result of superimposing visual timecode onto a digital media file.

WORK FOR HIRE
Receiving a single fee for your music composition with no future royalties. You essentially assign the copyright to the client.

People You Should Know

This industry is packed with creative people under tremendous stress, budgetary and time constraints, and other interfering forces. Their work can be very demanding, which requires them to use every ounce of their physical, mental, and creative faculties. When they hire a composer for their project, they want to make sure to get the best music possible. For many, this means relying on you for every aspect of the music composition and recording process. And that means you must have a collaborative relationship based on a single goal of mutual respect and trust.

In some cases, you work with the director/producer/head creative in charge of the production. Other times, your clients will have *their* clients to satisfy. When writing jingles, you almost always work directly with the advertising agency, rarely the actual client. Often, you never meet the people who are really paying your fee. Don't worry about these layers of bureaucracy. All you need to do is find out who approves your music and concentrate your effort at working alongside and pleasing that person or persons.

There are a lot of jobs related to a show's soundtrack. Sometimes multiple persons fill these positions, while other times one person wears many hats. For example, you may be music supervisor, music editor, composer, arranger, and orchestrator all in one. In either case, the demands of these positions are distinct and identifiable. Let's meet the people with whom you may be working.

AGENCY CREATIVES
The generic term for the people responsible for creating the commercial advertising spot. See *head creative.*

ARRANGER
This person takes the minimal sketches, such as a piano-only score, provided by a composer and expands them into a more comprehensive musical piece.

COMPOSER
The person who writes the music, i.e., *you*!

DIRECTOR
The primary creative force behind films. Contrarily, in television, they have production control, but often less creative control in post-production where the producer (and picture editors) rules. The same is often true for commercials, too.

EXISTENCE JUSTIFIERS
My favorite quote comes from Josh Billings, "Some people look so busy doing nothing that they seem indispensable." These are the people who make nitpicky comments and other suggestions only because they must justify their existence on the project. They really like what's happening, but feel they must make some contribution or risk being seen as useless and redundant. They have to earn their pay somehow. You'll find powerless control freaks in this gene pool.

GHOSTWRITERS (AKA UNDERWRITERS)
A little-known opportunity for many composers is to act as ghostwriters for bigger name composers. Often, the workload is too much for a single composer (typically so for episodic TV

and some films), and parts of the work may be outsourced. For example, Douglas Spotted Eagle's signature sound can be heard on several big feature films that have other composers taking the screen credit. Sometimes, a particular sequence or musical cue is so different from the rest of the score that it makes sense to have another composer do it. These underwriters, as they are sometimes known, usually go uncredited but earn their pay as part of the overall music budget and may also keep their writer's share for earning performance royalties. More often, though, these are work-for-hire projects—the ghostwriter gets a single fee, gives up all rights, and that's that.

HEAD CREATIVE (AKA "THE BIG GUY/GAL")

There is, hopefully, one person in charge of producing and delivering the commercial spot. Virtually everyone defers to this person's judgment. This head creative has the client's ear and ultimately makes the final decisions. He or she is also the person who takes all the credit when the spot does well and shifts the blame to underlings when it fails.

MUSIC EDITOR

The music editor creates the spotting notes following the music spotting sessions with the director, producer, music supervisor, and composer. These are essentially detailed written notes of where music should be in the finished show. From these notes, the music editor fashions cue sheets with specific timings of musical events. Composers work from these cue sheets when preparing the score. More often than not, the cue sheets reference SMPTE timecode numbers that have been superimposed (window burn) onto the digital file of the program.

The music editor may cut in temporary tracks as the picture edit progresses. These may be rough sketches from the composer, library music, or other music sources. Increasingly, this task falls to the picture editor, who may have a greater impact on the commercial/film/TV show's sound than the music supervisor or music editor.

Though you may score to picture, a music editor is often employed for films and TV to perform final tweaks matching the music to the picture. They will also edit source music and songs for inclusion if that applies. On occasion, this person will remix music from stems and create additional cues from those stems, too. These will then be cut into the show in places where no music was indicated during initial spotting notes. That means somebody changed his mind, or perhaps a song could not be successfully licensed, forcing a gap in the score that must be filled.

MUSIC SUPERVISOR

For films and TV, this is the one person in charge of the music. Typical duties of a music supervisor include going through the script and choosing where and where *not* to place music, creating and administering the music budget, working with composers on the original music score, finding other music (source music and songs) and clearing rights to those songs, supervising the final music mix and overseeing delivery, completing and filing music cue sheets for performance royalty statements, and other duties. Some supervisors work on the film/TV show only while others may work on the soundtrack album as well.

ORCHESTRATOR

This person takes the lead sheets from the composer and assigns the parts to specific instruments. For example, a composer may only do a 4-8-stave score. The orchestrator expands this to a full orchestra.

RE-RECORDING MIXER (AKA DUBBING MIXER)

This is the person who does the final audio mix for a film, TV show, or commercial spot. The term comes from the old technique where individual tracks (dialogue, music, and effects) were re-recorded or dubbed into a final mix on a film dubbing stage. The digital age antiquates this moniker, but the name remains, though often shortened to simply mixer.

PICTURE EDITOR (AKA CUTTER)

This is the creative mind who edits, or cuts, the film, TV show, or commercial. That person must take the myriad of takes shot in a studio and on location and weave together a visually cohesive and compelling story. Because of digital nonlinear editing (NLE) software , picture editors are increasingly asked to do more tasks beyond just editing. On the audio side, they cut in temp sound effects and music, and their choices can impact the production greatly. Be friendly with these fine people when you meet them because they have more power than might be readily apparent!

PRODUCER

These are the money people in film—the primary creative force in television and on commercials.

SUPERVISING SOUND EDITOR

The primary person in charge of the entire soundtrack for a film or TV show. This person oversees the dialogue and sound effects portion of the soundtrack. *See music supervisor.*

SYCOPHANTIC POOL

The lesser creatives and other hangers-on whose only purpose seems to be to agree with "the big guy/gal" on every issue. Be careful, as some may have hidden agendas and more power than you think.

Typical Project Formats

Projects come in all shapes, sizes, and lengths. Your job is to compose music based on the material the client provides. While there is an infinite number of possible variations and approaches, the vast majority of projects come in the following formats or hybrids of these scenarios.

IDEA- OR SCRIPT-BASED

The client asks you to score based on either an idea or a more concrete script. Either the idea is described, along with musical suggestions, or you get the script hard copy and begin the process soon after. You may eventually get a visual cut of the project with which to fine-tune your score, but not always.

Occasionally, you'll be in a competitive situation where you must compose your best music based on a few simple instructions. Pay attention to what your clients tell you and ask probing questions. They'll reveal what they are looking for (if they know it already). If they are just fishing—"we'll know it when we hear it"—recognize that you are doing their music research for them as part of your project.

TIME-BASED

You are asked to write music that conforms to a specific time or times. For example, the project might call for a 30-second upbeat tune. Occasionally, there are more precise timings, such as when the music must start out dark and somber and then turn more joyous at 12 seconds and then build to a big crescendo at 25 seconds and out by 29. Commercial spot producers often issue these kinds of directions.

STORYBOARD- OR ANIMATICS-BASED

There is a storyboard (a series of drawings representing the final project), sometimes as a digital video file, that you use to complete the score. The final project will match the storyboard (hopefully), so your music should fit the final editing version. For animation and game work, you may get animatics instead, essentially short, crudely animated movies that provide an overall feel. You may also be privy to works-in-progress of the game as it nears its final form.

Pre-visualization (pre-viz for short) is the new trend for media projects with substantial budgets. Using specially designed animation software, producers can create realistic versions of how a finished project will come together. Spending money at this stage can save a lot of money in the end for them. These animated storyboards can be rather sophisticated, complete with characters, sets, dialogue, camera moves, sound effects, and more. Scoring the pre-viz is not unusual, and it is more like a video-based project outlined below.

VIDEO-BASED

You receive a copy of the locked video that you can drop into your music composition software or DAW and score while watching the screen action, using your spotting notes and cue sheets for added reference. This is, by far, the more preferred method of working, especially on long-form projects.

MUSIC PACKAGE

Another common request is to provide a music package comprising several different cuts of music, often in different styles, timings, and instrumentation. The music you supply may be based on characters, situations, emotions/moods, or other client-supplied direction. These tracks are always free-form, free-standing tunes that are not locked to picture. In essence, you deliver a custom music library to a client that they can use and reuse as needed. You will typically provide alternate mixes and timings for the client and occasionally 8-track (or more) stems for client remixing. For example, this is how music gets used for ABC's *Extreme Makeover: Home Edition*. Producers have about 50 different pieces, including the show's distinctive theme, to use to fit the moods and emotions of scenes within the program. It's also how Brian Tarquin delivers much of his music for the daytime drama *All My Children*. There isn't time to score to picture, so instead, "songs" that can be easily slipped in are the order of the day. Needless to say, taking the master cue approach (discussed later) lets you deliver a large variety of thematically connected music to your client.

The Spotting Session

This is the all-important meeting between you and the client to discuss the music issues for a given project. Sometimes, these sessions go on forever and never seem to reach any concrete solutions. Other times, the client is better prepared and things go quickly. Work hard to get the answers you need to make the composition and approval process proceed smoothly.

Chances are your clients won't be very musically inclined. Assure them not to worry about the musical or technical terms. Encourage them to describe how they think the music should be and what it should sound like. Together, you can fill in the details as the project moves along.

Your role as the composer is to enhance and support two critical components: emotion and message. Musical scores are about emotion—how you want the audience to respond. And media projects are all about message—what you want people to remember. Often, the music is literal; sometimes nonliteral. But whatever musical choices you (or the client) make, the music must work to have an appropriate impact on the audience. Sometimes, the solution is a bold musical statement; other times your music's influence is subtle. Just recognize that you have an important role, so don't take your part lightly.

Therefore, communication between you and the people who will approve your music is vital. You want to make sure you are on the same musical page to prevent problems down the line. You can never get too specific at these meetings. Instead, the talk is often generic and unfocused. My suggestion is that you ask and keep asking these questions:

WHY ARE YOU USING MUSIC?

This is a fundamental question that may elicit some unique responses. Most media producers don't really think about this fundamental. Common answers are either "everybody uses music" or "we have to have music, that's all." I do find asking this question gets the client thinking a little more seriously and talking somewhat more candidly about the music they want for their project, though.

WHAT EMOTIONAL RESPONSE DO YOU DESIRE FROM THE MUSIC? THE AUDIENCE?

Since music to a certain extent is all about emotion, the answers to these questions can clue you in on the stylistic direction you should take with the score. "I want the audience crying" means you probably won't score synth pop. Make sure you get a feel for the range of emotions the client wants to convey; they may change with the dramatic arc of the story, documentary, or game.

WHAT DOES THE DIRECTOR/PRODUCER/CLIENT WANT TO SAY OR CONVEY?

This answer targets the message of the piece. It can give you greater insight into where to place the music, how, and why. Your music can make certain elements of a media presentation more memorable. Knowing what the client feels are these important points, and where they manifest themselves in the project, is crucial to delivering what the client wants.

WHO, SPECIFICALLY, IS THE AUDIENCE?

Defining the audience helps you better choose the right music that will appeal to them. You can use the information to make both stylistic and instrumentation decisions.

WHAT STYLE IS APPROPRIATE TO THIS AUDIENCE?

If you had told me a few years ago that using Led Zepplin to sell Cadillacs was a good idea, I would have laughed in your face. Well, guess what? The Zepplin generation is aging and now has the means to afford the popular luxury car. Therefore, the answers to this question and the next are the most crucial decisions to be made at the spotting session.

WHAT STYLE IS APPROPRIATE TO THE PROJECT'S MESSAGE?

How can the music you compose best convey the project's message? While one choice may appeal to the audience, it may not support the message satisfactorily. Or vice-versa. Careful thought must go into finding the right music for *both* the audience and the message.

Mentioning musical textures, as opposed to specific instruments, can be a better approach for the client with little musical knowledge. Andre Prévin tells the story of the client who insisted on French horns while feverishly pantomiming the unmistakable slide of a trombone.

Be careful about style discussions. What differentiates jazz from rock? Is it instrumentation or is it attitude? For example, your client says: "Give me dark and ominous." Here is how different musicians may interpret that statement:

▶ One composer writes for cello and bassoon.

▶ Another writes thick, analog synth bass drones.

▶ Another writes heavy drums swimming in reverb.

▶ And me, I write a children's lullaby—innocent and light—complete counterpoint to dark and ominous and maybe even scarier.

For jingle work, it's imperative to match the style to the audience and message. A classical piano piece probably won't work for selling a Corvette, but for a Jaguar, it may fit the image. A piece about a child care center could use a track of children humming and singing a popular children's song such as *London Bridge* or *Row, Row, Row Your Boat*. A nature preserve might try a folksy guitar piece or maybe solo flute (although sound effects like birds chirping, leaves rustling, and brooks babbling may make a more effective score). Yes, even sound effects are "musical instruments" when used appropriately.

HOW ARE YOU GOING TO USE MUSIC AND WHY?

Again, this is a question that probes the mind of the client. Is the music going to be diegetic or non-diegetic? In the background or up front? Will it be buried under sound effects or ?

Perhaps the music needs to evoke a time period, location, or event. Those factors may drive your stylistic and instrumentation choices. For example, use the sitar in the score. Does that evoke world music? What about the 60s? And, if so, the Beatles' 60s? Or Austin Powers?

There are three ways a score can work in a media production:

▶ Your music supports the real events/drama/emotion being shown. The music reflects what is actually happening. Most movies, especially blockbuster action flicks, follow this method. Don't confuse this with mickey-mousing, which is still a valid approach in some cases. Here the music mirrors the screen action, supports and complements the emotions, ideas, and messages, and doesn't detract from them.

▶ Your music enhances the subtext or underlying message instead. Here the music is different from the specific events/drama/emotion being shown, choosing instead to enhance the subtext of a scene and not what is actually happening. Often, this technique is used to portray a character's mindset and not what the person is specifically engaged in doing.

▶ Your music can play against either the first or second idea above. To illustrate this, think of a scene with extreme violence accompanied by a toy piano playing a children's lullaby.

WHERE AND WHERE NOT WILL YOU PLACE MUSIC?

Answering this query will take the bulk of the spotting session as you and the client go through the project and make these important decisions.

Take copious notes during the session; don't rely on your memory alone. Before you leave the spotting session, make sure you have consensus on the music. You want concrete decisions on the following information:

▶ Style or styles (if different sequences require distinct approaches).

▶ Instrumentation. Decide on the best way to represent the style. This may be a budgetary decision, too, so keep that in mind. You may want an orchestra, but your client can only afford a string quartet. You may need to prepare demo music for clients who possess absolutely no musical vision. Plan on it. It's often far easier to throw together a temp track and play it for them than to try to explain it!

▶ Placement. Detail all musical start and stop points and whether the music is source, underscore, or song. Indicate where single music events should sync with screen action (a hit point). Detail when multiple musical events need to match screen action. Multiple hits can quickly become cartoon-like mickey-mousing. Remind clients that silence can often be more powerful than sound/music. These spotting notes, as they are called, will act as your road map for the score. The more detailed version of the spotting notes, called cue sheets or timing notes, will provide more specifics when composing.

One other caveat. Watch out for those temp tracks! Clients may already have music synced up. The problem is, clients often become rather accustomed to—dare I say fond of?—these tracks. That makes your job more difficult to deliver music they will approve. Get a feel for how the client views these temps. Are they really sold on them? Or is it just something to cut to? If they are pushing you strongly in that direction, take note. There's no need to rip off the temp music, but the style, instrumentation, and beats per minute (BPM) might be something you need to follow to keep the client happy.

Spotting Session Techniques

While it is perfectly acceptable for clients to point to the screen and say "There. Start the music when the door opens." There is a better way. Ask for a digital file of the project with a timecode window burn or burn the timecode into the file yourself.

Timecode window burn.

My approach is to have the video on the timeline in Sony Vegas and place a timecode filter on the video. Also, make sure that the software timeline itself matches the timecode format used in the window burn. Then, sitting with the client, I go through the project and insert markers (or regions) at specific points and indicate what the client wants to happen musically at that moment. I also write this information down on paper. When the client leaves, I'm left with a digital cue sheet.

Alternately, though the process is a bit antiquated, you (or the music editor) will develop spotting notes and cue or timing sheets from which you can work. These are detailed written notes of scene action, music points, and more. I prefer my method whether the music is for a 30-second commercial or a feature-length film.

Getting Busy

As I said before, this isn't really a book about composing, arranging, or orchestrating your music; it's about selling your music. However, I would be remiss if I didn't include a little direction to hopefully help make sure your music meets your client's needs. Also, the interviews in this book provide additional insight into this creative process.

You can work, and many composers do, without a visual reference. You may use the spotting notes and timings to compose the score. Knowing how BPM translates into time, or perhaps using a stopwatch, is all you really need. You may be developing a stand-alone song or specific length cue where timing is less critical. The project may just call for a one-minute loop, such as in a game soundtrack. In these examples, it is perfectly acceptable to just compose in whatever way makes you comfortable.

Personally, I often put together sketches and ideas that later I will conform to precise timings. By adjusting tempo and time signature, even rather fleshed-out pieces can be shoehorned to match precise timings. Also, since I do audio-post, sound effects and sound design elements sometimes take the place of specific musical hits.

If you know a show will be sound-effects heavy, it really pays to communicate with the supervising sound editor. Otherwise, there may be conflicts during the mix, as your music and the sound effects fight for attention. It really is best to work it out *before* problems arise. If you know what those primary sounds will be, you can score around them. For example, if there are a lot of high frequency sounds, you could feature more mid-range and low-register instruments. That kind of orchestrating creates room for your score in a busy soundtrack mix.

Working with Video

Work from the same timecode video that you used during spotting. No matter what DAW or NLE you use, drop the video into a session and compose away.

I work with a combination of Sony Acid and Vegas, along with Reason (which I Rewire into Acid) and a bevy of other soft synths and samplers. I also record various acoustic instruments such as guitar, bass, and percussion. The timecode window burn comes up in Acid/Vegas so that I can work with the video and audio simultaneously. Immediately, I can see how my musical ideas fit with the video and can make adjustments in real time, instantly seeing and hearing the results. It is a great way to work, virtually seamless with little or no technical gremlins.

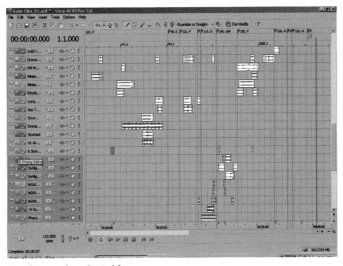

Scoring project in Acid.

More importantly, I can render quick video files for clients to see or hear, and they may come to the studio to listen and make suggestions. It's all very interactive and fast, which clients seem to appreciate.

Music as Color

My friend and fellow composer, Douglas Spotted Eagle (www.spottedeagle.com), offers this suggestion when you are mapping out a musical sequence. He suggests that you think visually with your music, specifically as colors, and choose instruments that reflect those colors. Look at the scene colors for which you are writing the music. If it is dark, think dark colors/sounds like cello, bass, and pad drones. Do mid-range colors dominate? Choose guitars, saxophone, and voice. Flutes, high piano notes, and cymbals represent bright colors. However, some sounds in the same color region may actually contrast with this idea. For example, compare the melancholy cello from *Crouching Tiger, Hidden Dragon* with the playful synth bass lines from *Seinfeld*. Both are bass instruments, but they couldn't be more polarized. Thinking of music as color is certainly an interesting approach that you may find inspiring.

Your Tools

As a composer, no matter what the project, you have certain musical tools available to you. Thanks to synthesizers and samplers, you have a myriad of choices for instrumentation, from convincing samples and emulations of real instruments to unusual sonic excursions. Despite such a wonderful palette of textures, don't forget about music fundamentals. My advice is to use everything you have at your disposal to craft the right music that works with the project, including the following:

► Tempo

► Time signature

► Key

► Melody

► Harmony

► Counterpoint

► Rhythm

► Unison

► Solo

► Ostinato

► Arrangement (introduction, verse, chorus, verse, chorus, bridge, chorus, ending)

► Themes

► Motif and leit motif

► Timbre (instrument choices)

► Pitch

► Dynamics

► Space

▶ Time

▶ And more

Developing the Master Cue

When you need to compose a lot of music for a project, such as a documentary, TV drama, or film, consider the master cue technique. Instead of writing all the music from scratch, develop a longer, fully orchestrated musical theme or tone poem and recycle it throughout your project. In short, create a theme and then compose variations on that theme. Better still, build variations into that single composition and then craft alternate mixes from it.

Jan Hammer applied this approach with his work on the ground-breaking television series *Miami Vice*. "What I do is use some piece of music more than once. It's not that I repeat them, but I record a lot more parts to each piece of music, so the variations are built in. Then I mix each cue differently in order to produce different cues. I flesh (the music) out to the extreme and then take things away. I might have 20 tracks on the master cue but only use three of them for a particular scene. So I spend more time on these master cues, which are them dissected into individual cues."

Thanks to the nonlinear world of today's music production environment, creating alternate versions is far easier than it was in Hammer's time. Your primary variations can be the following:

▶ Tempo—Radical changes to a song's tempo can create an entirely new feel.

▶ Key—A fresh key makes everything sound different.

▶ Length—Chop up sections, rearrange them, loop segments, and move to fit scenes better.

▶ Instrumentation/orchestration—Turn tracks on/off, assign different patches to the synth parts, and otherwise mix things up to sound different.

What's especially useful about this technique is that it allows you to write a great deal more music in a shorter time, and that same music follows identical thematic elements. There is a certain "sound" and symmetry to the score with the added variety in the music, making it interesting in different situations.

Here's an example: I was contracted to write the theme for a local TV show—a jazzy, up-tempo piece using drums, piano, bass, and saxophone. Since the show would sometimes deal with rather serious subjects, I decided to record a slower, darker version using lighter drums, a mellow electric piano, deep acoustic bass, and no burning sax solo. On still another version, I changed the sounds again and recorded a new flute line. This gave them a version for their end credits. Next, I took all three versions and chopped them up to create bumpers/stingers to use when going to and coming from commercial breaks.

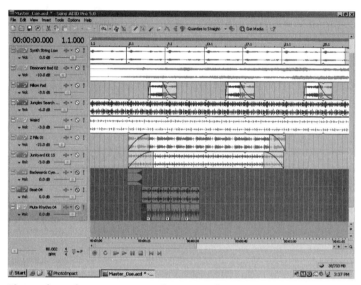

Pictured are the components of an example master cue. For a string interlude, tracks 1 and 2 are all that's needed. Shifting to a different key and slowing the tempo down makes the strings-only part different from the full version. Adding the muted tracks, a different drum loop, and bass line to the strings and increasing the tempo creates an upbeat version of the string theme. Muting those four parts and soloing the rest creates another variation. From this single short sequence, several minutes of music could be created; the possibilities are almost endless.

What's important about this is that *all* this music came from *a single* master recording. In this example, it was an entire MIDI score, so I just arranged and orchestrated the versions differently—essentially choosing different patches for my synths/samplers, changing key and tempo, and that's about it. I spent most of my time writing the main theme and then took a few extra hours to adapt the music to a variety of contexts and situations. The show producers not only got a bouncy opening, but also two separate and completely different arrangements based around the same theme. Add the bumpers, and it was a real bargain—much more music than they ever expected.

Other Time-savers

Music libraries can be a source for inspiration and a resource you can use in a creative pinch. When you are pressed for time or the client budget is painfully low, this might be an avenue to explore. Digital Juice (www.digitaljuice.com) has a new twist on the old buyout production music theme.

StackTraxx is their unique multitrack digital music, with unprecedented control over song content. Familiar with layers in Photoshop? StackTraxx applies that same concept to music. Each song includes up to seven individual song layers, called *stacks*, comprising elements such as drums, guitars, strings, and other musical parts. The tracks available vary by song. You use their free Juicer 2 software to preview and output the separate tracks to WAV or AIFF, import these separate tracks into your NLE/DAW, and remix the compositions, even adding your own unique parts.

Similarly, I sometimes use Sony Acid's Beatmapping feature on library music and then add new parts to create a whole new track. StackTraxx particularly lends itself to this technique, but other music library cuts work, too. Make sure you understand the licensing issues when you use library music in this way. By the way, there is a tutorial on my Web site (www.jeffreypfisher.com/stacks. html) about how to use Sony Acid to Beatmap tracks as described.

Acid Loop Libraries

And while we're on the subject, which Acid Loop libraries do I consider the most useful for scoring projects? I have a huge collection that resides on a hard drive and, frankly, pick and choose by ear and project, but I still find myself gravitating toward these desert island discs:

- Bill Laswell Sample Material (Sony)

- Brian Daly Modern Rock Construction Kit (Sony)

- David Torn Textural Elements (Sony)

- Junkyard Rhythms (Sony)

- Numina and Numina II (Sony)

- Underscore Pack (Hark Productions)

Nurture Your Musical Creativity

In this business, creativity rules. Follow these specific techniques and strategies to tap into your creative wellspring.

GET A WELL-ROUNDED EDUCATION

The more you know about a variety of subjects, the better prepared you are to use the material in your creative work. You have a bigger well from which to draw, and that can help you explore the deeper recesses of your creative spirit.

READ, WATCH, EXPERIENCE
Always keep expanding your knowledge and looking for new information and connections. Don't be surprised when seemingly unrelated material combines in a fresh way and sparks your muse. Feed your mind, and it will reward you with what you need to make your music better.

I train people as part of my association with VASST (www.vasst.com), traveling across the country. Travel can really make you tired, if that's your attitude. However, for me, travel is actually energizing because it offers additional experiences. I visit new places, meet new people, and learn more with each trip. I simply get a fresh perspective that enriches my life and tickles my muse. The reason I feel more creative is because travel takes me out of my routine. The ordinary gives way to challenges, some mundane (finding a taxi), and others virtually indescribable (seeing Mt. Hood from an airplane). I'm forced to use my knowledge and focus clearly on the days instead of the rote tasks that can sometimes comprise typical days back home. If you are stuck in a rut, consider taking a trip for the reasons cited. Get out of your element and soak in some scenery and people, letting it bathe and refresh you. Use this opportunity to improve your current status, to open your mind, and break up your routine. And while your body may indeed be tired after your trip, my personal experience is that your mind will be rested and ready to move forward on the tasks comprising your successful musical career and life. Where are you going to go?

WRITE
Keep a journal that helps you make sense of your world. All those things you read, see, and experience need focus and meaning to be useful. Record your thoughts, ideas, aspirations, and more on paper (or computer). Don't just file the journal away, though. Refer to it and use it as a creative tool.

CLEAR THE CLUTTER
Get rid of the physical and mental impediments to your creativity. A messy home/office/workspace coupled to an equally messy life will interfere with your ability to make music. Get your act (and life) together fast.

Specifically, clean out your workspace a couple of times each year. Things start to look messy and may make you feel disorganized. Plus, you might find it increasingly hard to find important material buried under the ever-growing stacks in your musical realm. These little spring cleanings help you "clean the slate" before moving on. It's best to use your downtime following a huge (or series of huge) project to clear all that tends to clutter up. Try rearranging the space a little, too. The fresh perspective can spark your creativity. This is something I've done regularly for my whole life, and few activities rejuvenate me more.

UNDERSTAND THE FOUR MAIN STEPS TO THE CREATIVE PROCESS
Not every piece you do will follow these steps exactly, but what you may discover is that overall, most creative people follow this process unconsciously. Knowing this can help you get through the "writer's block" we often face during step two (below).

1. Gather ideas. You usually jot ideas down, strum a few chords, maybe even the hint of a melody. This is often just playing around, the musical equivalent of doodling. You are usually unfocused and disorganized. When "doodling," many people feel guilty that nothing "real" is getting done. They confuse this crucial step with wasting time. It's not. Give yourself permission to "play" because out of the play can come some real, honest inspiration.

2. Do nothing and let everything percolate. You appear to be doing little, if anything. However, this is often the crucial step that lets ideas swim around in your brain waiting for the spark. You may feel frustrated at this point because you just can't seem to do anything good. This is where "writer's block" lives. It's often frustrating because you can't seem to find direction. Recognizing the importance of this stage can help you deal with the anguish of hoping for something good to happen.

3. Ah, the muse. Suddenly, a spark of inspiration hits, and the creativity flows from a higher place. Often, the work is effortless and productive. When inspiration strikes, we all welcome it with open hearts and minds. It is here where we'd all like to spend our days, in the throes of passionate creativity.

4. Perspiration. Now the hard work begins as you start pulling together what you made into a cohesive musical piece. Call upon all your skills to fashion something special from your creation and give it the polish it needs to be real. Once again, it's another place where we like to visit often.

All musicians have "bad days" where working on our music is unproductive, at least on the surface. This unproductive time is actually vitally important, as it leads to real productivity. Identify the ebb and flow of your creative process and use it to your advantage.

When you understand your creative moods, you can exploit them for your greater gain. Put the other stuff on the back burner and float downstream. Other days, know that the prospect of working on your music is farthest from your mind. It's a temporary dry spell. That's the day to catch up on all those other duties that pile up. This way you carefully balance your time away from intense creativity with time focused in the zone.

Don't force yourself on "bad days"; keep music around you, know that today's not the day, and don't worry about it. Look for other musical immersions. Listen to other artists. Throw in a CD of your works-in-progress as you drive to a day job or other appointments. Read a music publication. Practice your instrument of choice. Or simply play for pleasure. Take a minute to scribble a few ideas down about a song, lyric, production technique, or other idea. Even just take some time to promote your music in some small way—a quick call to a past client or a post to an Internet site. Whatever. My point is you can work on your music even when your creativity ebbs.

Eight Steps Toward Improving Your Composing Skills

"I've never known a musician who regretted being one. Whatever deceptions life may have in store for you, music itself is not going to let you down."—Virgil Thomson

You want your musical skills to get better and better, don't you? Of course you do. If you are nowhere close to reaching your peak performance, it's because you don't understand the *process* that helps you produce your best music *all the time*.

COMPOSE SOMETHING EVERY DAY

The best way to make sure you get the most from your talents is to use them. Write a piece of music every day. This doesn't need to be extravagant or even complete, rather just put your first thoughts down in some real form (paper, recording, etc.). Make composing part of your daily routine. Not everything you do will be good, but the exercise will yield some bits and pieces that you may later turn into something special.

Too many people believe they must be in a creative mood to compose. It's infinitely easier to procrastinate than to just start working. You can't be seduced by this unfortunate behavior. You must banish those "ifs" and "buts" and start writing. Don't worry about style or if you are composing something worthwhile. Write first to please yourself. If you let your inner voice of judgment interfere with your creative flow, you severely inhibit your work as an artist. Turn off the messages in your head and let go.

By far, the toughest part of writing commercial music is learning to be creative on demand. You can't always write just when you *feel* like it. Sometimes, you must write when asked. You must get instant inspiration and be able to compose, orchestrate, play, and record quickly. Music is both art and craft. You can learn and practice the craft aspects. Personally, I save up all my energy for when the muse is especially strong. This way I can sit down cold and write a score from scratch. If I composed and recorded all the time, I would find it difficult to create on short notice.

Get into a routine. Write at the same time each day. If you are especially strong in the morning, get up a little earlier and start composing. Late night your strength? Set aside an hour before going to sleep just so you can capture your energy in a musical sketch. You must find the method that works for you.

Regardless of your working method, make sure you practice, too. Don't confuse doodling around with being serious and truly creative. You must expend some energy and use this time to sharpen your skills. I play and goof around musically all the time. And I set aside time to seriously compose, too. I go back and listen to my doodles and transform them into stronger, more structured pieces. This keeps me fresh and original.

LISTEN TO MUSIC EVERY DAY

Oliver Wendell Holmes said it best: "Take a music bath once or twice a week, and you will find that it is to the soul what the water bath is to the body." Make sure you *do* take that oh-so-important music bath every single day. If you're like me you have tons of music in your collection from A to Z. Don't just play it in the background, though. Take time from each day to really sit down and *listen* to the music. Study it carefully and apply what you learn to your own work.

Will this affect your appreciation of your favorite tunes? I doubt it. You will gain a keen awareness of music composition and an even greater respect for other artists. For this to be a truly useful tool, you must scrutinize every note, every phrase. First ask yourself why and apply these answers to your own work: Why that progression? Why that instrument? Why a counter melody there? Why slapback echo here? Next, ask yourself how the composer used a certain technique, instrument, or phrase. Make sure you recognize what is art (why) and what is craft (how). Listen to the same piece repeatedly until you've exhausted every possibility; then put it away and don't listen again for a few weeks. Come back to it with fresh ears and see if you hear or feel anything new.

If you record music, first listen to the music and then concentrate on the recording techniques. Personally, I don't make the distinction between composing music and recording it. The two share a synergistic relationship. I feel composing and recording are integrated, not mutually exclusive. I can't write without hearing how the final version will sound.

IMITATE OTHER COMPOSERS BY WRITING IN THEIR STYLE

The easiest way to grow as an artist is to get inside another composer's head, first, by listening and second, through imitation. Many musicians learn by copying their favorite songs. While this is useful toward improving your *mechanical* skills, imitation is critical to improving your *composition* skills. Pick artists you admire and compose *in their style*. Don't just copy their songs. You must try to write a piece *as if you were* the artist. To imitate without directly copying is harder than it sounds. You should hear the influence, and the process should reveal both positive and negative aspects of your musical prowess. This exercise will help you learn from the masters first by listening, second by playing, and last through imitation. Then let go and use what you've learned to discover your own music. This won't happen overnight, but your critical study will pay off in time.

TRY OTHER STYLES AND FORMS OF COMPOSITION THAT YOU USUALLY IGNORE

OK, so you're a rocker. Nothing wrong with that. But have you considered composing for string quartet? No matter what your level of talent is, try this: Choose a simple tune like *Row Row Row Your Boat* and try to write multiple versions in various styles like hip hop, jazz, orchestral, new age, etc.

Choosing a simple, familiar tune means not having to worry about the melody. You are free to experiment with structure, chords, counter melodies, and so forth. Just because you don't like or aren't comfortable in a particular musical genre doesn't mean you shouldn't give it a whirl. Also, try playing an instrument you don't normally play. If you play keys, take up guitar. You'll gain useful, new perspectives.

Creativity means looking outside the boundaries. Don't stay tied to a single way of doing things. Try many different approaches. You'll find the solution if you open up your mind to all the infinite possibilities. Leaving your comfort zone is the doorway to your best work. You will find the true creativity within. Do you really want to risk shutting out this world and stifling your musical talent?

PLAY YOUR PIECES FOR FRIENDS AND ASSOCIATES AND ASK FOR CRITICISM

Find someone whose opinion you trust and ask for his help and candid, constructive ideas. You don't need a judge—you need help! Try to find someone you don't share a deeply *personal* relationship with. Because they don't want to upset you, many people will not be brutally honest. Let your music play all the way through and then ask open-ended, leading questions. Don't apologize for it and don't interrupt while it plays. Next, play the track again and analyze it in detail. Once you get opinions and advice, go back to the drawing board and put all you've learned to work and repeat the process again.

SEEK ADVICE FROM A RECOGNIZED EXPERT

Objective opinions, constructive criticism, and useful suggestions from a mentor will really open your eyes and give you insight into your work. Once again you are looking for constructive criticism. "That's good" just isn't what you need. You want *specific* information about how to make your work better and stronger. And you want to learn from your mistakes. Take advantage of expert knowledge and benefit from professional, objective expertise.

There are many ways to get this valuable information. You might try instructors at your local college or university. Maybe there's an area musician you admire who might evaluate your work. A songwriter's group might be another alternative. Consider sending your tape for review in magazines. You should *never* pay an agent, lawyer, or record company (or anyone for that matter) who *claims* to get your music published/recorded/etc. in exchange for your paying a substantial fee. However, I know it is useful to have a professional review your work and make useful suggestions. This professional would have no claims on your music or a vested interest beyond a desire to share his or her expertise with you. This kind of third-party opinion could save you mistakes you might unknowingly make. I equate this to having an accountant prepare your taxes. Sure you can do it yourself, but you may benefit from a professional's experience, and that is almost always worth the price you pay for the services.

PRODUCE YOUR DEMO AND SEND IT INTO THE MARKET

Once you've followed the above steps diligently, you will be ready to put together your best demo of your music and start promoting. This is the real test of your skills. Don't fret about rejection, use it to your advantage and make your work stronger.

EVALUATE YOUR PAST WORK

Don't let your old music fade away. Dust it off and give it a critical listen. Use this distance from your work to improve your past, present, and future music. I once discovered an old song on a long-forgotten tape, reworked, re-recorded, and turned it into a sale. Once you've let music sit for some time, the warts really stick out. Most of what you find will be coal. But once in a while, you'll uncover a gem.

Jingle Lyrics

Though the sung jingle that's *not* a popular song is rare, there may still be some opportunities to craft lyrics to accompany your music. For commercials, the lyrics may come from the ad agency; other times you may need to develop them. For jingles, try getting the client's promotional material—for example, brochures, advertisements, and so forth—and cull them for lyrical ideas.

For a local bank's jingle, I started with their slogan: "Proud to be a part of this great community." I also listened to their current jingle-less ads for other ideas they like to explore and grabbed some promotional material by simply visiting a branch. Here's what I came up with:

Verse:
We understand that life
Can sometimes throw a curve
You work to give your family
The comforts they deserve

Chorus:
At the (name of the bank)
We care about your every need
And we're proud to be a part
Of this great community

Verse 2:
From homes to cars and college
For business large and small
For everything in banking
(Name of the bank) has it all

(Repeat chorus)

Tag:
The name of the bank in name of town.

This format—verse-chorus-verse-chorus-tag—provides a lot of flexibility for developing different ads. The spot could be mostly narration and then close with the chorus-tag. The verses could be donuts for voice-over, leaving the choruses intact. Or the spot could be all VO with just the tag.

Overcoming Lyrical Writer's Block

For me, taking my wild ramblings and forcing them into a structure is one way to reach lyrical ideas. If you first write down what comes into your mind and then whittle, twist, and squeeze the words into a specific form, you will arrive at a new thought altogether. Try these two poetic forms: haiku and triolet.

HAIKU

Start writing some haiku. You remember, don't you? Three-line poems consisting of five syllables, seven syllables, and then five again. The economy of words creates a focused abstraction. And the rhythm of the words is instantly musical.

> *It's five seven five*
> *That's all you really need know*
> *As a path to use*

> *Stimulate your mind*
> *Look beyond the obvious*
> *Move along the road*

> *Creativity*
> *Discover your inner thoughts*
> *Unleash it right now*

Haiku is also an ideal format for promotional copy. The word rhythm makes the ideas flow. Load your words with benefits and format as haiku for maximum impact.

> *Stop paying too much.*
> *Get music you can afford.*
> *Call right now to save.*

TRIOLET

Another approach is the triolet poem form. This is an eight-line poem where the first line repeats as the fourth and seventh lines and the second line repeats as the eighth line. This form lets you tie otherwise different thoughts together into a more cohesive whole. And though the results may be as abstract as haiku, the activity should stimulate your thinking.

A place of sanctuary isolated and free
And the winds of change are cold
I couldn't live with their hate for love
A place of sanctuary isolated and free
I hate it when they try to possess me
It's only outside that our paths cross
A place of sanctuary isolated and free
And the winds of change are cold

And this leads to one conclusion
The winds of change are cold
They sting and scar our souls for life
And this leads to one conclusion
How cruel and inconsiderate they are
If only compassion was easier to afford
And this leads to one conclusion
The winds of change are cold

Chip McCarthy of Accentual Audio Productions shared this clever tip in my *Moneymaking Music Tip of the Week* email newsletter: "I get some of my best ideas for hooks and lyrics from ... fortune cookies! For example: 'Carve your name on your heart and not on marble.'"

While these exercises may not yield specific lyrics for you, they may produce something useful or, at the very least, open up your mind to possibilities.

Favorite Scores for Study

I felt it would be instructive to choose and comment on a few representative scores from the past century of film music. You'll learn more about the art and craft of media music by grabbing these DVDs and studying the music on them than by reading some history stuffed with old names and dates. This is by far an incomplete list, but it does represent a decent introduction to what's been done before so you can use what you learn to make your musical compositions better.

Many commercial DVDs carry bonus features that include documentaries on the film's music, including interviews with the composers. These are worth additional study as you augment your education.

OPENING TITLES/SHOW THEME

These musical sequences act as the overture for the film or TV show. The style as expressed in the instrumentation, themes, and motifs should prepare the audience for what they are about to see. These musical statements set the mood. Films such as *North by Northwest* (Bernard Herrmann) and

Halloween (John Carpenter) exemplify these concepts well. *NBNW* in particular lets you choose just the score as an audio track while watching the DVD. This disc alone will teach you more about writing for dramatic film than any other. Listen to how Herrmann revisits the main title theme in unique ways as the film progresses to its climax. Also of note, Herrmann was a master orchestrator; the colors he creates with his instrument choices are indeed worth studying.

MOTIF AND LEIT MOTIF

Motifs are reoccurring musical elements meant to enhance specific dramatic moments. One of the most infamous motifs is the shark's theme from *Jaws* (John Williams). I remember how frightening those two cello notes were when I first saw the movie as a kid. Leit motif differs only in that it applies to a specific character, such as *Lara's Theme* from *Dr. Zhivago* (Maurice Jarre) or the repeating trumpet figure from *Patton* (Jerry Goldsmith). These simple thematic elements can be very evocative and effective.

POV

Music can also help support a media presentation's point of view. For example, *Badlands* prominently features Carl Orff's mallet music for children. It's not children's music, *per se*, but rather music meant to teach children how to make music. This profound musical choice complements and reflects the main character's naiveté. Contrast that film to the simple, childlike approach taken for *To Kill a Mockingbird* (Elmer Bernstein).

BUILDING TENSION AND FORESHADOWING

Music plays an important role during this common dramatic device. *Psycho* (Bernard Herrmann) provides a strong example. After the character who has stolen money is confronted by a police officer for a minor traffic violation, she drives away with building paranoia about her deed. Play this scene without its soundtrack, and you'll see the intercutting of three shots: a CU of Janet Leigh's character, her POV out the car windshield, and her POV from the rear-view mirror as she is followed by the police car. Nothing actually happens in the scene. Now crank up the music and witness how Herrmann's score creates a sense of uneasiness, dread, and other strong emotions. Something is going to happen to this woman, and Mr. Hitchcock can thank Bennie for taking the audience there.

DIEGETIC TO NONDIEGETIC AND BACK

Amadeus (Mozart/Sir Neville Marriner) uses Mozart's music both as source music and dramatic underscore. While the entire movie moves back and forth with this technique, the sequence near the movie's end is especially effective. As Mozart dictates his *Requiem* to Salieri, we hear the music in his head (diegetic) as if the orchestra were in his bedroom. After fully orchestrating the piece, Mozart asks to see the score. As he begins to review what Salieri wrote down, the scene cuts away to Mozart's wife desperately trying to get back to her husband by carriage. The exact same music as heard before now transforms to dramatic underscore (nondiegetic) to the scene. I still get chills every time I hear it!

MUSIC AS SOUND EFFECT

Often music serves double-duty by being not only the score, but also used as sound design and sound effects. You often hear this in commercials where the line between score and effect is blurred. Two films employ this technique well. Near the end of *Terminator 2* (Brad Fiedel), after the T-1000 has been frozen and blown apart, the heat generated from the factory begins to bring the terminator back together. Listen carefully, and you'll notice that the atonal, pure sound design of the music takes the place of most of the sound effects in this sequence.

During the infamous shower sequence in *Psycho* (Bernard Herrmann), the shrieking violins provide a unique tonal color that sounds like a cross between screaming and bird cries. Using the strings this way makes the scene even more unnerving and horrible.

OFFBEAT, ATONAL MUSIC

Personally, I find fewer examples of composers taking unusual approaches with their scores. Today, there are either too many pop songs or big orchestral scores. Thankfully, a few composers have left some legacies. *Planet of the Apes* (Jerry Goldsmith) has a wonderful interlude during the first part of the film where the three astronauts cross the desert looking for life. There is a great deal of percussion, piano stabs, and atonal horn parts that bring an eerie and otherworldly feel to the sequence. And the percussion-driven fight sequences from Tan Dun on *Crouching Tiger, Hidden Dragon* interspersed with the plaintive cello melody are well worth further examination.

ELECTRONIC MUSIC

Electronic synthesizers and samplers are well used on many scores. Sometimes, they replace traditional instruments or bring new sounds and colors to the soundtrack. *Witness* (Maurice Jarre) has a unique twist, though. The music was scored and orchestrated in a traditional manner but realized entirely by electronic instruments. The film's director, Peter Weir, wanted something slightly askew, and replacing the orchestra with electronic simulations gave him the effect he wanted.

Listen carefully to the *Building the Barn* sequence in the movie. It's a beautiful musical moment that, to many untrained ears, really sounds like an orchestra. It's just a room of synths, giving the impression that something isn't quite right. Compare this to the version on the *Jarre by Jarre Films Themes of Maurice Jarre* audio CD, which features the same music played by a full orchestra.

TV MUSIC

In the past, TV movies and mini-series had big budgets that allowed for film-like scoring; however, rarely did an episodic show have that luxury. It was common practice to recycle themes for TV because there simply wasn't the budget to score individual episodes. Instead, composers put together various packages that could be used repeatedly at appropriate moments. Shows like *Mission Impossible*, *Wild Wild West*, and the original *Star Trek* stand out as examples of this methodology. The Vulcan neck pinch theme elicits a chuckle from me every time I hear it!

Then came *Miami Vice*. This show single-handedly revolutionized TV music. Michael Mann, the series producer, not only convinced big name talent to let him license their popular songs for the show, but he hired the capable Jan Hammer to compose and record an original score every week. Working from his own project studio, Hammer wrote as much as 40 minutes of original music per episode. The technological shift in the musical industry, driven by MIDI and new, cheaper recording equipment, made it possible. Today, many composers work on TV shows following the model of *Miami Vice*. For example, Mark Snow composed for the *X-Files* every week from his home-based studio. While many of these scores are electronics driven, some use hybrid techniques employing ensembles and even small orchestras.

Try This at Home

To further study how music can change the meaning of a visual sequence, grab a piece of video and then find five different music pieces. Play the video and switch between the music tracks to see how the meaning changes. Try it with some family and friends and then discuss each person's response to the different musical choices. People associate music with their own experiences. One particular piece may evoke positive emotions in one person, while the exact same piece holds only negative feelings for another. This fact can make scoring effectively difficult for composers. However, understanding the emotions of scoring is a critical step toward making your work better.

Getting Approval

As you complete rough compositions, play them for the client to make sure you are meeting their needs. Don't play mixes that are too rough, as many people don't have the vision-to-music/audio knowledge to make the necessary leap of faith to the finished score. Everything you play should be reasonably fleshed out and close to the final idea.

You may play these attempts in person at your studio or at the client's office. More often, you will email (or FTP) your files in some way, such as an MP3, WAV/AIFF, or even a video file. Don't skimp on quality here; there's no sense sending a garbled lo-fi encoded file to save upload/download time.

For some video projects, I've composed multiple variations for the same scene or sequence. In the past, I've provided separate versions, but that makes it difficult to do A/B comparisons. Instead, use the "alternate" audio tracks on a DVD. Depending on your DAW/NLE, render the video to the DVD format (MPEG-2) and then render the individual music mixes separately.

Use a DVD authoring program (such as Sony DVD-Architect) to assign the multiple audio tracks, up to eight, to play with the DVD. Burn the DVD and give it to the client. Now they can watch the video and quickly switch audio tracks using their DVD remote. You could even place 5.1 mixes and stereo mixes on the same disc.

The Approval Process

When you present your music, try to listen along with the director or creative team and make this review session a positive and constructive experience. Preface the playback by suggesting that they let go of expectations and self-imposed limitations and just listen to the music as it is all the way through. After this first hearing, listen again and start the conversation, paying closer attention to specifics. Start generally, then get more specific. Urge them to remember that constructive criticism benefits both of you and makes for a better project.

The client may make suggestions; listen carefully to what he or she says. If you've been following the strategies detailed in this chapter, revisions should be insignificant—minor tweaks here and there. If there is a demand for wholesale changes, then you didn't do your homework. Getting concrete answers during the spotting session will prevent misunderstandings at this stage. Playing rough versions throughout the scoring process and soliciting feedback will also make the approval process go smoother. If the music completely fails their objective, then work together to find the right solutions.

Don't forget that the client must be happy. You need to be an agreeable sort and willing to make changes that you may not agree with. Feel free to make your case, but don't come off as difficult to work with. In instances where you feel you have a better solution, but the client still insists on changes, do A/B versions: A is their idea, B is yours. Play them both and let the client choose. Live with the vote, though.

Delivering the Score

Finally, the clients signs off on the project, and all you need to do is deliver the master. You may simply send a stereo or 5.1 final mix or any number of variations. You may deliver multitrack stems comprising submixes of instrument combinations—drums, rhythm instruments, vocals, and so forth. Stems allow the re-recording mixer to adjust the relative balance of your music mix to better fit in the overall soundtrack. These stems may be as few as 8 tracks or as complex as 24+ tracks. Use care to make sure that stems are consistent from cue to cue. For example, have the drums on tracks 1 and 2, bass on 3, keyboard on 4 and 5, and so on.

Physical formats vary widely from audio CD and CD-ROMS of digital files to hard discs containing all the project files saved as a Pro Tools session. Make sure you and your client on are the right format, sample rate, and bit depth page. Find out specifically what the client needs before delivering the master.

Now all that's left for you to do is to collect the check and move on to your next project.

CHAPTER 4

Building Your Project Studio

"Your work is to discover your work and then with all your heart to give yourself to it."—Buddha

The Gear You Need for Success

Rummaging through some boxes recently, I excavated a picture of my studio circa the early 90s. My room was stuffed with gear—keyboards of all shapes and sizes, drum machines, effects, mixers, analog recorders, speakers, amps, instruments, and dozens of other gadgets all connected with a spaghetti mess of audio, MIDI, and power cables. Fast forward to the present, and you'll find only a couple of computers, a few well-chosen pieces of outboard gear, and some monitors. It may not look as impressive, but I can accomplish far more inside my current box than I ever could with a roomful of gear a dozen years or so ago.

Unequivocally, today is a great time to be a composer because the technology available allows you to craft amazingly complex and high-quality finished music with only a smattering of equipment. The startling emergence of home project studios, built primarily around computers, makes composing, playing, recording, mixing, and delivering your musical scores and jingles oh-so-easy.

However, few subjects elicit such diverse opinions as talk about gear does among musicians. We are passionate about gear. We defend *our* choices and often take great pleasure mocking the selections others have made. My favorite magazine, *Electronic Musician* (www.emusician.com) always has at least 20 pages of product reviews in every issue. Every month, 120+ page catalogs arrive from equipment suppliers such as American Musical Supply (www.americanmusical.com) chock full of gear—hardware, software, soundware, and every little thing in between. There's no doubt: Musicians have G.A.S. (Gear Acquisition Syndrome) really bad. While some of us can fight off the temptation, the rest of us succumb to its allure. When you are living off the proceeds your music generates, gear can be an expensive habit.

Gear, glorious gear! Nothing gets our collective hearts racing faster than the latest, greatest musical gizmo. We are convinced that our music will be better when we buy fill-in-the-blank, and so the quickest route to new sound Nirvana is to buy gear. Like the Sirens of Greek mythology, gear calls to us with its sweet, dulcet promise of musical inspiration. And if you are not cautious, you, too, will fall prey to G.A.S.'s Siren song. I used to have G.A.S. but have recovered (mostly!) from its destructive forces. I'm wary of anything new and instead meticulously follow a strategy before considering and buying equipment for my music business. More on this subject below.

What you need to do is assemble a personal project studio that has the capability to make, record, mix, master, and deliver high-quality digital finished music tracks. Though sometimes you may record in other studios and employ other players (e.g., an orchestra), the majority of your work you will do yourself. You will wear all the hats—composer, arranger, orchestrator, player, engineer, mixer, and so forth—and will need a gear list and environment conducive to getting all this done. To increase your earnings and keep your prices competitive, try to do everything yourself. The more you outsource, the less you make on a given gig. Match your equipment to your skills and then make prudent purchases that let you handle almost anything that comes your way. This will keep your operating costs (called overhead) low, which is a key to running a profitable music business, not a money pit.

Here's an important caveat: *You do not need everything in place before pursuing work.* Too many people stall their career with the fear that they don't have all the right gear. You can make money using a few basics. Pay attention to the projects and what your clients demand. Use your creativity to compose using what you have at hand, not what you wish you had (justified or not). You can and should add to your equipment as circumstances and resources allow. But *please* don't let G.A.S. or other feelings of inadequacy interfere with your initial career launch.

A single MIDI keyboard isn't enough to compete successfully in this area anymore. Most analog recording equipment, such as cassette-based recorders, won't cut it either. Computer-based sound creation, recording/mixing, and delivery are the standard. You'd better embrace it. Chances are that you already have some equipment, even a fully stocked project studio, ready to do your work. Skim the first half of this chapter anyway to see where you might be lacking and to gain a clear strategy for future purposes. If you are starting out or your gear list is painfully small, then study the following information scrupulously. Always remember that you can rent equipment or use another studio when your personal capabilities fall short.

Being able to play some keyboard greatly improves your chances at working in this field. While you don't need to be a piano protégé, you won't get by with the one-finger approach either. Playing other instruments besides keys gives you a distinct advantage, though. You can always find a partner or use outside players to fill in gaps in your skills.

I call my particular approach to scoring an electro-acoustic hybrid. My sound palette combines samples, synthetic textures, and real instruments that I play myself (guitars, bass, and percussion) and that I get from loops. When my clients need rock, jazz, new age, hip hop, world, exotic, or out there, I'm ready to go. I can do some rather convincing orchestral stuff, too.

Avoid Musical Gear Buying Mistakes

Virtually all of us have bought equipment that we really didn't need or didn't work the way we expected. We all make mistakes. You were probably caught up in the moment and didn't fully evaluate your needs or follow some basic purchasing guidelines. You just said, "Charge it!" And now your dirty little secret gathers dust in a back closet (or fails to solicit any bids on e-Bay).

Before you rush out to your local gear palace and part with your hard-earned cash, take a step back. Carefully evaluate your situation and follow this four-step process. You will save both money and the regret that comes from making bad music equipment purchasing decisions.

DEVELOP A GAME PLAN

Take a few minutes to objectively examine your situation. Draft a plan that details what it is you want to do and what you need equipment-wise to accomplish those goals. Planning also protects you from falling prey to G.A.S. and helps you make better equipment choices and purchases. Build some flexibility into your plan that lets you adapt to changing circumstances. Don't get caught spending a gazillion dollars soundproofing your studio only to find you have to move in a month.

As you choose the path for your music business, bring along only those essential items that will let you travel that path easily. As experienced world travelers always say: Pack lightly. Why burden yourself, or your bank account, with excessive musical stuff you don't/won't need? Instead, pare your needs down to the bone. Quit fretting about stuff you don't have and start focusing on what you can do with the gear you already own (or with a few carefully chosen additional items).

There are additional benefits to this approach. You'll have less equipment to learn and maintain. You'll be able to master a few tools and focus on being more creative with them. Some of the greatest music was written with quill pen and parchment. Do you feel Mozart would have composed better music if he'd had a gel roller pen or a computer instead?

Ask and answer these questions: What do you do (or what do you want to do)? What equipment do you already have that lets you do what you do? Are there any gaps in your gear list? If no, stop. You're done! If yes, what gear do you *really* need right now? And now for the biggie. Ask and answer this final question before going on: Why do you need that new piece(s) of musical gear?

Good answers to this question include: Your gear is broken and needs replacing, the new gear will help you make more money, or clients are demanding an upgrade that you don't currently offer (5.1 surround, for instance). Let this appraisal be based on fact, not emotion. Use your logical mind to reduce or maybe even avoid impulsive decisions altogether.

DO YOUR HOMEWORK

Convinced yourself that you jus-gotta-hav-da-next-big-thang? Start to research the gear possibilities. First, check the music magazines by looking at ads and then reviews. Second, check the Internet for information and reviews. Harmony-Central (www.harmony-central.com) is a good starting place, as are the myriad Internet forums available. For example, equipment queries are common threads on the Acid, Sound Forge, and Vegas forums I co-host on DMN-Digital Media Net (www.dmnforums.com).

Third, ask your peers what equipment they use and why. Specifically target other people who are doing what you do or plan to do. That's why I asked the all-important gear question of the people interviewed for this book.

Fourth, equipment manufacturers' Web sites can be helpful for comparing features but tend to be useless for the unbiased opinions. Last, stop by your local gear palace and give the gear a test-drive. Don't pull out the card yet; you're still kicking tires at this point. Leave the card at home if the ephemeral moment fills you with trepidation. You may be able to rent the gear and take it back to your studio for a more rigorous workout. On high-priced items, the minute rental fee can be money well spent.

Be reasonably wary of untested technology or trendy items. It's wiser to choose either timeless gear or technology with a clear upgrade path. Quality instruments, mics, and other fundamental components are usually worth their extra investment. Software-based tools offer the flexibility of upgrades and expansion, while many synths have soundware you can purchase to expand your sonic palette easily.

Always compare price to features—the features *you* need. There are often less expensive alternatives to the top-of-the-line that still have up to 75% of the same feature set. In many cases, this inexpensive alternative will suffice for your needs. And if your research didn't reveal these alternatives, you didn't look hard enough

The Web makes comparing prices a snap. Don't forget to include shipping in the equation when evaluating online prices. Also, depending on the retailer and state in which you live, you may save sales tax when you shop online. Still, buying locally means you get local service when there are problems. That fact may make paying a little more worth it.

Two more price-shopping tips. One, consider buying used from local retailers or e-Bay. Two, look for closeout prices right before or after the NAMM shows in January and July. Dealers often have an incentive to close out the old line to make room for all the new stuff. Last year's merchandise still does what it always did. It might not be the latest and greatest, but if it gets the job done and still allows you to sell more music, it's worth the price.

SET WHEN AND HOW

Needs? Check. Research? Check. Now you must plan the acquisition specifics. I've talked with many people about this issue, and we all agree that having a detailed action plan of what to get, when, and how reduces buyer's remorse significantly.

When the equipment you're considering allows you to make some money directly through its use, figure out how much you will charge for using it (or how you will recover its cost). Calculating the payback eliminates some of the guesswork from your purchasing timeline. If you are adding to your general equipment list, you will need to prioritize which pieces you will buy now and which must wait.

The "when" purchasing decision is almost always driven by the how you are going to pay for it answer. Cash is always the ideal way to control your spending. If you only use money you already have, you won't go over budget or into debt. Start a rainy day fund and set aside 5–10% of what you earn from your music and earmark it for new purchases. When you've saved enough cash, buy what you need. Alternately, have a yard/garage sale. Scour your home for stuff you no longer need or want. Price your things at about 10 to 15% of their original purchase price, take out an ad in your local paper, make a few signs, and spend a Saturday earning some easy money. If you prefer, e-Bay some items instead. Use the proceeds to finance the gear you need.

Personally, I often pitch clients on ideas that will pay enough money to buy new gear. I rarely buy any large-ticket items unless I can pay for them quickly through a single project. This method helps keep the gear lust at bay and also helps ensure you don't spend money on things you might not need (or never use).

Don't finance your purchases through high-interest credit card debt. However, there are alternatives such as the "same-as-cash" deals offered by many companies. This is essentially an interest-free payment plan. You order the product for something akin to three payments of equal amounts. The company takes your credit card number and charges you equal installments spread over time, usually once a month for three months. They bill you the same day each month until the amount is paid in full. Combine this technique with the grace period on your card, and you get gear or supplies today and easily pay for them over time. You also won't incur finance charges or inter-est, provided you pay the balance each month. Similarly, some major retailers, such as Best Buy and Circuit City, regularly promote great financing deals on computers, such as no interest for up to 24 months. This way you get a new box for well under $100 a month with *no* finance charges, provided you pay it in full in 24 months.

You might try leasing gear in certain circumstances. However, unless it is a major capital pur-chase, not many equipment dealers will set up lease terms for you. Also, consider renting instead of buying. For example, short-term renting lets me use high-end, high-quality gear at a small price. I've had to rent mixdown decks to accommodate client demands; there was no reason for me to own it. I then charge back the rental fee to the client. Find a local rental house and see what they have available. That way, when you need a fancy mic, preamp, or other cool gear, you can get what you need, use it, and pay a smaller rental charge—always significantly lower than buying and maintaining the gear yourself.

DECIDE TO BUY... OR NOT

This diligence pays off because now you know what is best for your particular enterprise. If it's a go, grab what you need and move on to the next step in your plan. It's also acceptable to pass this time around and move on without opening your wallet. Every time you contemplate a new equipment purchase, ask yourself those questions from step one. *Only* after you've answered them should you consider going shopping.

One final tip: If your decision means buying the new musical gizmo, take another 48 hours to mull it over anyway. If you're still hot after two days, your decision is sound. If you've cooled a little, perhaps you should reconsider.

Essential Items for Every Studio

While I advocate trying to get the most bang for your buck with every equipment purchase, there are a few areas where you shouldn't cut corners. It is worth the extra expense to invest in these few key components.

FRONT-END

If you will be recording numerous acoustic performances (instruments and voice), you need a decent collection of quality mics and mic preamps. Consider buying both large and small diaphragm condenser mics and a few dynamics along with both tube-based and solid state preamps.

The cheap soundcard that came with your computer simply won't do for professional work, either. Purchase a high-quality soundcard with solid A-D converters (analog to digital). There are both internal (PCI, Cardbus) and external (USB, Firewire) choices. Choose the soundcard that supports the number of inputs and outputs you need. For example, there must be six outputs for surround sound. Also, make sure your DAW/NLE can talk to the soundcard effectively.

INSIDE THE BOX

Not only do you need sound-producing software, you also need sound-shaping tools to make your compositions and final mixes sound their best. Many DAWs/NLEs include these effects, and while most included options are adequate, there are many far better tools from third-party vendors. You need effects in these categories:

▶ Tonal (equalization or EQ)

▶ Space/Time (reverb, delay)

▶ Modulation (phasing, flanging, chorusing)

▶ Dynamics (compression, de-essing)

▶ Pitch (bend and to fix out-of-tune performances)

▶ Timbre altering (distortion, lo-fi)

▶ Noise reduction (gates, audio restoration)

I consider EQ and dynamics processing to be the most useful and necessary tools. Don't skimp here. Whether you buy hardware- or software-based versions (or both), these will be your go-to tools for a lot of your recording and mixing chores. You won't ever regret your purchase of a compressor (or more). You simply can't get a modern rhythm section sounding right without one. They are, by far, the most useful special effects devices you can own. I prefer having at least two versions of these tools:

▶ EQ(s) and compressor(s) that work but don't color the sound

▶ EQ(s) and compressors(s) that have a signature sound all their own

BACK-END
The speakers you use to monitor your music recording and mixing must accurately reflect the finished sound. It's crucial to have a monitor system that has a flat, extended frequency response so that your mixes translate well outside your studio. Whether you choose passive speakers with a separate amplifier or powered speakers (active monitors), they must be accurate. Be careful if you elect smaller speakers because they may not reproduce the bass sufficiently. Make sure you check the bass content on bigger, fuller-range systems. Contrarily, 2.1 systems (stereo with a subwoofer) can exaggerate the bass. What sounds big in the studio may sound thin on a standard stereo system because there really was no bass, just the sub kicking air around your room.

Until you really know what you are doing, it pays to check your mixes on a variety of systems Besides the main monitors, check on as many other systems as you can—car, boom box, a typical home system, and even an MP3 player with headphones. You probably have most of these already. It might surprise you how different a track can sound. Always check mono compatibility and stereo downmix if working with 5.1 surround, too.

I use my main monitors, double-check on the LX-4 surround system (in stereo), take mixes to my car, friends/family houses, school, and more. I've been known to listen to mixes at the local electronics superstore where I can put my CD in 10–12 different units, taking notes the whole time. Sure, it takes a little more time to make sure your soundtrack works on many different systems, but it's worth it. After all, it is *your* name on the credits!

POWER CONDITIONER

If you've made a substantial investment in your gear, don't let it get ruined by common electricity hazards such as voltage fluctuations, surges, and line noise. You want a very high-quality voltage regulator, surge suppresser, line stabilizer, noise-filtering, RFI-reducing, uninterruptible power supply with battery backup. Protect yourself... or suffer the consequences.

Your Successful Studio

My project studio has undergone tremendous changes through the years—from dozens of individual hardware pieces to almost completely software-based. Ironically, as the amount of physical gear minimizes, the quality of my output, both technically and compositionally continues to go up. While I still record guitars, percussion, and vocals using mics with my isolation booth, the majority of my work stays "in the box" (inside the computer).

The following information provides insight into the relatively simple, effective, workable, and profitable project studio that I use for audio production, scoring soundtracks and jingles, and even both audio and video post-production. You may have a more extensive setup; nothing wrong with that. You may be getting by with less; good for you. For those starting out, notice the few key pieces (computer, music composition software, and sound-making devices, acoustic and electronic) that you must have.

HARDWARE

▶ Sony P4 with DVD/CD-writer. This is my primary music, sound, and video production tool. It has gobs of RAM, a dual head video card to drive two 17" monitors, and both internal and external hard drives for holding media.

▶ Universal Audio UAD-1 DSP card and plug-ins (I can't live without Nigel for guitar re-amping and the wonderful emulations of the LA-2A and Fairchild compressors and the go-to Pultec EQ). This card is in the main computer along with its VST/DX plug-ins.

▶ An old PIII that I use for business tasks: Writing, bookkeeping, Web site maintenance, email, CD burning, printing (labels, promotional materials, products for sale, etc.), and so forth.

▶ Sony P4 laptop for use on the road (and increasingly in the studio, too). This box mirrors the primary media creation computer; it has the same software.

▶ Contour Design ShuttlePRO V2 used for software navigation with its 15 fully programmable buttons and a jog/shuttle wheel that greatly speeds up many music and video editing tasks.

▶ PreSonus Firepod audio interface with eight mic/line inputs and eight outputs, enough to drive two separate monitor systems (one stereo, the other 5.1 surround).

▶ ADS Pyro A/V link with Panasonic broadcast monitor (TV). This converts digital video (DV) from the computer into an analog signal that displays on the external video monitor. I can watch video on a bigger screen (positioned between my stereo monitors) while I compose and mix.

▶ Johnson J-station guitar/bass amp modeling and effects. I can dial up so many sounds that I haven't used a physical amp in over a decade (I re-amp with UAD's Nigel and iZotope's Trash, too).

▶ Line 6 DL4 delay stompbox for creating guitar loops.

▶ M-Audio Oxygen 8 USB-based MIDI keyboard controller for getting MIDI notes into the computer. I also take this on the road with my laptop for remote composition and client presentations.

▶ Event 20/20 monitor speakers with Hafler amp for checking mixes.

▶ M-Audio LX-4 5.1 self-powered surround monitor system.

▶ Marshall MXL-2003, MXL-2001, MXL-990, and D.R.K. mics along with Shure SM57 and Audio-Technica 831b lavaliere (for acoustic guitar).

▶ Stands, shock mounts, cables, and such.

▶ Various headphones.

SOFTWARE

▶ Sony Acid Pro 5.0, Sony CD Architect 5.2, Sony DVD Architect 3.0, Sony Sound Forge 8.0, and Sony Vegas 6.0.

▶ Nero 6 for data CD/DVD burning.

▶ Ulead DVD Workshop 2 for DVD authoring.

▶ Propellerhead's Reason 2.5 "virtual" rack of software synths, samplers, and drums.

▶ Various soft-synths from Native Instruments and Ultimate Sound Bank.

▶ iZotope Ozone 3, Trash, Spectron, and Vinyl.

▶ RBC Voice Tweaker (automatic pitch tuners).

▶ T-racks mastering software.

▶ Dozens of DirectX and VST effects plug-ins and VST synths (freeware, shareware, and purchased).

▶ A rather large collection of Loops for Acid sample CDs (from Sony, Hark Productions, Cycling 74, QUp Arts, and others).

MUSICAL INSTRUMENTS

▶ Ibanez electric guitars (Strat and 335 copies).

▶ Aria six-string acoustic guitar.

▶ Casio CZ-101 (it was my first synth, so I keep it around for sentimental reasons).

▶ Dozens of ethnic/world percussion instruments (drums, shakers, etc.).

▶ Flutes, recorder, unusual stringed instruments, and other noisemakers.

▶ My voice.

Double Your Computer/Double Your Productivity

Your computer serves as a major component of your music business. You use it for email, Web surfing, composing, recording, and otherwise managing your career. If you're like me, that computer is also a little production factory—burning CDs and DVDs, printing promotional material, mailing labels, and checks, and generally helping you get done what needs to happen. In short, your computer helps you do more in less time.

Rely on your computer to help keep you organized. Store all the information you need just a few mouse clicks away. Keep contact information for your clients, prospects, media, and more. Track your financials. Use it to stay in contact with fans via email and the Web. Your computer often becomes the indispensable "staff" you can't do without.

Have you ever thought about having more computers? Well, I did, and at first I felt it was rather decadent to have more than one gracing my office. Instead, expanding my computing power turned out to be one of the best decisions I ever made. Investing in a second and third computer has increased my productivity dramatically.

From a financial standpoint, the extra expense was quickly recouped. Before I spent a dime, I tallied my hours wasted waiting for my single computer to finish what I'd assigned. I multiplied those hours by my hourly rate and realized that in about a month, I'd get enough additional work done to justify the new purchase. I was right… and then some!

I've reserved the second powerful computer as my central production workhorse. I use it for composing, music and sound recording, mastering, video editing, and CD and DVD production. It only has the software needed for those tasks, with everything else happily jettisoned. This computer isn't even connected to the Web. A primary benefit to the dedicated production computer is that you can optimize it for the work you do. I've tweaked my box so that the programs I use run very well. I suffer fewer crashes and virtually no data loss.

I've relegated my original computer to Internet duties, Web site maintenance, writing, book-keeping, and a few other business chores. The third computer, a laptop, serves as my office away from the studio with a combination of media creation tools and business productivity applications. Firewire- and USB-based hard drives enable moving project data between workstations to be a snap, too.

In the past, when rendering a video project, burning a CD, or downloading a file, I could do little else. This scenario was a real time waster. Now I can be working at one computer while the other chugs away in the background. Typically, I might work on a music project on one, burn DVDs/CDs on the other, and even press the third into service at times. If one computer is tied up video rendering, I can still get my email and surf the Web using another.

Spaced Out

You also need an area in which to set up your equipment, compose, record, and mix. One additional benefit of having fewer component parts is that your need for space to hold it all is significantly less. Working from your own home is not quite the radical idea it once was. There are great tax, environmental, and lifestyle benefits to a home-based studio. It comes with greater flexibility, letting you work when you are at your best. Personally, I'm sluggish in the morning, turbo-charged from one to eight, and zonked by ten. After being home based for 15+ years, I can truly attest that there will be more time for work or play, less stress, and far more comfortable surroundings. I would find it very hard to give up my 10-second commute.

Consider working from home during the initial phases of your commercial music business. The advantages mentioned above and the money you save can really make the difference when first starting out. Of course, you'll need to check zoning and with your landlord (if applicable) before you work at home, but we'll discuss that later.

My project studio is a combined studio and control room in one corner of my basement . It is a surprisingly quiet space that only needed acoustic control and not any major soundproofing. I've tweaked the arrangement of its 225 square feet over the past few years and am rather fond of the current setup. It's actually open on two ends into bigger spaces, one being my home theater.

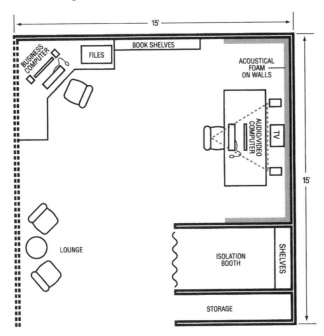

Fisher's studio layout.

One desk holds my business computer with printer nearby. Everything I need for daily business functions is within arm's reach, as is the telephone. This computer also connects to the Web. Try to keep your business as paper-free as possible. By keeping most files on your computer, you'll need very few traditional paper file cabinets. About the only paper you'll need to keep are signed contracts, receipts, and check stubs that match invoices. Keep everything else in the box, but make sure you have a sufficient backup strategy, though!

Another desk holds the primary media CPU, soundcard, dual-monitors, keyboard, and other equipment needed for composition, recording, editing, mixing, and mastering. Once again, everything I need is within easy reach or on nearby bookshelves. My acoustic instruments serve as decoration for the space and are literally all around the room.

The small isolation booth has a mic stand and mic/headphone tie lines to the main recording computer. It also has a bookshelf for additional storage of material less used but still needed (paper, envelopes, books, manuals, and such). Long-term storage is adjacent to the booth. The lounge area is for meeting with clients and relaxing away from the computer screens.

And on those rare occasions when a project demands capabilities beyond my space, I journey to a bigger studio to work on tracks. It's easy to save money here when you plan ahead, buy off-peak studio time for less, do as much as you can in your own studio before/after the higher-priced studio time, and prepare lead sheets/scores for outside players.

The number one complaint from home workers is they don't care to have strangers traipsing about their personal space. It's not been a problem for me, though. Clients rarely visit my project studio. I make it a point to meet them on their turf or send files via the Web (email and FTP). I do, however, invite clients to outside sessions at commercial facilities and often meet for lunch at convenient restaurants.

Maybe you don't care for the idea of working at home. Perhaps there are too many distractions or other problems. If you don't want to or can't locate your project studio in your home, you have three other choices: rent office space, work with another recording studio, or get an office in a studio complex.

RENT OFFICE SPACE

This is, by far, your most expensive option. Paying rent and other utilities can zap your precious resources quickly. If you don't have enough start-up money to support your business (or enough savings for your personal life) for six to eight months, stay home. Frankly, this idea is foreign to me. Unless you are getting into the recording studio business, with clients coming and going at all hours, I don't see the need for an outside office. You'll handle most of your daily business at a keyboard (faux ivory or QWERTY). If you meet your clients at their place, you really have no need for an office at all.

WORK WITH A RECORDING STUDIO OR PRODUCTION FACILITY

Strike up a deal with an existing recording facility or production house where you become a kind of staff composer. They give you an office in exchange for your doing all recordings at their facility. They get the benefit of a professional composer (you), while you get exposed to a client base you might not otherwise meet.

OFFICE IN STUDIO COMPLEX

This is similar to the above arrangement, differing only in the number of area composers. In Chicago, there are several communities of composers centered around a well-equipped multiple studio complex. This, too, helps you get many other clients to which you might not otherwise have access. The downside is that your direct competition surrounds you.

Finding and Using Other Musicians

Occasionally, you may need help. Where do you get it? If you are in a band, enlist the other members to cover parts or try these resources:

▶ Music stores. Place notices or get numbers of solo and group musicians. Many stores have an ad hoc referral service. Use it.

▶ Telephone book under musicians or entertainment.

▶ Musician's union.

▶ Bridal shops (many bands leave their cards there).

▶ Find magazines and newsletters that list musicians and other talent in your area. Many cities have a monthly, sometimes weekly, entertainment magazine that may help you find the right information.

From a business standpoint, you'll be subcontracting their services. This doesn't require anything special. Hire them, get them to play, pay them, have them sign a release. To sweeten the deal, throw in a free copy of the finished project, primarily if they are featured performers.

Find the help you need *before* you need it, though. Making friends with a few versatile creatives can go a long way toward making your music better, not to mention meeting deadlines. Once you get a pool of musicians to draw from, you should be ready for just about any situation that comes up. Treat them well and stay in contact regularly.

Also, it really pays to find a single-source, local equipment supplier that can handle almost everything you need. Find two or three alternate suppliers and one or two studios that can help you when an eventuality pops up. Do it now and start to build relationships with these vendors *before* you desperately need their help.

Composition and Technology

The commercial music business requires you to be creative on demand. Dealing with that stress is often difficult. My tip is for you to keep the composing process hassle-free and keep the main steps mutually exclusive. There are essentially two steps in all creative endeavors: Get the idea down quick and dirty and then go back and edit your idea relentlessly and turn it into a solid piece. Don't expect to get everything right the first time. The real work is in the transformation from sketch to full-blown song or score. Take care of the routine. Don't let the technology interfere with your creative process. Your mind will find the true creativity within. And your music will be much better, believe me!

Organize your technology first. Make sure that the tools you use to create and record are playing well together. Get the latest software updates and drivers to keep your system glitch free. Take time to organize sounds, MIDI channels, effects programs, everything. *And write it down.* You should be able to configure your system with just a few button presses. This way you're up and running quickly and optimally.

The more sophisticated the project, the more you need to be organized. Start by building folders on the hard drive for the project and using subfolders wisely to hold raw takes, edited versions, and works-in-progress. Backups are crucial. Make sure you back up multiple times to multiple places. Don't just back up to the same drive you use—go out to another drive and perhaps CD/DVD, too. I burn a single CD backup of my files once a month. Audio (and video) files and session notes go to DVDs with their expanded storage. I also use several external Firewire drives to hold my projects. On crucial projects, make multiple backups and store a set off-site.

Create song templates that use specific sound palettes. Use several different templates, each geared to a particular style of music, rock/pop, orchestral, and so forth. Have ready-to-use sounds already assigned to instruments, tracks, and so forth. You can always tweak these things later, but for now you want to compose fast with the technology as transparent as possible. Make sure instruments always come up on the same tracks/channels, too, e.g., drums on 1–6, bass on 7, guitar on 8–9, etc.

Keep composing separate from recording and mixing. Never start editing, tweaking, or mixing your composition until you finish writing it. You can start editing after the composition is in reasonable sketch form. Avoid looking for special sounds until the song structure is complete. Don't start with the effects until all the editing is complete.

After the track is down, then you can start editing. Sure you may re-record a part, replace a part or a sound, or go in a different direction altogether. That's fine. But do it after you've first tried writing what you thought was good. Don't record a drum part and then tweak and quantize it to death before moving on to the bass. Use a preset drum pattern or loop, drop in a bass line, move on to chords, etc. Build up the sketch and then stop. Take a short break and then go back to your composition and start editing. Once you finish editing, then it's time to mix, balance, and do all those fancy things you do to breathe life into your music.

Arrange your workstation for maximum efficiency. The way you set up your room can have a great impact on your productivity, both positive and negative. Constant hassles from your technology interfere with your creativity. Keep the stuff you use most often within easy reach. This includes the computer, sample CDs, keyboard, manuals, whatever it is you use.

Learn your gear inside and out. It's oh-so-tempting to grab every new toy that comes out. I suggest instead that you concentrate on mastering a few tools. The more you know about your equipment, the more you'll be able to get out of it. I keep it simple by using Reason, Acid Pro, and Vegas as my main tools, along with a few soft synths and my guitar. Also, make sure that everything is in good working order. Have a maintenance plan. Draft a signal flow diagram to help you manage gear.

There is no need to clean up after every session as a commercial studio must do. If you find the right sound, don't risk losing it. Leave your gear set up and ready to use. You never know when inspiration might strike. You don't want to be hunting for a cable when you should be hitting Record. With everything close at hand and ready to go, you can grab what you need and start creating your best music.

Find the best settings, too. Spend some time getting good sounds from your gear, and then leave the knobs alone or save those presets. You can plug in and record and be assured of getting the tone right. At the very least, find a way to save those settings. For example, keep a notebook of your favorite settings so you can easily dial up the sounds you want when your memory fails. Don't take chances with your valuable data, either. Set up a backup strategy and stick to it.

Set aside work time and keep it sacrosanct. It's easy to be distracted when you should be working. Find the best time when you are your most creative. Don't let anything interfere with that time. Turn off the phone; get voice mail. Stop surfing the Web. Close the door. Ask not to be disturbed. And then use your peak time to your best advantage.

Recording Techniques

While entire books address how to record music and musical instruments, I find most of them rather loquacious. It is my opinion that mixing is far more important than recording. The only purpose of recording is to capture the performance and the instrument's natural tone with enough volume that maximizes the signal to noise ratio. To do this effectively you need accomplished players, a few decent mics and preamps, a quiet acoustical space in which to record, and the ability to set good recording levels. What about mic technique? Use your ears to find the place where the instrument sounds its best and then stick a mic there. If your sound-creating tools are synths and samplers, they are mostly plug and play, and all this talk goes away.

Inside Mixing Techniques

There's little doubt that you will need to mix your music before delivering it to your clients. Whether you provide a stereo mix, multichannel stems, or do the entire audio post-production yourself, develop your balancing and mixing skills. The production process combines both art and craft, and neither is easily mastered. Here's some useful advice for handling matters both technically and more creatively.

Learn to listen with a critical ear. When composing, you focus on the music, but when mixing, your attention must be on how the music sounds and present it at its best. Listen to mixes of similar styles by other people and emulate what you hear. Choose a track that's similar to what you're doing and compare your mix to this track. A/B-ing your mix to another is an additional learning technique.

Listen to the whole piece with all tracks full up. Listen for what's there. Then go back through track by track and make decisions about what parts to keep, lose, feature, and relegate to supporting roles. Look for the essence of the music and do what it takes to bring that out. Get help for the mix. Take those mixes to others places and other people for insight. You can easily collaborate long distance by emailing roughs to a peer and asking for his comments.

Start in mono and work to get a great mix before doing any stereo work. It's hard to make a mono mix sound fantastic, but when you do, the conversion to stereo will be even better.

Carve out a place for everything. You don't want parts stepping all over one another in a jumbled mess. Fill the entire audible frequency range with deep lows, crisp highs, and a well-distributed mid range. Your mix shouldn't be boomy, harsh, or brittle. Embrace contrast.

In his book *Practical Techniques for the Recording Engineer*, Sherman Keene offered his viewpoint of what comprises a successful mix. Decades later, his ideas remain especially poignant. "A good mix includes: powerful and solid lows, proper use of mid range, clear and clean highs, proper, but not overburdening effects, real acoustic information, not just electronic reverbs and delays, dimension with a sense of depth, motion and movement of the instruments, and one true stereo track, preferably up front." To that wonderful advice I would add that every track should have some *ear candy*—a few audio moments that stick in the minds of the listeners.

Get busy with the controls you have. Use volume level, EQ, pan (stereo/surround position), effects wet/dry balance (wetter sounds move tracks back into a mix; dry sounds move parts forward), and more to craft a power mix.

Play those faders (the software equivalents are volume, pan, and effects envelopes). As you begin mixing your music, keep moving the faders up and down and all around. Often, I'll diddle with EQ and effects sends and returns. Even some subtle panning works well. This approach brings a little extra motion to your mix through these subtle manipulations.

Vary your tempo. You can be subtle by pushing ahead a few clocks and falling behind occasionally. Or be more intrusive by jumping tempo in greater leaps.

Don't forget about dynamics. I hear a lot of music that lacks dynamics. Get soft. Get loud. Swell. Fade. Mix it up. Subtract some instruments from the mix. Add in everything, including the kitchen sink sample. If you don't know what I mean, listen to orchestral music, specifically try Mahler's *Adagio* to his *Tenth Symphony*. You'll quickly learn what dynamics really are!

My favorite trick is to double a part and offset one in time slightly by a few milliseconds and then hard pan the two sounds. This makes for a wide stereo spread, opening up room in the center for other performances. It's perfect for guitars, piano, and strings. Also, double bass parts an octave lower (no stereo panning, though). The regular bass line has the articulation, while the doubled, an octave lower, provides the thump.

Remember that less is sometimes more. Today's technology makes it very tempting to add layer upon layer. The side effect is that your song or production gets rather dense and cluttered. Sometimes, you must step back, reevaluate, and strip it down. Heed the advice of award-winning recording and mixing engineer Ed Cherney: "Listen to what's there, see where the song is, [and] eliminate things to find the heart of the song. Ultimately, mixing is about heart, not equipment. Nobody dances to what kind of gear you used."

Take frequent breaks while mixing because
Tired Ears = Bad Mix!

Reverb sounding muddy? Don't send so much bass to the reverb. On vocals particularly, use EQ before the reverb and take out everything below 3,000Hz. This gives a nice, bright splash on the plosives and hard consonant sounds. Also, this can make the words more intelligible in a busy mix. Alternately, add a delay before your reverb and set it to a 100% short delay with no feedback. Send a vocal line to the delay and then on to the reverb. In the mix, you'll first hear the dry vocal. The delay line then creates a gap before the reverb begins. This makes the room seem bigger, without needing a long (read: muddy) reverb time. Adjust the delay time to fit your music. On choppy vocals it's cool. Dry sound... silence... reverb splash.

Occasionally, your music may be used as source (nondiegetic) on a project. If you are handling the mixing chores, try these ways to make it more realistic. For music coming from a radio or boom box, use the equalization controls to cut the highs and lows from the music. By reducing about 8–10 dB at 10kHz and 500kHz, you get a boxy, cheap radio sound. If the music is coming from earbud headphones, cut all the lows and mid range and boost the highs slightly. The result is that tinny sound everyone recognizes. Make a clean studio recording sound like it's coming from a live performance of a band or orchestra by adding a little slapback echo or reverb to the music. Another effective strategy is to cross-fade source music with dramatic music. You must work this out in advance. You can create an interesting transition caused when the two music pieces overlap.

Layer your guitar parts using different brands. Each axe (and amp for that matter) has its own unique quality. Or try this trick: Record a rhythm part using standard tuning and then track a second part using a capo a few frets up. Adjust the song key accordingly, of course. This works great on acoustic guitar parts. Often, I'll pan the two tracks hard left and right. That opens up space in the middle for vocals and other instruments.

If you really want your synth to sound like a guitar, run your lead patches through a guitar combo amp and mic it up or use the appropriate amp plug-in. Guitar power chords are usually just the root, fifth, and octave. No thirds, that's why they work in both major and minor keys. Guitarists *tend* to play monophonic leads and bend notes a half-step *up* generally. However, David Gilmour bends his guitar notes 2 1/2 steps up on *Comfortably Numb*! A guitar player cannot bend a note *down*. To do that, the string must already be bent up, struck, and then released. Start with the pitch wheel up, press the key, and release the wheel so it springs back to pitch.

Search for and use equipment, especially synths and outboard gear that others don't usually use. Old gear can give you a very distinctive sound.

Don't forget that EQ can be *cut* to affect tonal quality, not just boosted. Do you want a deeper bass? Cut everything from 5K on up on the bass track. Cutting the highs keeps all the sound in the lower register without getting too dark or flabby.

Flange or chorus ride and crash cymbals. Make sure to use a noise gate to eliminate the noise of the chorus or flanger when the cymbals are silent. This way the effect kicks in when the cymbals are struck with a unique wobbly sound.

Put a speaker and mic in your garage, basement, or tiled bathroom. Place them at opposite ends so you pick up the most room sound. Send instrument tracks to the speaker and then re-record the result, essentially adding *real reverb* to your mix.

You might need to mix more sound design than music. Follow this workflow. Ask yourself what you are trying to create and what the "sound" of the creation is. Then think about what kinds of things make that sound or components of it. Finally, figure out how to create that sound. I often start with a raw sound and then use various tools in Sound Forge to tweak the sound into something new.

The fine folks at iZotope (www.izotope.com) offer a free PDF guide called Mastering with Ozone. *Although this resource is Ozone-specific, there is still plenty of general and applicable advice in the booklet to make downloading it worthwhile.*

A final mix is *not* a master. Use mastering hardware or software to add the final sweetening to the stereo mix. However, don't overprocess too much. Mastering programs makes it way too easy to push the sonic integrity of a piece. Often, a little low-end whump and high-end sizzle, coupled with some light compression to raise the overall level, coupled with peak limiting to prevent digital distortion, is all you need. Use your favorite CDs as a reference when mixing and mastering. Alternately, hire a professional mastering engineer who brings experience and fresh ears to your project.

Keep a notebook of your tricks and tips and compile your own personal bag of tricks that brings your music alive.

Consult these resources for help in building and maintaining your project studio and for insight into making your music sound better: Electronic Musician *and* Mix *(www.emusician.com and www.mixonline.com).*

Mixing Voice and Music

Dialogue and vocals rule. It's very easy to get "used" to the voice and push it back in your mix. First-time listeners will struggle to understand what's being said/sung. When your music has to share the listener's ear with voice (dialogue and narration), there are several tricks to employ to make sure that the voice is clear and understandable and your music isn't too low in volume. If you simply reduce the volume of the music in relation to the voice track, it will sound too low when the voice stops. Too much music volume, and the audience struggles to understand what's being said. Here are some solutions.

ORCHESTRATE BETTER

Some musical instruments fight with the intelligibility of speech. For the male voice, the lower mid-range instruments, like acoustic guitar, tenor sax, and the middle of the piano, are the culprits. For the female voice, the upper-range instruments, such as alto sax, flute, solo violin, and screaming guitar solos, tend to cover up and mask intelligibility. Any music track that predominantly features one of these instruments will conflict with the associated male or female voice.

Compose your music without these interfering frequencies so there is space for the voice track. For example, if you are using a female voice, avoid music with a hot guitar solo. It might help you to think of the voice track as another solo instrument and select appropriate music that lets you feature it predominantly in the track.

STRIP LAYERS AWAY

High-powered, high-density tracks work well for visual sequences, but they fight for space (and audience attention) when used under a voice track. In general, the less-is-more school of music is best. Choose music that is full range—tight low end and crisp highs—but with a somewhat reduced midrange.

USE STEREO/SURROUND

If you're working in stereo, create a hole in the center stereo field for the voice track by leaving solo and midrange instruments *out* of the stereo center and balancing them to either the left or right speaker. With surround sound, the center speaker carries voice, so the stereo and surrounds are perfect for the music.

USE EQ

Create a hole for the voice by removing the music track's troublesome midrange frequencies with an equalizer. The frequency band that most affects speech intelligibility (male and female) is between 3–5 kHz. Reduce the music track by 4–6dB at those frequencies and correspondingly boost the same frequencies by 2–4dB on the voice track. This takes some experimentation to work exactly right, but a little knob diddling and careful listening will show you the way.

DUCK THE MUSIC

By far the best way to make sure the music and voice tracks don't interfere is to reduce the volume of the music significantly during the voice passages. Called *ducking*, because you duck the music out of the way, this technique makes for a perceptibly louder music track and a far more intelligible voice part. In your DAW/NLE, simply use a volume envelope to control music levels in relation to on-camera dialogue or narration. Here the music "ducks" down under the voice track.

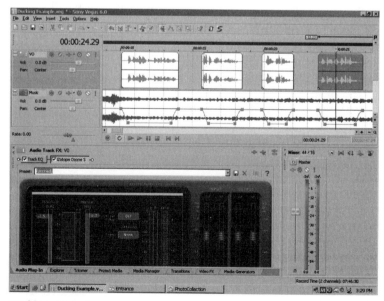

Ducking example.

Surround Secrets

As high-definition grows, so does high-definition sound. As people increasingly add home theaters, the demand for surround sound increases. You may be asked to deliver your music, indeed entire soundtracks, in the 5.1 format. Even though surround was initially developed for film sound, it is being embraced for TV, DTV, games, music, and more.

Surround sound or 5.1 comprises stereo L/R channels, dedicated center channel, surround or rear channels L/R, and a low frequency enhancement channel (LFE) that is 1/10th the bandwidth of the other five (hence .1). Surround mixes collapse (known as *downmix*) to stereo and even mono for those who lack surround listening capabilities.

To work in surround, you need a surround sound authoring program, DAW or NLE, the Dolby AC-3 and/or DTS encoder (hardware or software), a multichannel soundcard (capable of providing six discrete outputs), five matching full-range speakers, and one subwoofer capable of reproducing 20–120 Hz. The room setup follows the ITU Rec.775 specifications with the front stereo the same height and distance from the listening position, 30 degrees away from center. Place the rears 110 degrees away from center and the LFE subwoofer speaker in front, near the center. Calibrate the speakers using pink noise at –20 dbFS RMS into each speaker to read 83dBc on a sound pressure meter (c-weighted, slow).

There are no rules for mixing surround sound. Picture the soundscape as it relates to the visual and position music sounds accordingly. Decide whether to immerse your audience *in* the experience or not. Use surround panning to position sounds in the 5.1 speaker array. Generally, put dialogue in the center speaker. The LFE is a bass enhancement channel, not the place for all the bass. That's why the five speakers are full range. A consumer playback system may use bass management that essentially routes bass from the LCRLsRs to the sub because the satellite speakers are too small to reproduce bass effectively. Don't confuse the two!

For more information on surround, consult these resources:

- Instant Surround Sound (VASST/CMP Books) by Jeffrey P. Fisher.

- Dolby (www.dolby.com)

- The Recording Academy's Producers and Engineering wing (www.grammy.com) guidelines: Recommendations for Surround Sound Production free PDF download.

Equipment's Last Stand

Setting up your studio is a complicated issue, and I've only provided the essentials. You don't need the newest equipment to make it scoring soundtracks and jingles. Your composition skills will always outweigh your equipment list. As long as you can craft a clean, quality recording, you'll be successful because the real skill is in the writing, *not* your equipment. Music equipment is only as good as the person using it. Equipment does not supplant ignorance of music theory. It's as if I gave you oil paints and canvas and said create a piece of art. If you don't know how to paint, what good is it?

I admire people who push the limits of their imagination, creativity, and resources. That's my whole philosophy. Too many people rely on technology because it is far, far easier than making do with a few simple tools. Don't fret about having the latest, greatest toys. Get the most out of some basic gear, and you'll have a lot more fun. And be much more successful. Besides, you can never own everything you need or want. Build a system that works for your particular strengths. You can always rent equipment when necessary or just pack up your gear and head out to a commercial studio to record.

INDUSTRY INSIGHT

Eric Beheim
Cine-Phonic Music Service, San Diego, CA
cinephonic@aol.com

Recent credits/past projects:
Music scores: *Unseen Cinema* series (Anthology Film Archives/British Film Institute DVD), *Old Wives for New* (Image Entertainment DVD), *The Cat and the Canary* (Image Entertainment DVD, 2005), *Victory/The Wicked Darling* (Image Entertainment DVD, 2004), *Coney Island* (featured in *The Best Arbuckle Keaton Collection*, Film Preservation Associates DVD, 2002), *The Sheik/The Son of the Sheik* (Image Entertainment DVD, 2002), *World War I Films of the Silent Era* (Image Entertainment DVD, 2001), *Civil War Films of the Silent Era* (Image Entertainment DVD, 2000), *The Indian Tomb* (Water Bearer Films, 2000), *Go West* (Kino-on-Video DVD, 1999), *The Plastic Age* (Kino-on-Video/Image Entertainment DVD, 1999), *Slapstick Encyclopedia* (Kino-on-Video/Image Entertainment, 1998), *The Bells* (Kino-on-Video, 1998), *The Toll Gate* (Kino-on-Video, 1998), *Here Comes the General* (Film Preservation Associates, 1998), *The Strong Man* (Kino-on-Video, 1997), *America* (Kino-on-Video, 1996), *Douglas Fairbanks in Robin Hood* (Kino-on-Video, 1996).

Why did you choose this career (and how did you get started)?

I've always had an interest in music and film. Between 1989 and 1992, I managed and conducted a small professional orchestra that performed live accompaniments for screenings of classic silent films, using scores that I'd compiled. I bought my first MIDI equipment in 1993 with the intention of using it in my "day gig" as an informational video producer.

What was your first project and how did you land it?

In 1996, a producer who was aware of the work that I'd been doing with my silent film orchestra contacted me about preparing and recording a film score using MIDI equipment. Coming up with the music was no problem, but at the time, I only had a small, very basic MIDI rig that I didn't feel was adequate for doing a commercial project. However, he needed the score right away, and his budget didn't allow for recording it using live musicians. With some misgivings, I agreed to take on his project. (After I'd worked on it for about two weeks, I realized that I'd found my calling!) I met his deadline, and he immediately hired me to do a second score. Most of the fee that I'd earned on the first project was reinvested into more equipment, and my home studio was launched.

What are you working on now and how did you get this current project?

I've just finished providing about two hours' worth of music for *Unseen Cinema*: a 7-DVD 20-hour anthology of American avant-garde films produced between 1898 and 1941. (I was referred to the producer by one of my longtime "anchor" clients.)

What gear do you use?

Intel p4 PC running Windows XP, Finale 2004 software, Kawai MDK 61 MIDI keyboard, Edirol UM-550 MIDI interface, a collection of E-MU hardware samplers and Proteus modules, augmented by Garritan Personal Orchestra software samples, T. C. Electronic M300 dual engine processor, T.C. Electronic M-One XL dual effects processor, Mackie 1402-VLZ mixer, M-Audio Studiophile BX8 monitors, Beyerdynamic DT931 headphones, Furman PL-Plus power conditioner. Audio Recording DAW: Intel p4 PC running Windows XP, SAWStudio Basic software, M-Audio Delta 66 audio Interface Tascam DA-88 Digital Multitrack Recorder (used for recording master copies for final delivery), and Tascam DA-20MKII DAT deck (used for recording master copies for final delivery).

Explain your promotional strategies (what works and why)?

First, I identify potential clients who need the type of music services that I offer. Then I contact these potential clients and acquaint them with the benefits my studio can provide them: service that is good, fast, and relatively inexpensive. (Of these three criteria, most studios only offer them a choice of two!) I also take great pains to ensure that any projects I do for a new client meet or exceed her expectations. This is probably why most of my work is repeat business from a select group of "anchor clients."

What skills do you feel someone needs to succeed in the area?

Obviously, a certain degree of musical knowledge is required, as well as the ability to use a computer and a basic understanding of MIDI studio equipment and digital recording and editing procedures. Writing and communication skills are a must if you plan to handle your own promotions. And some knowledge of small business bookkeeping and financial management will be a big help, particularly if you're operating your studio on a tight budget. Success with a home studio also requires the self-discipline to manage your daily workload so that the projects you accept are completed on time and on budget.

How do you approach projects, technically or creatively?

I like to approach projects creatively, although I also have to spend time studying the technical aspects of my equipment so that it will help me achieve the end result I'm striving for. Typically, work begins when the client sends me a timecoded work tape. I use this to break down the screen action into sections, or cues, based on the various moods I feel the film is trying to convey. Using the time code, I prepare a cue sheet, which lists each section and its running time, expressed in hours:minutes:seconds:video frames. I then compose music that matches the mood of each cue and edit it to conform to the cue's running time. During the process of selecting the music, I frequently play back music and visuals in rough sync to get a feel for how well they work together. Sometimes, I go through several revisions before I feel that it matches the visuals.

I use a second digital audio workstation (DAW) for audio recording and editing. I record each cue on its own and then edit them together using the cue sheet timecode information. For frame-on accuracy, the edited audio must conform to the SMPTE format of the work tape, e.g., 30 Drop Frame format. After the music is assembled, I add any required sound effects. Once the producer approves the composite soundtrack, I create the master copy for use during the final layback session.

There is a terrific article by Eric that explains his whole approach in greater detail: http://www.digitalprosound. com/2001/03_mar/features/maharajah1.htm.

How do you get paid (typical pay for projects, royalties, etc.)?

Typically, I charge my clients a flat fee for doing their projects. I base this fee on the total number of minutes' worth of music I have to provide. This fee includes computerizing, editing, and recording the music, as well as assembling the various soundtrack elements (music, narration, sfx, etc.), preparing a master copy for final delivery, the cost of materials and postage, etc. If one of my clients needs something changed in the middle of the project and it's not too complicated, I try to accommodate them at no extra charge.

What do you wish you'd known then that you know now?

Looking back, I wish I'd known from the start how to better utilize my effects processors so that my mixes sounded more like they'd been performed by live musicians rather than electronic gear. This had to be learned mostly through trial and error and over a long period of time. (Whenever I listen to one of my earlier projects, I wish it could be recalled and redone to the standards I'm achieving today.)

What are your plans for the future?

Thanks to a happy set of circumstances, I was recently able to take an early retirement from my day gig. I'm now looking forward to devoting more time to taking on additional work from my anchor clients, as well as identifying and cultivating new clients.

Can you comment on financial strategies you used to start and run your career and business?

My home studio began as a part-time business. As each project was completed, I made it a point to invest a portion of the earnings back into new hardware and software or make upgrades and improvements to my existing gear. In this manner, my studio grew and evolved over a period of time and literally paid for itself. Equipment-wise, it is now to a point where very little else needs to be acquired, and the income that it generates is mostly profit.

Can you comment on using employees, partners, and outsourcing?

I use outsourcing for those services that I can't perform myself: computer servicing, equipment repairs, graphics work, printing, etc.

Is there anything else you'd like to comment on that you feel is important?

In operating my own home studio, it has never been my goal to aspire to become one of the "fat cats" within the electronic music field who get the plum TV and film scoring gigs. Thanks primarily to a faithful cadre of anchor clients, I've been able to work on a number of interesting and challenging projects that have proved to be both personally, as well as financially, rewarding. If I've learned anything, it is that when you are working at something you thoroughly enjoy, the money aspect is secondary.

CHAPTER 5

Demo Success Secrets

"The good composer is slowly discovered, the bad composer is slowly found out."
— Sir Ernest Newman

If you are more concerned with getting a good drum sound recorded than getting your finished music into a buyer's hands, you'd better listen up. Producers of multimedia content know the power and impact that music can make on their work. Your music functions as the solution to their problems. And your music demo is one way that you show how you can help them achieve the results that they want and need.

What comprises the best demo? I could be flippant and simply say: good music. There is a little more than that involved. While your demo must showcase your best work, obviously, it also functions as your calling card of sorts and therefore often makes the first impression. You want to make sure that first impression sticks in people's minds so that they consider you for their projects. You never get a second chance to make that first impression. So, make sure your music knocks their socks off!

Your demo may convince someone you can do music, but it won't make the sale. Your demo is really only a means to an end, typically the final justification on a sale already closed. That means people make decisions about the composers they hire often *before* they actually hear the music. Clients want to know if they can work with you, if you will listen to their ideas, and if you can translate their needs into the music they feel is right.

Your ability to meet with prospects and clients, focus on their projects, and then offer musical solutions is a far greater skill than your knack of crafting a decent music demo. In short, you must sell *yourself* and then your music. That doesn't mean your demo is irrelevant; on the contrary, it's not. But do realize that it isn't the most important aspect of getting gigs.

Your car breaks down and the mechanic informs you of what needs to be fixed. Unless you have some car knowledge, you're forced to do what the mechanic says. This person is a mandarin who knows far more than you. You are but a humble person at this person's mercy. Unfortunately, composers are rarely, if ever, in the position of mandarin when it comes to music choices. Virtually everybody you work with already has some idea of what makes for good music. They know what they want, and it's up to you to deliver it exactly how they hear it. You can't tell your clients what *you* think is best, and they bow to your all-knowing status. Instead, you are often forced to work with them on their terms, whether what they say is right in your mind or not. Therefore, demos are the audio equivalent of a sales brochure. It is just another part of the overall sales equation. Its function should be to generate leads to people who are good prospects for buying your music. It should reassure these prospects that you can indeed compose and deliver music. And it should help you close the sale.

General vs. Custom

Although it is mandatory to have a demo of your best overall work in the styles that you have mastered, it is equally acceptable to have numerous demos to cover special circumstances. For example, you may have a demo centered on your soundtrack work, another for advertising jingles, and still another that showcases other music outside those two genres.

The worst part of a generic demo is that some narrow-minded listeners will not hear exactly what they need on your demo. And since they don't hear it, they don't hire you. It doesn't matter if you can cover a variety of styles; they don't understand that. The only way to overcome this is to make sure you tailor every demo to the precise needs of those who request it.

Often, a prospect is looking for a specific musical style. Rather than give them a generic demo that covers a wide range of skills, send a demo of music only in the style they requested. Though I do have a general demo of my work (it's my *Melomania* music library), I usually prepare custom demos for prospects using only existing tracks that meet the specifications they mention. I find that by asking a few questions of the prospect or doing a little research about the project, I can deliver music that is closer, if not right on, to what they are looking for. This greatly improves my chances of securing the gig.

Sometimes, people will want specific music that is not on your demo. Whip something up for them and send that. Programs like Sony Acid make it a snap to put something together fast. Plus, the very fact that you quickly tried to write a custom piece for the prospect may really impress them.

You may be asked to compose in a style with which you are unfamiliar. Get on the Web or travel to your local CD store and buy up a bunch of music in that style. Listen carefully to these tracks.

Dissect them to discover the essence and then emulate what you've learned. In some cases, bringing in an outside composer or musician who is familiar with the style can help you work through this better. Also, sometimes you just need to compose the flavor of a style. And that might be just as simple as using the right instruments.

You may be tempted to write complete songs when what the client really needs is a simple music bed to hold under some visual or narration. Don't overwrite when it's not really necessary. How will the music be used? Background music doesn't need to be fully fleshed out as a foreground performance. Always remember that your music is about emotion and message. Do what must be done to have the emotional impact desired and underscore the message appropriately and effectively.

Watch out for the speculative demo, though. Prospects may ask you to compose specific music for them. If they like what they hear, they'll hire you. This is in *addition* to your usual music demo. It's up to you whether you want to put time and energy into such a speculative venture where there is no guarantee you'll get the gig. Try to draw from your existing creative wellspring first. If they insist on a custom speculative demo, quote them a token fee that covers your basic costs. To sweeten the deal, tell them you will deduct the demo composition costs from your full fee *when* they hire you for their production.

Recently, I was asked to submit a demo for a horror film-composing gig. After talking at length about the project with the producer, I threw together a DVD of some recent similar work. On the DVD were both audio-only segments and a few video segments from similar films that featured my music. I even composed a brief new theme based on my conversation with the director. I customized the DVD to this project, burned it, and overnighted the package. Here's an excerpt from the letter that accompanied the disc:

Great talking with you about your film, [insert horror movie title]. Your passion and exuberance are contagious! Thank you for giving me the opportunity to demo my music. I've enclosed a DVD with recent music that showcases my dark, ambient style. There are both music-only cuts and video scenes from a low-budget indie on the DVD.

The first music track was inspired by your need for a [insert horror movie title] "love theme." I composed it this weekend, combining a slightly melancholy approach with a darker edge. I hope you find this fits the message and emotion of what you are trying to say. I'll make sure to meet your needs exactly and give you music that works for your vision and sounds great. If you need more information, or additional musical ideas, do not hesitate to ask.

Of course, it takes some time to put these together, but far less than you might imagine. I have mixes of music in a lot of styles that I keep in folders on my hard drive. When a demo request comes in, I probe for information that helps me put together the right combination of tracks. Then I pick from my extensive library and either burn a quick CD/DVD or edit together an MP3 that I can email (or both!).

The Competitive Demo

In the TV theme and advertising jingle world, the demo has a different connotation. Here you are in a competition. You haven't been hired but just asked to create a speculative demo for the project. It's not uncommon for larger agencies handling the accounts of big advertisers to pay you for this demo contribution. These demo fees, as they are known, can range from a few hundred bucks to a couple of thousand dollars. The fees lean toward the lower end these days, though.

Ad agencies understand that it doesn't cost you very much to produce these demos, and so the fee they pay is usually a small token fee to cover production costs and little else. The catch-22 of this situation is that you can't cut back on either the composition or the production quality. The whole job hinges on how good your speculative demo is. You must do a first-class job because you are judged by the quality of this single composition.

If your track gets selected, you will earn the larger fee when the advertiser buys out your music. If your music is destined for a TV broadcast, your money will mostly come from performance royalties. If you don't land the gig, you still keep the demo fee to cover your time and expenses putting together the demo.

There was a time when these fees were substantial enough to keep you in business—even if you never sold the final. Today, agencies want to pay less and less for you to prepare a custom demo. They figure competition is healthy, and if you win the contract, the fees paid for the final more than make up for the demo costs you incur. However, you can't skimp on the demo; it must be really good! With so much money at stake, there is some rather strong competition for these dollars. It is the way the jingle world still works—that is, when they aren't licensing already existing songs from record labels. Make sure you understand what you are up against.

Who Is the Demo For?

There are essentially three buyers of original music composition services:

▶ Advertising agencies

▶ Production companies (video, film, games, radio, TV stations, etc.)

▶ Direct to buyers (advertisers, end-users, etc.)

Ad agencies typically commission scores and jingles on behalf of their clients. You work directly with the agency to produce the music they need for a particular project or ad campaign. When working with a production company, you and the director discuss the various music cues and other technicalities. You may never meet the actual client because the production company works directly with them, and you are the music subcontractor. Often, an advertising agency hires a production company that in turn hires you. Rarely will the actual client commission you to write music for their projects and ad campaigns. However, it does happen, especially on small local jingles where you work directly with the client.

The point is that you must target your demo to the specific audience. If you plan to sell jingles, put lots of short jingles on your tape. Try for a variety of styles, singers, and genres. If you plan to sell to other music houses or direct to production houses, you must grab attention and show your versatility. Also, you can prepare custom demos for your super hot prospects, as mentioned earlier.

Prepare Your Best Demo

You may have personal notions when it comes to music, but the purpose of your demo is to show clients that you can do the job. Therefore, your demo must contain your best music, well-recorded, and presented in a neat, professional package. Your demo must be very high quality, feature your originality and composition skills, demonstrate your versatility at covering many styles, and do all this in less than 10 minutes, preferably less than two!

Here's the most important aspect of every demo you use: grab attention, hold on to it, and keep the energy up. The second-most important point to clarify: use contrast. Unless you are targeting a specific niche, it's crucial that you showcase your talent range. And that means many styles, instrumentation, and so forth. Mix it up! I've heard way too many music demos that sound the same from track to track. Part of this is an equipment issue where a single synth/sampler results in a certain "sound" to all tracks. The other part is a lack of compositional prowess; all the songs *sound* the same because they essentially *are* the same.

This happens with soundtrack music demos where the music is rather boring without its visual accompaniment. If you write music that needs the visual adjunct to work, put together a video demo instead. Otherwise, your music demo must contain very strong soundtrack music of the opening title variety.

Don't prepare just one demo and use it forever. After you get the first one down, start on your next. As you get some clients under your belt, you'll have new music to add to the mix. Building your demo of your best music is a constant, never-ending process.

As you begin to put together your demo(s), here are the methods that consistently work: several complete tracks, a montage comprising snippets from several tracks, and free samples.

DEMO WITH COMPLETE TRACKS

The demo with five to seven complete cuts works well. I recommend you include a rocker, something urban, a little jazzy track, an orchestral piece, an ambient/new age/sound design piece, and something unusual—the most popular music styles.

Always lead with your best track and style! The slow track that takes two minutes to get to your ripping sax solo does not make for a good demo. You want tracks with impact and that leave a strong impression. If you specialize in one particular style, you can limit your demo to just your specialty. But you also will limit your clients. Most are looking for versatility. Show them you can cover a variety of styles, and you'll be more successful, generally.

DEMO MONTAGE

This innovative method is the *de facto* standard for general music demos. Put a montage of short snippets from several songs together. For one of my demos, I wove 16 songs into a two-minute montage that included only the best parts of each track. The best tactic is lots of little snippets—including jingle stingers such as a station ID: W-F-C-G!—carefully woven together into two or three minutes of high-powered music. Don't let any track last longer than 15 seconds. I *highly* recommend you consider this format. It's the smartest way to present your skills. A montage of your best music grabs attention, makes a solid impression, and helps you stand above the crowd.

There is a drawback. Many music buyers want to hear longer pieces to see how well you maintain interest with your music. To accommodate this request, put a few longer pieces after the opening montage. In short, lead with the montage and follow with a few extended cuts. That makes the best demo.

While you should draw from your best existing tracks for the montage, you may need to write pieces that bring the montage together into a seamless whole. Alternately, look for ways to edit tracks together, such as a cymbal crash on a rock track becoming the opening to an orchestral piece. Listen to how the chicken squawk on *Good Morning, Good Morning* matches the guitar note introduction to the *Sgt. Pepper Reprise* on the Beatles landmark album.

SAMPLES

The last option is a somewhat radical idea. While I recommend that you have a demo CD/DVD/MP3 of your latest, greatest music, I also suggest that you prepare samples that you give away. This technique is much like when the cookie store lets you try their latest culinary delight. They hope that you'll come back for more. Try the same approach with your music.

One of my promotions (a very successful one, I might add) offered five free music tracks to anyone who requested my demo. While a demo just screams: "Here's what I did," a free sample says: "Here's something for you to use to make your work better. And if you want more of this, just call." The demo gets listened to and then sits on the shelf. Your sample gets used, stays on the prospect's mind, and gets you the jobs. Yes, you are giving your music away for free. But you hope they like what they hear and come back to *pay you* for more.

Face reality. People just aren't interested in your music. They're only interested in what your music can do for them. Position yourself to help them. Show how your music solves their problems. This is how you get the work. Get it? Sell the sizzle (better video, more effective message), *not* the steak (music). Are you seeing the difference? Instead of giving them a CD to listen to, you are giving them music *they can use.*

To make this sample work, you need a few music cuts in different styles. This must be music you own *all rights* to and music that you are willing to give up completely to the world. Make sure that you are *very* clear about how people can use your music. You might invite them to contact you and tell you where and how they used your tracks. If you allow them to use the free samples for broadcast, make sure you insist that producers file cue sheets so you get paid your performance royalties.

Interestingly, Freeplay Music (www.freeplaymusic.com) follows this business model. They essentially give away their music tracks for broadcast use as long as the producers agree to music cue sheet compliance. In other words, they (and their composers) earn money from performance royalties through the PROs (BMI, ASCAP, and SESAC). Content producers and broadcasters must fill out cue sheets for all music they use in their broadcast productions (radio/TV). This information determines the money paid out. According to Freeplay Music, they have 570 Web downloadable tracks (and are always looking for new composers!—wink, wink) that have been heard on over 1,000 network broadcasts. They have different licensing for nonbroadcast use, though.

The sample music tape makes an ideal promotional offer. Consider how you can grab attention with something like this: "*Get FREE music for your projects.*" You then offer your samples to those who respond to the offer. This concept is unique, and it creates lots of interest… so be prepared for the inquiries. Once I sent this promotion to 20 prospects, generated four leads (20%), and got one client!

JINGLE "SAMPLES"

Jingle composers can use a twist on the samples idea. Again, you still need a demo of your best jingle work. Additionally, write a few jingles that are somewhat generic, ones you can re-lyric easily by slipping in a different company or product name.

Listen to the radio or watch local television for advertisers who don't use jingles. Visit this business and get some of their promotional material. Write the words to your generic jingle using important points about this prospective client. Add the new vocal track and make a demo. Contact this client and ask for the marketing or advertising manager. Tell them you've heard or seen their ads and wondered if they ever considered using a jingle. Tell them you have prepared a sample jingle especially for them and set up an appointment to play the jingle.

In other words, you compose a jingle specifically for the client, customized to their needs, and use this speculative work to secure the project. Or you can write several generic jingles that can be easily customized and updated through new lyrics. Offer to do a custom jingle or, for a cut-rate price, you can rewrite the generic jingle just for them. Only grant a *local* license to the jingle, which frees you to sell the music many times over across the country. This is the secret to what's known as jingle syndication.

NARRATE OR NOT?

You can consider adding narration to your demo. An intro and outro are all that's required. You don't want to step on the music, so keep it short and simple. Here's an idea:

> *You know original music makes a difference in your productions. And you shouldn't have to settle for something that almost fits. Now, you don't need to compromise your creativity. You get the music you need—music with impact, music that works—at a price you can afford. Just listen to this musical montage of my latest work. I'll be back in two minutes with more details."*

While it's not necessary, the narration *can* reinforce your promotion and sales message, help guide the listener through the selections, introduce sections, profile different services, make an offer (call now to get the music you need), and provide the necessary follow-up information (address, phone, email, etc.).

NO TRACK RECORD?

Nobody has a completely blank slate. You don't wake up one morning and decide to compose soundtracks or write jingles. You must have music already available that would be suitable for your demo. Use what you have as your demo of your best work. They may not be *real* credits, but they'll work for now until such time as you can replace them with real credit.

LEARN FROM OTHERS

Not sure what goes into a successful demo? Get demos from other composers. Usually, a visit to a few Web sites will give you an idea of what's out there. Study what your competition is doing and learn from their best approaches (and their mistakes).

Demo Formats

You need to present your demo in several different formats.

CD

Distributing your music on the ubiquitous audio CD is still the primary way to demo your skills. Prospects and clients will listen in their car, at home, on a boombox, and occasionally on a decent sound system. It's portable, high quality, and still demonstrates your professionalism.

There's no need to make hundreds of copies, though. Burn them as needed. I keep a few generic demos ready for a moment's notice, but, I burn custom CDs more often than not. The technology for making CDs is rather commonplace, so I won't go into details here. Most computers include CD writers and ship with rudimentary CD authoring software. Essentially, you use the software to select music clips, insert a blank CD-R, and then burn the files to the finished disc. Make sure you "close" the disc so that it can be played on any CD player. All that's left is to print a label or print directly on the disc, pop it in a case, and send it on its way with a cover letter.

MP3

Make your demo available in MP3 for both Web downloads and to send as email attachments. What's great about this approach is you can have montages, full cuts, and free samples all at the same time on your Web site. When you need to send a demo, you can send the prospect the link to your download page. Be aware that emailing files with over 1MB attachments get rejected by many ISPs.

Technically, you use sound software, such as Sony Sound Forge, to convert or encode your music files to the lossy MP3 format. MP3 uses psycho-acoustic masking to decrease file size. It essentially allocates encoding bits to the most prominent sound, which masks or covers up other sounds. The other information is thrown out with our brains filling in what's missing. It gets rid of sound/data, so it adversely affects your music. Don't skimp on quality here to reduce files sizes. Use the 128kpbs encode setting at the very least. This translates to about 10:1 compression; one minute of music will be about 1MB.

To make your MP3 encodes sound better, take these steps. Use EQ to roll off the lows and highs, below 100Hz and above 10,000Hz. The extreme lows and highs can fool the encoder, resulting in a less than ideal finished sound. This radical EQ does take some of the deep bass from your tracks, but they sound better overall. The extreme high frequencies contribute to MP3's "swirly" nature, so eliminating them reduces that side effect significantly. Next, apply some light compression, 3:1 or less, to reduce the dynamic range a little. Normalize the music to about a 95–98% volume level on the peaks. And finally, encode the MP3 using the 128kpbs stereo setting. Add your contact information to the ID3 settings that can be included with your MP3.

The problem with the MP3/download approach is that you lose a little control over the promotional process. I prefer a more proactive approach to selling my music. Prospects may visit your page, listen to your tracks, and disappear. You wouldn't even know it and couldn't begin to follow up. Additionally, you may send a link but not know if it was listened to or not. And if there was a problem with your Web site, the person may just give up.

Podcasting might be a variation worth considering, too. This relatively new phenomenon lets people download MP3-based audio files from the Web, transfer them to an MP3 player, and then listen to the content anytime, any place. It's a terrific way to promote, train, talk to like-minded people, and of course, entertain. Think of it as your own little "radio station." Create the recording,

MP3 encode it, upload it to a server, and then get people to download what you present. It's just another way to deliver the musical solutions that you offer. Check out these popular directories: www.podcastalley.com, www.podcastcentral.com, and www.thepodcastnetwork.com.

VIDEO / DVD

If you have several video clips that use your music, a video demo is a terrific idea. You can prepare the video demo as a download, streaming clip, and DVD versions. The same rules apply: lead with a short montage and follow it with longer sequences from as many different sources as possible.

Stick with online video formats—Flash, QuickTime, or Windows Media—that don't force people to get esoteric plug-ins. Mind the bandwidth issue; don't put up huge files that few people will download. Instead, offer a few options, depending on the prospect's connection speed.

DVD demo.

Putting together a DVD is not nearly as difficult as it once was. NLE software lets you edit video together and even create video titles to use as backgrounds for audio-only sections. DVD authoring software gives you the tools to create and burn the final DVD. Of course, you need the proper DVD hardware on your computer to go along with the software. There isn't space in this book to talk about this subject in the detail it deserves. Video is fast becoming the demo format of choice, so it is in your best interest to learn more about the technology.

Even if you don't use visuals, per se, in your demo, you can use a video format for your online demo. Add a still frame, maybe just your logo and contact information, and then encode the video and music. It's basically an MP3 with a "cover." When your file plays on a prospect's computer, he hears your music and sees your contact information. You can even make the video a clickable link (or force it automatically) that takes the client to your Web site. An added benefit to using a still frame is that the file size will be small.

CD face.

Packaging the Demo

Now that you have picked and recorded the right music, it's time to duplicate and package it. Keep the physical packaging simple and professional. A printed label or printing direct on the CD is all that's required. Your Web site design and layout (discussed later in the book) are the packaging for your downloadable demo(s).

Make sure to print your name and contact information (telephone and email) on the label/CD face. Make sure it is easy to read. Discs get separated from their packaging, so printing on the disc itself is mandatory. Throw a business card into the case that holds the disc, too.

When sending a demo CD to a prospect who specifically requested it, use a slim-line CD case or even a paper envelope. If you are sending your demo cold, use a full-size CD case and add a tray card that has your name big and bold on the spine. If your CD is in a stack, your case will stand out from the crowd. Get empty CD cases from stores that carry computer and office supplies.

Get Creative

You may need to go an extra step to get your music noticed. I've heard many stories of the great lengths some music houses go to get their demos into the hands of prospects. Some have had their demos delivered to prospects by costumed performers. Others have sent food or other novelty items with the music. These were fun and may still work in some circumstances but are a little passé today.

However, to a few very important prospects, I sent my commercial music demo tape inside a portable cassette player with headphones. I bought the tape players from a bargain bin for less than $5 each. I created a specific mix that sounded good on the tape deck and headphones.

After installing batteries, I cued up the tape so the package was ready to roll and mailed it. The idea was to get them to listen to my music with a minimum of fuss. I also put a sticker with my logo and contact information on the tape player (and on the tape, of course). There was a cover letter, too, that essentially said "Press play and hear how I can help you today!" I followed up the promotion with a phone call. It was a novel approach that generated some great interest at the time. The cost was relatively cheap compared to some promotions (about $10 per prospect). While I would *never* send a tape today (and an MP3 player is a little pricey), hopefully the idea still sparks your imagination for possible ways to get recognized.

Industry Insight

David Was
Los Angeles, CA
wasomatic@hotmail

Recent credits/past projects:
Founding member of the rock group Was (not Was), with five albums and four top-ten singles in Europe/U.S. Producer for Rickie Lee Jones' *Pop Pop*, Holly Cole Trio, *Don't Smoke in Bed*, and co-producer (with Don Was) of Bob Dylan's *Under the Red Sky*. Commercial composer for Acura, Infinity, Toyota, Coke, Microsoft, Canon, Jiffy Lube, and Subway. TV scores: *The Education of Max Bickford* (CBS), first eight episodes, *That Was Then*, (ABC), six episodes. Music supervisor for a few movies, including *the X-Files Movie: Fight the Future, American Werewolf in Paris* (producer), and *The Big Tease* (co-producer). Album Executive Producer for *Songs In The Key Of X: Music From And Inspired By The X-Files.* The show's theme song actually went to #1 in some places, and the album sold over a million copies. All the artists who contributed were big fans of the show, so the project was a delight. Composer for the 2002 Academy Awards broadcast, a score he did, to some controversy, using only Sony Acid!

What was and how did you land your first project?
An ad agency was looking for Thomas Dolby to score a commercial. They called Capitol Records and reached my brother who convinced them to call me. I got the gig after sending them a cassette demo. I had no idea what I was doing but was fortunate to have understanding agency creatives who held my hand through the whole process.

To a certain extent, getting into the commercial market was easy. Having some bold face ink attached to your name gives people confidence. Your name and reputation is a name they can hang their hat on: "I got the guy from Was (not Was)." So having that cachet really helped initially. Then word of mouth kicked in, and I could bank on that for a while.

However, once that initial cachet wore off, I found myself without an agent, and the ad agencies who'd been hiring me had pretty well cycled through me and were on to something new. So, I started looking for an agent. And it was the old Hollywood conundrum: You need a reel to get an agent and an agent to get a reel.

I decided to pound the pavement myself first and took my demo (on ¾" U-matic tape, no less) to a young, aggressive ad agency. They politely sat through my reel, but at the end asked if I had anything new. Right then, I realized the newest piece on the reel was five years old. I said to them, name a genre, and I can cover it. They never called.

What this comes down to is understanding that the half-life of the ad guys is so brief and ephemeral. You blink, and they're gone. So, you must struggle to keep your name in front of those who hire you. Just keeping track of them, where they go, is hard enough. Thankfully, for me this has paid off, and the past clients started calling me again and business picked up. My advice? Keep that demo up-to-date with your freshest tracks and keep your name and face in front of those who sign the checks.

What are you working on now and how did you get this current project?
For the most part, I do instrumental music for TV spots with lyrics only once in a while. I'm presently working on the soundtrack to an indie film, doing a few commercials, and putting together another Was (not Was) album with my partner, Don Was.

One real trend I'm seeing at ad agencies is bringing music supervisors in-house. These people are charged with finding music, clearing licenses, commissioning and working with composers, and more. One idea I've considered pitching to ad agencies is to be their contract composer on a monthly retainer. I'd be available to do the demos and projects they need for a set fee. If a project gets picked up, there would be the usual package/creative deal. A $5,000 a month retainer would be cheap to the agency and a good, steady gig for the music composer.

Another trend I see, and this is unusual, has composers putting together a speculative commercial spot in the hopes of selling it outright to the advertiser or agency. Some just remove the soundtrack from an existing commercial, add their own sounds, and use that as their demo. Others put the whole thing together and pitch it. They are spending a lot of money on these speculative ventures.

When it's TV pilot season in Hollywood, everybody scrambles to score show themes because if the series and theme get picked up, the music royalties are substantial. However, instead of getting paid to write the music, some music houses, and well-known composers, *pay* to have their music in the competition. It's a crazy turn of events that I won't participate in at all.

To add to that problem, TV producers often have nepotistic ideas about hiring composers. They seem to say, "We're using this guy and not listening to new stuff." They tend to bring in their own people, leaving music supervisors with little control over hiring. And composers like me are out of consideration.

What do you feel makes a good music score (or jingle)?

You are writing the music to a 30-second picture that may already have a million dollars invested in it. If you give them the right music that makes it all gel, it's a magical thing. However, it may take a lot of effort on your part to satisfy the client. But when it works, it really can be a magical moment. It's like when I've written a song and then you hear people singing your lyrics and melody. You've made a connection that makes you feel what you're doing is important, and that you've had a positive effect on someone. As a record maker, I looked down on commercial music. Now, years later, I realize it is a very difficult thing to do, and it can be just as satisfying.

Almost anything helps a picture; it soaks up music like a sponge. I find it really funny how people react to music when synced to picture. At one point, through complete serendipity, the music will exactly match up to the action, and people watching this will focus on that single moment of symmetry, disregarding everything else that doesn't match. Composers should never feel everything has to match, because one well-chosen moment will stick in the minds of the viewers.

Personally, I see picture editors as very important. They often lay in the first music temp track, and the choices they make at this juncture can drive the whole project. Editors are some of the hippest people in the commercial field; they choose the freshest, most contemporary cuts. As is typical, what's cool in the music world takes about seven months to hit the commercials. It pays to stay current and slightly ahead of the game, as it were.

If you come into a project with a temp track in place, no matter what you compose, take the beats per minute (BPM) as gospel. Find out what the tempo is of that temp track, steal it, and use it! Also, find out if there are any concrete ideas on the agency side. If there are, use them, too. Otherwise, you are usually faced with one of two challenges:

▶ They know exactly what they want and essentially would like you to plagiarize it.

▶ They have absolutely no idea what they want and, therefore, provide little or no direction.

You know, music is universal, and virtually everybody feels that they are a music expert to some degree. They know what they like but have trouble expressing it. As a composer, you have no advantage of being the expert in charge. You will find a sophisticate occasionally who knows what she wants and can express it. That is the exception, not the rule, though. And once in a very long while, they give you carte blanche and let you run with it.

What gear do you use?

I'm primarily Mac-based using Logic, Reason, and Ableton Live. I also have a PC for Acid, though lately I've been bringing in the Acid loops to Reason's NN-19 sample player and chopping them up. This way, I play the loops, and parts of loops, as samples to get around their "loopy" nature. Reason is a very amazing program, especially their new mastering stage, which lets me do everything in the computer. My keyboard controller is an Equinox, and I use some Hafler monitors, but check mixes on other systems, too.

What skills do you feel someone needs to succeed in the area?

In a nutshell, I stole my business model from a book on screenwriting by Kenneth Atchity. He lists four attributes that you need for success:

▶ Connections. Typically, it is who you know that brings you a modicum of success. I feel it really can help you to be the son of the nephew of the guy who runs the company that you want to score for.

▶ Likeability. How well do you get along with people? Do you have the right look, appropriate social manners, and so forth. For example, I worked with a guy who I consider to be a musical genius—great talent, real technology expert, and such. However, he had no people skills; he was a punk, and the ad guys were scared of him. You must possess the personal touch that makes people feel warm and cuddly and know they are in good hands.

▶ Persistence. You simply can't give up too easily.

▶ Talent. If you truly are Mozart, then connections probably don't matter as much. However, if you are well connected, then having talent doesn't matter as much at all, either.

You can't possess only one of those attributes, you must have a little of everything to make it. At the end of day, the golden mean prevails: moderation in *all* things. A little talent, a little personal touch, and a willingness to work hard to make those invaluable connections. That's what gets you on the radar.

How do you get paid (typical pay for projects, royalties, etc.)?

The fee that composers get for commercials sometimes shocks people. There is a lot of competition and agency capriciousness, so winning the gig is akin to winning the lottery. And so, because of the hard work, client interference, and endless revisions involved, the money you charge really fits the job description. You receive a fee for being driven crazy by the client. The $15,000 you get isn't for your music; it's for the suffering you incur to satisfy the client.

Specifically, the commercials I write are typically a buyout with no royalties. I'm my own publisher on those deals, so I get the whole thing. They are package deals, too, where production costs often comes out of the single fee.

Don't take this next piece of advice lightly! This business can drive you bananas just trying to get your pay. Believe me, only you can be responsible for collection. For example, I was watching TV and heard a car commercial with one of the Holly Cole Trio tracks I'd produced. Nobody had called me about it, but I thought I must be owed some money for it. Consequently, I called my publisher, EMI licensing, and they essentially said, "Yes, we owe you money, and we have a check, but not a current address." That's music-speak for: If you hadn't asked, you wouldn't get paid! Turns out the check was for $25,000, which is more than I got paid for doing the whole album.

When you get to this level, realize that often nobody pays you unless you go hunting for your money. My partner, Don Was, told me that Bonnie Raitt takes her accounting team in every 2–3 years to check the books. Then there is the common practice of cross-collateralizing records, which essentially robs Peter to pay Paul. Instead of paying what's owed, the label renegotiates royalties and future payments, shifting the dollars to be paid to some date down the line.

A well-known TV network asked for 38 submissions for a TV show. Some big names contributed because the money can be really good if you win the competition. Of course, the demos have to be fully produced, too. The problem is, what the client is doing is making the composers be their R&D department. They use you to refine their idea. Anyway, I made it to the top three recently, but none of us won. The show licensed an existing track instead. However, they still used my piece on the end credits for foreign release and offered only $500 for all my time and effort. I'd never heard such an outrageously low fee for such a use ever. $5,000 maybe, but $500?

Now I work with a collaborator, a young kid I heard in a Sam Ash music store playing jazz organ. I asked him if he liked his job, and he said no. I offered him $1,000/week to be my assistant composer. He thought about it for a moment and then said, "Will you put that in writing?" And I did.

A few months after the aforementioned TV debacle, my collaborator calls to ask if I received my ASCAP check for the foreign themes, amounting to $1,600. Now I'm the co-composer, but I didn't get a check. Turns out I had to log in to the ASCAP Web site and make sure my name was linked to the theme, or I won't get paid. I do this and then finally get the money.

What do you wish you'd known then that you know now?
Beware of temp tracks because sometimes the client wants you to cover the tune as closely as possible to the temp without getting sued. Here's what happened to me. I was hired to do a car commercial and went through the process of several rewrites. I kept getting conflicting input from the creatives and ended up doing several different scores. Finally, or so I thought, they signed off on the track. I literally screamed when the session was over. The next morning the phone rang. There was a

new cut of the commercial, and they'd temp tracked in Chris Isaak's *Wicked Game*. And, of course, they asked if I would redo the music.

I put together a different feel to the track using my Ensoniq SD-1. My partner Don Was changed the bass line to more closely capture the *Wicked Game* feel and then we brought in T-Bone Burnett to do the guitar. At the studio session, I laid down the keyboard tracks before they arrived (so they didn't know the bulk of the track was from one keyboard). And the agency loved it.

A few days later, a registered mail letter arrives from some 1880 law firm saying that Chris Isaak is suing and the ad agency is indemnified from the action because of the Purchase Order I signed. Now I'm a one-man operation with no agent or lawyer. I start doing some digging myself and find out that the agency originally offered Isaac $150,000 for the original song, and he turned them down. I also realized that I never signed the so-called PO. The agency decided to fight the case, brought in a musicologist, and then it leaked to the papers. The car company hated the exposure, so they paid Isaak and pulled the spot.

After the dust settled, the agency called me again and asked if I'd redo the music. However, there was only half the budget, $7,500 instead of $15,000. I said yes and finished the commercial. At that point, I'm sure, they would have put anything on the spot!

Is there anything else you'd like to comment on that you feel is important?
Make sure you get far enough into this industry based on those four attributes I mentioned. Exploit those skills you do have. This is a creative industry. Nothing is done by the book. Be willing to be a little different.

Create your own luck. Take action when there is an opportunity. Because suddenly an opportunity presents itself, and are you prepared when it happens? Opportunity is abundant. If you can do the job, you'll find the opportunity somehow. And when you find that door, give the impression you're in control, even if you have to learn on the job.

CHAPTER 6

Finding the People Who Buy Original Music

"The foolish seek happiness in the distance, the wise grow it under their feet."—James Oppenheim

There are many opportunities for selling your original music, but where do you find leads, prospects, and ultimately clients? It used to take some major detective work to hunt down prospects through the labyrinthine business and creative world. Now it's amazing how easy it really is to find people and get in contact with people via email or telephone.

Your job is to find the *specific* names, addresses, email, and telephone numbers of all the creative people at audiovisual, video, and film production companies, cable companies, game developers, educational publishers, Web design firms, advertising agencies, radio/TV stations in your area, and around the world. If you plan to sell direct to companies and people, you need to get the proper contact information there, too.

Finding this information is a snap, thanks to the Internet search engines. With some carefully entered keywords and other search criteria, you should be able to find the information you need fast. There are even Web sites to visit where prospects solicit for music for their productions. And, best of all, you can be listed on these sites (and in the search engines) so that people looking for music find you, as well. There are also several directories published, online and in print, that also provide contacts,. Some of these are detailed below.

If you are just starting out, work locally and search for smaller, budget-conscious productions. Use this market to learn the business, earn a reputation, augment a demo reel, and build some success before you pursue those bigger projects. Many smaller producers go on to bigger and better projects, taking you along as they move up the ladder. Small gigs today pay off for you down the road.

Have your sights set on the big time? Lofty goals are fine, but don't neglect the success right in front of you. Consider that you might do better staying local. For instance, you can control your promotion by leveraging local contacts. By concentrating on who you know and where you know to go, you can often create a great success in a smaller geographic region. One recent caller told me about how all his old college buddies ran the local radio stations. He has an "in" there for whatever work he pursues. Getting popular in your local area is often easier to achieve than going for the gold. You may then choose to stay local or expand as interest increases.

Finding those few clients who are willing to use you for the majority, if not *all*, of their projects is the real secret to this business. Building those relationships takes time and the talent to deliver the music that keeps them coming back for more. But just because you have a few anchor clients doesn't mean that your prospecting should stop there. Always keep looking for new business!

Finding Contacts

What follows is a partial listing of ways to find possible sales leads. There is probably a whole heap of other sites and resources that I haven't even mentioned. They are out there for you to find and benefit from. It's up to you to uncover your own little secret ingress into the commercial music world. If you find a really good resource, consider sharing it with others via my email newsletter.

ADVERTISING AGENCIES

These businesses buy music for the advertisers they represent. The music is then used in radio and TV commercials, on the Web, and in other presentations produced by and for the client. Use the several available guides to the agencies and advertisers. They contain comprehensive listings of all the advertising agencies that handle larger budgets.

▶ Advertising Red Books (www.redbooks.com). These are not inexpensive books; a good local or university reference library may have a copy.

▶ Peter Glenn Publications (www.pgdirect.com) also publishes a few use- ful directories of people and companies in the advertising field, mostly East coast, though.

Not all advertising agencies buy music. Many specialize in print or Web and not radio/TV pro- duction. The directories don't always differentiate. However, usually by looking at their clients, you can determine if the agencies are a suitable prospect. Additionally, you can always call and ask, "Does your agency buy commercial music for your clients?" If the answer is yes, ask to speak to the people in charge of acquiring music. Talk details with the person to whom you get connected.

Want to go national with your jingle business? You have to find the ad agencies that handle the big national accounts. Where? Read the media (Web sites and magazines) that serve the advertis- ing community. There will be plenty of stories about which agencies are handling what accounts.

Then you'll need to sleuth the contact information for those who directly control those accounts. Send your demo and ask how you can be considered for upcoming campaigns. Offer to send in a speculative demo based on their needs. This isn't the easiest market to break, but your willingness to research the information you need, your talent to craft a top-notch demo, and some perseverance might just help you land that big account.

▶ *Advertising Age* (www.adage.com)

▶ *Adweek* (www.adweek.com)

ANIMATION

This is really just a subset of the TV world that I've singled out because, despite a few shows on Fox and Cartoon Network's *Adult Swim*, most animation is aimed at younger audiences. Surprisingly, I hear some rather sophisticated soundtracks on the cartoons my son, Adam, watches (*Teen Titans* and *Totally Spies*, for example). Technology has made animation less expensive to produce. There's a lot of content out there, and more on the way, all needing quality music. Look for music supervisors'/editors' names on the credits, along with the production companies they work for, and then use the Web to find contact information. Some of this information may be in the *Film & Television Music Guide* mentioned under the "Hollywood Films" section later in this chapter.

AUDIO BOOKS/SPOKEN WORD

Books on "tape" are still very popular (along with their modern sibling, Podcasting). Do they use original music for these productions? You, betcha. Contact the book publishers or the production companies listed in the credits. I did a quick Google search and discovered several possibilities.

CD-ROMS (AND OTHER MEDIA-RICH CONTENT)

Educational publishers and many special interest publishers continue to distribute content via CD-ROMs (and even DVDs). Visit the library or a software store to see what's out there and, more importantly, who is creating this content. You may run across some major publishers that will take some work to contact; however, the few smaller fish out there may be far easier to get in touch with and pitch your music services. They may be more receptive to working with you over their conglomerate counterparts.

CONVENTIONS, WORKSHOPS, AND OTHER INDUSTRY EVENTS

Although the specifics of relationship building are the subject of another chapter, suffice it to say here that meeting people who are in a position to hire you at industry events is a prime way to find work. Actively participate in whatever is going on and meet with as many people as you can. Discuss their projects, what they need, and how you can help. Attending big industry shows, such as The National Association of Broadcasters (NAB), Sundance Film Festival, Siggraph, and Electronic Entertainment Expo, is important toward taking your career to the next level. As a bonus, attendees often get directories of participants and vendors complete with contact information (very handy for follow-up!).

CORPORATE PRESENTATIONS

Whether they are approaching clients, prospects, or their own employees, companies use video, CD-ROMs, PowerPoint, live events, and the Internet to deliver their messages. Many of these productions need music (and sound design) that you can provide. Corporate videos are sometimes called *industrials*, but not by anybody I know; nonbroadcast is the more typical term. Although a company may have an in-house production department, they might still outsource to production firms specializing in their particular needs. Both producers are candidates for your music.

Make contact, by phone or email, with the marketing or advertising department. Find out if they have in-house content producers or with whom they work on the outside. It really pays to do a little research here, as opposed to cold calling. Find those companies that produce this kind of material first. Ask around, surf the Net, whatever it takes to gather useful intelligence. To a certain extent, just about any decent-sized company that talks to the public will be producing some kind of multimedia content. They are not all candidates for your music, but why risk not finding *the one* by not calling?

CREATIVE DIRECTORIES

Most major cites have a directory of creative talent or resource of some kind that lists possible prospects, including their complete contact information. In Chicago, there are two such directories: The *Screen Production Bible* and the *FILM Illinois Production Guide*. You might contact your local Chamber of Commerce or Advertising Council to find out how to get one. Also, contact your state's film office; they may have or can direct you to such local resources. Don't forget about your local library, for assistance.

▶ *Screen Magazine* is the Chicago and midwest industry guide (www. screenmag.tv).

▶ The Producer's Masterguide (www.producers.masterguide.com).

▶ LA411 (www.la411.com) and NY411 (www.newyork411.com).

▶ Craig's List serves a variety of cities (www.craigslist.org, chicago.craigslist.org).

▶ State of Illinois Film Office (www.illinoisbiz.biz/film/film_production.asp).

The best part of a local directory of creative talent is that you can (and should) list there, too. Listings in both *Screen* and the *FILM Illinois Production Guide* are free. I'm listed as a composer and producer in the "Music and Sound" section of both directories. If a listing isn't free, it is usually very affordable. Contact your local directory to see how to list, when, and how much it costs.

And so as I was writing this book, the phone rang with a major music scoring project for me. I spoke with the producer/director for a few minutes about the project. I then had the opportunity to ask him where he'd heard of me, and he said he saw my name in the *FILM Illinois Production Guide*. I've been in there for many years, and this was the first time a project came to me from that resource. I'm not complaining, rather I'm quite happy with the fact that I've always kept my information updated in this annual guide. You just never know when someone might see what you are up to and give you a call. And while you already know I prefer proactive promotion, there's nothing wrong with a little passive promotion thrown into the mix.

CURRENT AND PAST CLIENTS

Don't forget that anybody who has bought music from you in the past is a real candidate for buying from you again. However, creative people move around a lot, so you may need to spend some energy keeping track of them. Staying in regular contact is the only sure-fire way to keep your work in front of them no matter where they go. Plan to spend part of your time monitoring the whereabouts of past buyers.

DOCUMENTARY PRODUCTIONS/PRODUCERS

Docs are hot right now. Many of them are produced by small production companies and independent producers. My experience says that these people are more open to listening to new talent than other similar content producers. They don't often have big budgets, though. Contact them using the same methods for production companies mentioned below.

EDUCATIONAL PRODUCTIONS (AIMED AT SCHOOL AUDIENCES)

There are content publishers and independent production companies that produce for the educational market. How do you find out about these productions? Ask your local school librarians. You should be able to get leads to prospects by finding out who produces the material and then touching base with them.

Also, colleges and universities often have media divisions responsible for producing programming and capturing academic and student activities for both internal and external broadcast. For example, at the College of DuPage where I teach, the Multimedia Services division offers various media services such as producing video programs, satellite teleconferencing, CD-ROM and DVD authoring, PowerPoint production, and streaming media. All of this production work benefits from music. It's worth your time to research possible avenues and make appropriate introductions.

GAMES

This dynamic field has grown tremendously in the past decade and shows no sign of letting up. New games are released at a steady rate, and while there are some big companies releasing content, there are upstarts breaking in all the time. The Internet carries a wealth of information about this area. Here is a partial listing of resources.

▶ Game Audio Network Guild (www.audiogang.org)

▶ International Game Developers Association (www.igda.org)

▶ *Game Developer's Magazine* (www.gdmag.com)

▶ www.gamasutra.com

▶ www.gamedev.net

▶ Electronic Entertainment Expo (www.e3expo.com)

HOLLYWOOD FILMS

"I want to write movie music!" We all live by that mantra. Few actually do it. Hollywood doesn't take chances (indie filmmakers do, though) and tends to hire the known quantity, i.e., the proven composer. There are some big names out there who seem to get all the work. Fresh faces and sounds are very rare. Occasionally, a rock/pop star makes the successful transition—Danny Elfmann, BT, for example. Unfortunately, breaking in as an unknown is virtually impossible.

However, there is a path. Work on little, independent productions and build relationships with the directors and producers. They may be small fish today, but they may be bigger fish later and take *you* with them. Don't just work on the music and leave. Become part of the team and work to promote the small productions as a partner in the hopes of something bigger happening down the line.

Don't think this path works? Here are some director/composer teams that started out that exact way: Carter Burwell and the Coen Brothers, Terence Blanchard and Spike Lee, and Angelo Badalmenti and David Lynch. Convinced this is worth pursuing yet?

Thankfully, there are some top-notch resources that will help you get your foot in the door. Start with these:

▶ One of the best resources for finding solid prospects is the *Film & Television Music Guide* published by The Music Business Registry, Inc. (www.musicregistry.com). The directory provides the complete contact information for *the* people in the film/TV music world, such as movie studio, TV networks, and independent production company music departments, music supervisors currently working in film/TV, film composers, music clearance companies, music editors, and more.

▶ The *Hollywood Music Industry Directory* published by the Hollywood Creative Directory (www.hcdonline.com) is another resource complete with contact information.

▶ The *Hollywood Reporter* (www.hollywoodreporter.com) lists films and TV shows currently in production. Nearly every issue is a gold mine of ideas, leads, contacts, and more.

▶ The Film Music Channel (www.filmmusicchannel.com) is another resource—actually several different resources—that you should consult.

▶ There are links galore at this useful site (www.johnbraheny.com).

▶ Internet Movie Database (www.imdb.com) provides a wealth of information about past productions. Their companion fee-based site (www.imdbpro.com) has info on current projects, but you must join to get contact details and demo submission guidelines.

▶ Another fee-based site is www.filmmusicjobs.com, where people seeking music post for free, but you pay to see the details.

INDEPENDENT FILMS

Whether documentary or narrative, the same kind of technology that made music production easier and cheaper has done the same for video. Armed with a mini-DV camera, mic, and NLE software, just about anyone can make a movie today. There is quite a low-budget/no-budget movement in the film/video world today. A lot of this work is purely speculative ("we hope to sell it to HBO") or just for art's sake.

Contrarily, some "independent" films have surprisingly large budgets complete with big-name talent, both in front of and behind the camera. In either case, hanging out where indie filmmakers congregate is one way to reach prospects. These films tend to be labors of love produced by a close-knit group. Becoming part of that coterie is the way to score these pictures. This world is cliquish, so working to entrench yourself in the right clique is vital.

There are a couple of magazines that serve this market—*Filmmaker* (www.filmmakermagazine.com) and *Independent Film* (www.ifmagazine.com)—and several major and minor film festivals, such as Sundance, Tribeca, and South by Southwest. Again, reading credits and tracking down the proper contact information is the way to find people. Make your introductions and see where it takes you.

Although working on these smaller films may not pay well, I guarantee you will have more creative freedom while having an absolute blast working on them. I speak from experience, having composed for several small student and indie films, not for the money, but for the investment in the future and the sheer joy of doing it, of pursuing creative ideas that the mainstream would balk at.

*Try the music for your film Web site (http://www.
musicforyourfilm.com). It's actually for filmmakers to
find and connect with composers.*

LIBRARY MUSIC SUPPLIERS

Most music you hear on radio, TV, and nonbroadcast productions is not written specifically for
the production. Producers rely on production or library music to supply many of the tracks they
need for their projects. There are dozens of companies delivering music for both broadcast and
nonbroadcast use. Perhaps you have what it takes to compose, record, and deliver a library music
CD that people want to buy. To supplement your income, consider composing production library
music that you either produce and sell yourself or by pitching to one of the established companies.
Because this is so important, there is more detailed information about this subject in a later chapter.

Meanwhile, if you want to learn more about library music, check out the many companies that
supply buyout library music to the audiovisual industry, such as two of my favorites:

▶ Fresh Music (www.freshmusic.com)

▶ Digital Juice (www.digitaljuice.com)

LOCAL CABLE COMPANIES

You may not realize it, but many of the local commercials you see running on your favorite basic
cable channels are produced by your local cable company. Cable companies also produce a lot of
local programming, including sports, talk, public affairs, and so on. They need music for both
areas. Call your local/regional office and ask for the local production department, for example, the
people who produce both local programming and local advertising. If that doesn't work, ask for the
advertising department. Also, watch some local programming and look for producers' names on the
credits. Contact them directly through the production department or their own production firm (if
that applies). I cut my teeth working this market; there are still opportunities to learn *and* earn.

MEDIA

Another group that you will depend upon for the success of your musical endeavors is the media.
You need to identify *all* the possible media—print, broadcast, and Web—that reach the same people you are trying to reach. You'll need specific contact information and names of editors. You will
be sending your news releases, pitching articles, and so forth to these people. The publicity you earn
is just one more way to promote to your prospects and clients. Chances are that you already have a
good idea of the media available to you. That doesn't mean you shouldn't do a little more research,
too. For information about media, try these publications and Web sites.

▶ *Gale Directory of Publications and Broadcast Media*, published by
Thomson Gale (www.gale.com)

▶ Media Finder by Oxbridge Communications (www.mediafinder.com)

After you find suitable contacts, call the advertising department. Tell them you are investigating them as a possible outlet for your advertising dollars. Ask for detailed information, and you will usually get sample issues (if print), ad rates and specifications, and the most important data—very informative marketing research and demographics about their audience. You'd pay a lot of money for this information, but this is how you get it for free. If you are considering writing for the publication, talk to the editorial department about writer's guidelines (or you may find them on the Web).

MUSICAL DIRECTORIES

Resources devoted to the traditional music industry can still be useful. For example, the Mix Master Directory has listings for quite a few audio production companies and music houses, including the following:

▶ Recording Industry Sourcebook (www.artistpro.com).

▶ Mix Master Directory (www.mixonline.com).

▶ Musician's Atlas (www.musiciansatlas.com).

▶ The Berklee School of Music (www.berkleemusic.com) has online job opportunities that may be worth checking out.

NETWORKED IN

Another option is networking. Don't be afraid to ask others about possibilities. All the people you know have connections, and those connections have further connections. By exploiting these relationships, you can often discover what you need. Occasionally, you may be put in *direct* contact with the people you are trying to reach. For example, you need to talk to the school librarian but don't have any kids in school. Neighbors have kids? Perhaps the parents can get you the information you need about educational content producers.

One assignment may lead to another. For example, you may work with an animation firm from whom you find out about a video production company. While you should never "steal" clients away from people who have already hired you, there's nothing wrong with getting introduced and networked into a gig. This kind of thing happens regularly. One person with whom you work on one show mentions you to somebody else doing another, similar project. It's really just word of mouth, but with a minor twist. Treat the people who help you this way generously; try to return the favor. You have to let people know that you are looking for specific work; otherwise, they might not remember you when the opportunity arises. Try the following resources:

▶ Local Chambers of Commerce, other business organizations, and clubs

▶ Local chapters of national organizations such as NARAS (www.grammy. com), BMI/ASCAP, or the Musician's Union (AFM)

▶ Who's Who in Entertainment (www.marquiswhoswho.com)

NEWS FEATURES/PUBLIC AFFAIRS CONTENT

Your local TV station news department produces mini-documentaries and other public affairs programs for broadcast. While they tend to grab library music, you need to convince them that at times, they could make a greater impact with your original music. Don't necessarily pursue the Executive Producer. Instead, find the regular show producer(s)— again look for a title, such as segment producer or something similar, in the credits and contact them through the news division.

ONLINE FORUMS, CHAT, AND SUCH

There remains a huge collection of Web-based forums and IRC channels that service specific topics, including narrative, documentary, and commercial audiovisual productions and gaming. You should mine these for leads to possible projects. On the DMN where I co-host several forums, there are many appeals for help on various issues. Positioning yourself as a genuine assistant and not as somebody there to make a buck is just one more way to build your reputation.

OTHER MUSIC HOUSES

They may be competition, but that doesn't mean they aren't also prospects for you. A music production company can get overloaded and need to outsource some work. You want to be the one they call when this happens. Make contact, get them a demo of what you can do, and stay in touch regularly. These projects usually are all about timing. You call on the one day they need somebody fast. Make the call!

PRODUCTION COMPANIES

Production companies run the gamut and include audio, video, and multimedia firms that put together a variety of audiovisual content, such as training, educational, promotional projects, games, software, and so forth. Read the credits of the media productions where you'd like your music to be considered. Contact the producers, directors, or music supervisors/editors by looking for production company names and then doing a little sleuthing.

For example, if you watch PBS, Discovery, TLC, and their ilk, you'll see many of the same companies producing many of the shows. Some of these companies produce a staggering number of hours every year, and they consume music at an equally astonishing rate. Where are they getting this music? You, perhaps? Not if they don't know about you first!

Here is a listing of some of the top resources for finding and connecting with production companies of all sorts. Refer the previous and subsequent listings for even more possible outlets.

► Mandy (www.mandy.com) is a directory of creative talent and companies.

► The Production Hub (www.productionhub.com) is similar to Mandy.

► *Post* magazine (www.postmagazine.com) is all about post-production. Since music is a primary post thing, this magazine is invaluable.

► Entertainment Jobs (www.eej.com) is another great resource.

► Check the film music directory (www.filmmusicdirectory.com) as another possibility.

► See "Creative Directories" and "Hollywood Films" for other details.

RADIO AND TV COMMERCIALS (LOCAL, CABLE, REGIONAL, AND NATIONAL)

Obviously, there are still opportunities to craft soundtracks and jingles to accompany advertisements. You reach these opportunities by approaching a business directly, through advertising agencies, and production houses, and even by contacting the radio/TV station itself. Ad agencies and production firms are covered elsewhere.

Compile a list of the radio stations in your local area (within 50 miles). Get the name and phone of the heads of production or the advertising sales manager. Make the calls; you could become their in-house composer.

► Find stations at radio locator (www.radio-locator.com).

► This site (www.quadphonic.com) lists college radio and TV stations.

► *Bacon's Radio/TV/Cable Directory* and *Broadcasting and Cable Marketplace* (see "TV Programs," later in this chapter, for details).

► *Billboard* (www.billboard.com) carries a wealth of information.

One caveat about your local radio stations. They love to produce ad spots in-house because it is cheap. Plus, they almost never charge their advertisers for production. What they really sell is air time. So, they'll go to an advertiser and say "You buy 100 spots, and we'll do your commercial for *free.*" That makes it rather hard to compete on your end. When the radio station throws everything in for free, you will have a difficult time selling your production and music services to them.

I suggest bypassing the radio stations and going directly to the advertisers. Though you'll face some tough obstacles, you must work to convince them that your contribution will make their ad stand out and be more memorable. I find that most ads produced by radio stations start to sound alike. If an advertiser really wants to be heard above the din, you must give them the tools to do that. That means good writing, good talent, good music, great production values—exactly what you provide.

Something I've done is to prepare a generic jingle that I can re-lyric easily. I then visit a radio advertiser that is not using a jingle, collect some of their promotional material, return to the studio, and write/record a "demo" jingle that uses their promotional message, name, etc. Next, approach the advertiser and play that demo. They will be impressed that you took the time to make a "custom" jingle for them. It's the way to make a sale and not much trouble on your part. If you don't make the sale, choose another prospect, re-lyric the same jingle, and start again.

SAMPLE LIBRARIES

Another possible income stream is to pitch your services to those companies that sell soundware—samples, synth patches, loops, and such. Since the dawn of MIDI, the soundware market has grown exponentially. You can buy patches for your synths, samples for your samplers, and loops aplenty for your DAW. There is a wide range of material already available, but hungry electronic musicians are always open to fresh ideas. Perhaps you have what it takes to produce a sample CD volume that people want to buy. You will want to contact the makers of the soundware you already buy. There's more on this subject in the "Diversify and Thrive" chapter later in this book.

SONGWRITER'S MARKET

Another source for companies that buy original music is the annual *Songwriter's Market*. They have a complete section devoted to audiovisual producers. But be forewarned. The competition is fierce. I've heard horror stories about a single listing getting hundreds of demos! Go for it if you have the chops and like playing the musical equivalent of lotto. These jobs are more luck than skill alone.

▶ Look for *Songwriter's Market* at www.writersdigest.com.

TELEPHONE BOOK

The business section is a good initial source. Look under audiovisual, video production and post-production, and advertising agencies. You'll get the telephone numbers easily but not a name. You'll need to call each place listed and ask to whom you should talk regarding custom music. It's that easy to get off and running. When you call, simply say:

> *Hi, this is Jeffrey Fisher. I run a music production company in town and I'm calling to find out who usually buys music for your company.*

THEATER AND DANCE

There are small theater companies and dance troops out there that may need music for their shows. Do some research and see what's going on around your area. If these groups are doing original material (plays, recitals), they may be possible prospects. Contact the artistic director directly. Don't expect much pay, but you could build credits and experience, and that's not a bad investment.

TV PROGRAMS

Whether you want to write for TV sitcoms, dramas, reality, or any other format out there, there's no denying the *huge* demand for music. And there's no denying the even larger pool of competition for those dollars. You will be competing against some of the biggest and brightest the music world has to offer. It's not an easy market to crack, but well worth pursuing. Understand that although networks and cable stations use music, most programming comes from production companies who make their own music deals for the shows they produce. (See "Production Companies," earlier in this chapter.)

Find the contacts at TV stations around the globe using these resources:

▶ *Bacon's Radio/TV/Cable Directory* (www.bacons.com/research/ radiotvcable.htm).

▶ *Broadcasting and Cable Marketplace* (www.broadcastingcable.com).

▶ National Association of Broadcasters (www.nab.org).

▶ American Women in Radio and TV (www.awrt.org).

▶ See the resources under "Hollywood Films," earlier in this chapter.

VANITY PROJECTS

Schools, churches, and even individuals may use your expertise for fundraising or commercial projects. Keep your ears open, ask around, and pitch your own ideas to the right people.

WEB

Your music may be used on a Web page, streaming video, in Flash presentations, Podcasts, other downloadable or streaming presentations, and any technology to be invented later and delivered via the Web. Web design firms especially, along with advertising agencies and production companies, are the prospects for this work.

STILL CAN'T FIND IT?

Can't find resources and publications that serve the area you are trying to reach? Ask around. When you visit a client or prospect, look to see what they're reading. Local business publications have sections devoted to advertising and audiovisual production. Put on your Sherlock Holmes hat and start researching. You'll soon have what you need. And don't forget that your venerable local library is always a wealth of information, too. So, *use* it!

Check out Directories in Print, *published by Thomson Gale (www.galegroup.com). This guide lists over 15,000 directories published today. If you can't find it here, what you need probably doesn't exist.*

Competitive Issues

What about competition? In smaller towns and rural areas, there are usually only a few small music companies to worry about or other musicians looking to supplement their income. In big cities (like Chicago, where I live), the competition is fierce. But there's more work to go around, too. If you live in a remote area, don't be discouraged. There is enough work within a 100-mile radius of your home. You may just need to widen your reach somewhat. There will be less competition, and you just might find one or two production companies that will give you *all* their work.

Of course, the Internet makes this business a global market, so you have the potential to work with anyone, anywhere in the world. Technology, including telephone, fax, email, Web, FTP, and overnight mail, lets you compose music for clients located virtually anywhere in the world. It isn't always easy, as some people just refuse to work this way and prefer face-to-face. Others are more forward thinking. That same global marketplace may bring added competition from unexpected places.

Want to know what your competition is doing? Just listen to the radio, or TV, or cable. Go to the movies, especially smaller films and indie festivals. Check out educational and business videos and CD-ROMs from your local library. Pick up the latest games. Surf the Web and visit your competition's Web sites. Listen to their demos. Visit the popular music sites. Get demos from library music producers and from your competitors. Once you know what all your competition is doing, you can position your music composition services accordingly.

The best way to discover information about your nearby competitors is to ask for it. While I'm not advocating lying and misrepresenting yourself, you may need to use a little competitive deception to get the information you need. Call your competition and request their latest demo and promotional materials. Tell them you are new in the area and are interested in their services. While some may catch on to your story, others will give you what you need. If you don't feel comfortable asking for this information, have a friend or colleague do the dirty work and get the information sent to her office. Study what your competition is doing and learn from their mistakes. After collecting from a few, you'll know exactly what you need to do to compete in your market.

Win Against Your Competition

Small companies like yours can outwit your competition in several ways.

EXPLOIT NICHE MARKETS

Go after the smaller budgets and companies that the big guys pass up. Diversify your service line to offer a variety of music and recording services to those people who (wrongly) think they can't afford such professional work. Carve out a position in your market and promote your particular strengths.

GET CLOSE AND PERSONAL

Stay in contact with your clients and be available to meet their needs. Don't put barriers between you and them. Answer your own phone, follow up promptly, and concentrate on their local, parochial needs and desires.

USE TECHNOLOGY WISELY

Today's computers will give you a distinct edge. They become your company support staff and allow you to store, monitor, and use vast amounts of data. They handle your routine, freeing you to promote and create.

LISTEN TO YOUR CLIENTS AND PROSPECTS

They will tell you what they are looking for in music. What styles do they use or prefer? How much music do they need? What budgets do they have? These questions are educational for both them and you. The answers will help you sell more of your music. After you find out what your clients need, you are in an ideal position to give it to them.

Industry Insight

Winifred Phillips
Generations Productions LLC, NYC area
www.winifredphillips.com

Recent credits /past projects:
Composer, "Charlie and the Chocolate Factory" videogame (Global Star/Take Two Interactive/ Warner Bros.), Composer, "God of War" videogame (Sony Computer Entertainment America), Composer, "Radio Tales" drama series (National Public Radio/XM Satellite Radio). These programs include *Arabian Nights Trilogy, Beowulf, Dracula's Guest, Dr. Jekyll and Mr. Hyde, The Fall of the House of Usher, Frankenstein, Gulliver's Travels, Homer's Odyssey, The Hunchback of Notre Dame, The Invisible Man, The Island of Dr. Moreau, Jason and the Argonauts, Journey to the Center of the Earth, The Lost World, Phantom of the Opera, The Pit and the Pendulum, Sleepy Hollow, The Tell-Tale Heart, The Time Machine, 20,000 Leagues Under the Sea, War of the Worlds*, and many more.

Why did you choose this career (and how did you get started)?
I think the career of a composer is not something you choose. Rather, you're driven to it by an insatiable need to create music. The career of a composer is challenging on many levels, which makes passion for the work and a steadfast belief in your own abilities incredibly important. I was fortunate in that my first project turned into an extended relationship with an organization that believed

in me and supported my early creative efforts. That opportunity gave me the chance to grow and learn as I worked.

What was and how did you land your first project?

I started as a composer for National Public Radio. NPR offered a weekly national forum for drama at the time, which was called *NPR Playhouse*. A lot of great dramas received their national debuts on *NPR Playhouse*, including the *Star Wars* dramas. I approached NPR with my work, and they took me into their fold. I'm immensely grateful to them for all the support and encouragement they gave to me. I worked on a series for NPR called *Radio Tales*, which adapted classic works of science fiction, fantasy, and horror using wall-to-wall music. I wrote music for over a hundred programs for NPR. It was a great experience. NPR's artistic standards were very high, and the production schedule was challenging, so it really taught me a lot about working efficiently.

What are you working on now and how did you get this current project?

After NPR it was a natural progression to writing music for video games. I'd always been a gamer, and games are similar to radio drama in that they both rely on music to relate vital information to the audience. With radio drama, the music needs to replace the missing visual content. With games, the music needs to let the players know how they are doing while playing. I've just finished up work on the "Charlie and the Chocolate Factory" video game. I got the job by patiently researching the industry and sending out demos until I found a company that liked what I do and wanted my sound to be a part of their game. It was also helpful that I was able to meet with them at E3—the Electronic Entertainment Expo held every year in Los Angeles. I strongly feel that face-to-face contact is irreplaceable.

What do you feel makes a good music score (or jingle)?

It's hard to generalize about that because underscore is so dependent on the nature of the drama for which it is written. Some projects work very well with music that is relatively nonreactive to the action on-screen, serving instead to set a general mood and give the characters a sense of overall identity. Other projects absolutely need a very sensitive, changeable, reactive score that moves fluidly with the action and enhances every dramatic moment. Both approaches are viable choices. I think a media composer needs to be a storyteller at heart because the music must first and foremost serve the story.

What gear do you use?

I work with Pro Tools, Kontakt 2, a PC2x keyboard, and loads of plug-ins and sample libraries. I also rely on lots of vintage outboard gear (sound modules and effects processors).

Explain your promotional strategies (what works and why)?

Research works. It may not seem to do the trick right away, but in the long run it is the most effective promotional strategy available to a composer. The Internet is a gold mine of information about where composers might find their next project. Web sites like Mandy.com and ShootingPeople.org provide opportunities to find work and make contacts in the film and television industries. In the field of video games, Gamasutra.com and AudioGang.org provide valuable networking and informational resources. Sites like Music4Games.net and Soundtrack.net are great places to become more familiar with who's who in the industry. *Game Developer Magazine* is the leading trade publication of the video game industry, filled with news regarding technological and artistic developments in the field. Starting in this business is always frustrating at first, and no single strategy will allow you to sidestep that entirely, but knowledge of what is happening in the industry will give you a definite advantage.

What skills do you feel someone needs to succeed in the area?

Apart from musical skills, media composers need to cultivate written and speech communication skills. Often, we are judged by our ability to communicate, both verbally and in written form. We're evaluated based on how well we'll be able to bounce ideas back and forth with the game developer. The concept of the taciturn composer who expresses him or herself through music alone is one that won't succeed in this business. The most successful composers are able to speak eloquently about music, relate their passion and their inspiration to the developer, and show the developer that they understand and are committed to the overall goals of the project.

How do you approach projects, technically or creatively?

Each project is different, and I approach each one differently. At the beginning, I pay very close attention to the direction of the game developer and then research musical genres and styles that embody that direction most effectively. Whether I rely on that research or discard it entirely in the process of creation, I think that research always serves to define the musical scope of a project when it is first begun.

How do you get paid (typical pay for projects, royalties, etc.)?

For my radio work, I was paid by the project. For my game work, I am paid for each minute of finished score, which is fairly typical of the video game industry as a whole.

What do you wish you'd known then that you know now?

The technology of music creation is continually growing. If there were anything I could have done better in my early days, it would have been to aggressively avail myself of every tool that music technology had to offer. The field of media composition is tremendously competitive, and none of us can afford to fall behind technologically. When I started, I didn't understand that as well as I do now. Of course, keeping up with the state of the art doesn't have to mean breaking the bank. There are alternatives that can help a composer early in his or her career. But there is no way around the fact that media composition is an expensive field to enter, requiring a substantial investment in equipment and supplies. Staying educated in technological developments in the field is now a prerequisite to success.

What are your plans for the future?

I plan to keep writing music for games and other media. I really enjoy my work. I feel privileged to be a part of these inspired projects. Now is a great time to be a media composer.

CHAPTER 7

Turning Prospects into Paying Music Clients

"An ounce of action is worth a ton of theory."—Friedrich Engels

There are four crucial keys to building and sustaining your career composing soundtracks and jingles:

▶ Finding and contacting possible buyers.

▶ Bringing your benefits to these prospects.

▶ Closing sales.

▶ Staying in contact with current and past clients (to make additional sales).

This isn't a one-time process. You will check off these four steps repeatedly as your pursuit of this work continues. Promotion is the *most important* part of succeeding in the commercial music business. Sure, you must have talent, but if the world doesn't know about your talent, you'll fail. Promotion isn't something you take lightly or do occasionally. In good times and in bad, you must always be out there promoting and selling what you do. Period. End of discussion.

I probably spend about 30–40% of my time promoting, 20% taking care of business matters, and about 30–40% actually doing what I sell. Does that shock you? It's nevertheless quite true. When you are first starting out, you may spend 90–95% of your time promoting. I know I did, and I still hear from a lot of readers who have been down a similar road. Here's the lesson: Your next client is *at least* three months away. Can you afford to wait?

Recently a peer quipped, "I'm really busy today, but who knows about tomorrow." That observation struck a chord with me. It's a typically entrepreneurial thing to say. You might be busy right now, but you might be twiddling your thumbs in a few days. Those of us who work on our own tend to take on any and all work that comes along. Turning down a project just isn't in our psyche. Why do many of us feel this way? Because you never know what might happen next. Your next gig might be weeks or months away. Of course, not refusing some work can find you overloaded at times (and risking burnout). What's key is striking a balance. Make sure you keep promoting and selling to bring in a steady stream of business. Take on enough work to keep you comfortable and find ways to outsource the overload when that happens.

Too many people confuse promotion and advertising; advertising is only one aspect of the whole promotional mix. Advertising costs money, but many promotional opportunities are free or very inexpensive. Promotion does take some of your time, though, so there is a cost. But without this investment in your business, you'll have little work to do.

Remember that every aspect of your daily business is a promotional opportunity:

▶ How you answer your phone.

▶ What you say on the telephone and in-person meetings.

▶ The look of your promotional materials (Web site, letterhead/business cards, CD/DVD label, etc.).

▶ The quality and versatility of your demo(s).

▶ How you follow up.

▶ How well you use publicity.

▶ And, yes, your advertising.

For you to have any chance at making it in the commercial music world, you must develop an image and build and sustain it through every little thing that you do. Establishing an image as a creative music professional willing and able to help people use music more effectively takes considerable effort on your part. Once in place, you continually promote that image to further build the reputation that people buy. It's a long road that you'll rarely traverse easily. But the payoff for your hard work makes this toil worthwhile. Don't take this burden lightly, and don't blow it needlessly.

For example, I once called an equipment rental house, and whoever picked up the phone said, "Yeah, rental house here. Whaddya want?" When I asked whether he had a certain piece of equipment to rent, he replied, "Uh, I think so. It's 50 a day plus delivery. When d'ya want it?" He wasn't the least bit interested in my needs, so I hung up. Needless to say, his dubious phone demeanor cost him this and all my future sales.

Don't run your business the way this poor fool does. Be polite, understanding, accommodating, and genuinely interested in everyone with whom you have contact. You *do* want to help people through your music, don't you? Make sure this comes across with everything—and *I do mean everything*—that you do. That is what effective promotion is all about.

Seven Steps to Promotional Success

You need to formulate a general promotional plan that you will follow as a road map for finding and reaching out to possible music buyers. You also need to generate a specific action plan for *every single project* you want to land. In both cases, ask and answer seven basic questions. First, ask the questions and answer generally. This becomes an overall approach to promotion for you to follow. Then ask and answer these seven questions again for every project that you decide to pursue. It only takes a few minutes to do this, but ultimately it improves your chances exponentially.

1) WHAT DO YOU SELL?

General: You don't sell a feature (e.g., music). You sell benefits—what your music brings to media content producers (e.g., mood and emotion). This is what clients really buy. Decide what it is you truly bring to buyers. This answer becomes the primary purpose of your business and will serve as the major thrust of your promotional efforts.
Specific: For a particular project, narrow down the focus, such as music for a video game to make the player's experience more enjoyable.

2) WHAT GIG DO YOU WANT TO LAND?

General: Identify what it is you want to do. First, think about the kind of music you want to write. Do you want to write jingles? Score long-form indie films? Next, look for the places where your music fits, such as in commercials, dramatic films and videos, computer games, and so forth. Finally, find the people who create these productions (and eventually let them know you can solve their music problems).
Specific: Define a possible outlet or a particular gig, such as Ms. Director's next indie film score.

3) WHAT DOES IT TAKE TO GET THE SALE?

General: You need to discover those hot buttons that when pressed will motivate people to buy what you sell. Essentially, there are two approaches to take: get rid of pain or promote a gain. Pain = scene lacks emotion (your music helps). Gain = producer wants music (you have the music they need). Don't forget that all-important distinction that you will be selling yourself along with your music.
Specific: You defined the gig you want; now figure out how you are going to land it. Do you know Ms. Director or someone who does? Will you approach her at a screening? What, where, and how?

4) ARE THERE ANY OBSTACLES OR DRAWBACKS?

General: Consider all the downsides that may interfere with your pursuing this kind of work. This may be skills you lack, equipment, competition, and so forth. Uncover what it will take to overcome these challenges.

Specific: What definitely is in your way? How you can move those impediments aside?

5) WHO IS RESPONSIBLE FOR BUYING?

General: Research the field to uncover those who are the best candidates for what you've decided to do in steps 1 and 2 above. Follow the advice in the previous chapter for tracking down prospects and compile a list of contact information.

Specific: Locate the actual contact information of the prospect who has the power to hire you.

6) HOW DO YOU MAKE CONTACT?

General: Develop the promotional material and tactics you will use to promote yourself, your music, and how you can help people make their productions better. You will need material that you can mail, email, and post to your promotional Web site. What goes into these missives is the subject of the next chapter.

Specific: Decide which promotional tactics you will employ for the person identified in step 5. Will you telephone or email? Try to set up a meeting at an industry event? Or any number of other possible ideas. You will need a cogent follow-up strategy, too.

7) WHAT WILL THE PITCH BE?

General: Formulate several offers that promote the benefits you determined buyers want.

Specific: Decide and then present the offer or pitch when you make contact with your prospect.

Promotional Tools

You will need some basic promotional material that highlights your skills, capabilities, past work, and credentials. As mentioned previously, the material you develop will need to work in standard mail format, in an email, on your Web site, and in other forms. It makes good sense to prepare most of this material right away. It is even more important to keep your promotional material updated. As you complete projects and earn additional credentials, swap these out for outdated, and less impressive, data. And remember that the material you use is often the first contact someone has with you. Make sure yours makes your best impression.

Don't create any of this material until you read and understand the chapter about preparing promotional material later in this book. You will save tons of time, energy, and money that you would otherwise waste on materials that don't work to sell your music.

Here's what you need:

BIOGRAPHY

Prepare a one-page professional biography to help people better understand your musical background. This isn't your life story; it functions as narrative résumé. Tell what you are about, where you came from, and what is happening now. Consider writing it as a short feature that a media source would use when profiling you and your work.

Also, prepare a short, 50 words or so, version that you can use in letters, emails, on the phone, for publicity, and other opportunities. Here's an example:

Jeffrey P. Fisher provides music, sound, writing, video, training, and media production services for broadcast and nonbroadcast clients. His music appears on dozens of productions and the Fresh Music library, Dark New Age. Jeffrey writes about music, sound, and video, including nine books, and teaches at the College of DuPage Motion Picture/Television department. Contact him at www.jeffreypfisher.com.

BROCHURE

Take a piece of paper and fold it into thirds. This fits neatly in a standard #10 business envelope and gives you a cover, an address panel, and four inside panels to promote yourself and your music. Try including a picture on the cover along with a strong benefit headline. Use the fold-in panel for project listings and testimonials from satisfied clients. Use the three inside sections to profile what you've done and more importantly what you can do. Include the short bio, if there's room. Place your contact information on the back panel. Design your brochure so the back panel carries an address panel and can be mailed on its own.

Having a printed brochure shows you are a serious professional. It also makes it easier to supply information to people quickly during in-person situations and when you mail information. The same content can be cut and pasted into emails. Of course, having your brochure match the look and feel of your Web site ties your promotional image together quite nicely. The same content used for the brochure goes on the Web site, too.

BUSINESS CARDS

Business cards are the easiest way to give somebody your contact information. I give every worthwhile contact my business card. And my cards ride along with nearly every piece of mail that leaves my office. Keep your cards updated should your contact information change. Choose a design that matches your letterhead, brochure, and Web site.

CD

We've covered creating and packaging your demo in a previous chapter. This—or rather the music on it—is your #2 promotional tool. (Who is #1? You are!)

INTRODUCTORY LETTER

Develop a letter that introduces the benefits of doing business with you. You may need to develop several versions, depending on the projects and people you pursue. Make sure you focus on what your prospects want (good music that reinforces their message, on time, and on budget) and how you have the credentials to deliver what they need. While most of this letter will be generic, always customize it to fit particular situations, people, and projects. Update the lead paragraph to address specifics and then follow with your standard promotional verbiage. This letter makes for the perfect introductory page on your Web site, is great pasted into an email, and can be mailed after printing on your letterhead.

CREDENTIALS

Gather the credentials that serve to build your reputation. You will want lists of recent projects and especially prominent client names. If you've received special press coverage, other recognition, and awards, you need to feature these. Place these credentials on your brochure and Web site and slip them into emails.

Also, consider writing short case studies about projects. They dress up other promotions nicely and often serve as the basis of media releases used for publicity. Take the problem/solution angle where you essentially solve a client's problem with your music. These are success stories that say: "So-and-so benefited from our help, we can do the same for you."

DON'T FIX WHAT AIN'T BROKE

When it comes to successful promotions—those that result in gigs and cash—don't meddle with those that still work. If a said promotion brought in the business, don't change for change's sake. Run the promotion again and keep at it until it fails to generate the response you want. If your promotions are working locally, there's no reason to think they won't work on a larger scale. Apply what you do in other areas, and hopefully your hard work will pay off.

ELEVATOR PITCH

Practice describing what you do in 25 words or less. I call this promotional blurb your "elevator pitch," pretending that you are in an elevator with a prospect and you have only a few seconds to tell your story.

EMAIL

Today, a primary way you will connect with prospects and clients is via email. It is a wonderfully efficient and productive communications tool. Using it, however, demands that you master some rudimentary writing skills. Learn how to organize your thoughts succinctly and get to the point fast. Master grammar essentials and always check your spelling before clicking Send. DON'T TYPE IN ALL UPPERCASE LETTERS. Most of all, use your email contact as a means to secure more work. More tips on this subject in a later chapter.

EMAIL SIGNATURE

Develop suitable promotional blurbs that appear at the end of every email that leaves your computer. I have several different versions that I use for specific situations. Include your name, contact information (email and phone), a line about what you do, and a link to your Web site. If you can make the link clickable, so much the better.

FLYER/POSTCARD

Don't neglect the lowly flyer or its sibling, the postcard. A mass emailing would be the online equivalent. Use these simple tools to profile a recent project, especially if it something readily available for past clients and prospects to see or listen to. Alternately, announce upcoming projects or events, deliver general promotional information, or even make a special offer of some kind. Mail your flyers or postcards and add them as pages to your Web site. Postcards are particularly effective and inexpensive reminders for clients and recent prospects.

FOLLOW-UP

Here's a single equation that summarizes the importance of this step: Leads + Follow-up = $ales. No matter how flashy your promotional material is or how incredible your demo sounds, your attempts will fail miserably if you don't follow up. Get on the phone, send emails, mail another letter or postcard, and reconnect. It should come as no surprise that follow-up and follow-through are crucial to building and sustaining your business. I've seen many instances where people have dropped the ball when they should have known better. Don't let that be you. People get busy and forget about you. It is your job to remind them that you are ready, willing, and able to help them right now!

For example, people contact me with ideas, and I'm usually quite open to them. However, I'm often busy and ask the people to contact me again at some later date to pursue the idea further. I effectively shift the burden of follow-up to them (which makes my life easier). I'll notice that the vast majority of these people who contact me in the first place rarely approach me again. They just let a good idea die. This is unfortunate when simply entering a reminder in a PDA or calendar is all it takes to keep the process flowing.

FREQUENTLY ASKED QUESTIONS (FAQ)

I love this format, especially for Web pages. It's easily created and quickly conveys answers to all the fundamental questions people ask you about your music and doing business with you. There's a sample in the next chapter.

LOGO

You may want to develop a logo for your business. This may be as simple as a typestyle that you use for the company name or a more traditional approach. Although not a crucial item, consistently using it increases name retention.

MEDIA COVERAGE

When you and your music have appeared in print and on the Web, such as in feature stories, interviews, and reviews, get reprints that you can mail and post on your Web site. For the Web, a link to the original article is sufficient. Including this material provides third-party validation of your work. Ideas on how to secure free publicity are detailed in another chapter.

MP3
As mentioned in the previous chapter, encode your music demo to MP3 for online downloading and emailing.

OTHER GOODIES
Items that carry your logo/company name on them, such as mouse pads, mugs, and a myriad of other possibilities, can be an interesting promotional gimmick. While a bit passé these days, promotional items used in moderation may still work as a way to thank clients and carefully spread the word in certain circumstances. If you take this tactic, be sure this item is useful and of good quality. You want the prospect to think highly of you every time they pick it up or use it. Of course, make sure your name, phone number, and email address are clearly visible along with an indication of what you do, for example, original music scores.

PACKAGING
Letterhead is mandatory; you'll use it for everything from letters and quotes to contracts and invoices. Choose letterhead, matching envelopes, and business cards that coordinate with your brochure, CD labels, and Web site.

PHOTOS
Consider getting two photos: a decent head shot and one of you working in your project studio. If you've scored a major client, a two-shot of you and this prominent individual is a must. Promotional material from projects you've worked on, such as the poster for the movie you've scored, the cover of the game you worked on, and similar elements, make for useful graphics to accompany your promotional push on the Web and in print. These graphics also make wonderful decorations for your studio.

PROMO KIT
Assemble and mail your introductory letter, brochure, business card, and demo CD together for a powerful promotional package. The contents of the letter, an email signature, and a link to your online demo are the email equivalent of this important promotional approach.

SALES LETTER(S)
See the information under "Introductory Letter" above. Essentially, these contain the words (along with other items such as testimonials, awards, recent clients, and such) that you use in a variety of promotional means—telephone calls, emails, chat rooms, Web pages, online forums, and more.

TELEPHONE
This is another crucial way to connect with people. Master the details later in this chapter.

TESTIMONIALS
Endorsements, letters of recommendation, and other testimonials from happy, satisfied clients are also useful additions to your general promotional campaigns.

VOICE MAIL MESSAGE

Record a brief, professional announcement that people will hear when contacting you by telephone. This is often the first real contact people may have with you. Set the tone right for this first impression.

You've reached Joe Pro Music. I can't get your call right now because I'm currently helping other clients get the music they need. Please leave a message, and I'll get back to you.

WEB SITE

You will need an online presence, and we'll discuss its details later. For now, visit www.winifredphillips.com for the prototypical example of a professional composer's Web site.

Crucial Insider Knowledge

Don't send out your demo unsolicited. Repeat this phrase ten times out loud, *"I will never send my demo to anyone without first making contact!"*

Advertising agencies, video production companies, game developers, radio/TV stations, and others get assaulted by audio and video demos every single day. It's hard to stand out from the crowd, so you end up getting buried alive. *Screen* magazine once reported that a single blurb that ran in their pages resulted in a small production company getting over 400 demo submissions in one week!

When you send demos to people who aren't expecting it, you give up the primary power of promotion, which is control. You want to control your contact with people, to lead the sales process. Sending demos is far too passive when you *must* be proactive and in charge.

There are two exceptions to this rule. One, it is acceptable for people to hear your demo on your Web site, provided you got them there in the first place. Additionally, you could devise a way to capture the contact information (email addresses) of those who do visit your site and listen. Two, it is fine to send new music to past clients as a way to reconnect and encourage them to buy more music from you.

Sadly, most unsolicited demos are *not* listened to or are not listened to with much attention or enthusiasm. My mailbox gets its fair share, but unless I have an immediate need, this stuff gets filed away (polite for canned, as in garbage). I simply don't have the time to listen to all that arrive, and few busy creatives do either. Such is the fate of most, if not all, unsolicited demo submissions. *Do you understand this?* It might not seem fair, but it's the harsh reality of the commercial music world.

When you don't take the time to make contact first and determine a buyer's needs and how your music can specifically meet those needs, you risk being ignored. I once received a demo from a jingle singer with a sticky note attached that read, "Next time you need a great singer, you know whom to call." Oh really? He wasted his money. Doesn't this seem selfish, foolish, arrogant, and just plain stupid? It is. So don't do it.

What you really want to do is promote an image of success and of helping other people realize their goals. Promotion can't be all about you, you, you. It must be about what people get from you and your music. So take proactive control of the sales process, not a passive attitude. Go after the projects you want to do and make contact with the people with whom you want to work. Don't wait for the phone to ring and don't send your promotional material out into the world in the hopes that people will notice. When you *do* take charge, good things happen. And while it might not be over-night, your dogged determination will eventually pay off.

Getting to a position where people really want to hear your music is where you want to be. You don't just dump stuff on people and hope for the best. Those who are anticipating your music are more likely to listen to it intently. And then buy. Contact people and discover whether they need music, and if so, how you can help. Part of this process is weeding out the cold prospects, those who have no need or will never buy music from you, from the good, warm prospects with whom you have a shot. Occasionally, you'll have a hot prospect that has an immediate need. Strike fast!

Commit right now to spending the majority of your time, energy, and money on the warm and hot prospects you uncover. Of course, you'll also need to stay in regular contact with current and past clients with the purpose of generating new business.

Qualifying Prospects

Your first step toward finding whether people are true candidates is with your research that reveals them in the first place. For example, don't bother calling an advertising agency that only does print. Once you have a narrow list of potential soundtrack and jingle music buyers, it's time to qualify them further. You have two choices: call them or send them an email/letter. I used to be a big fan of using the mail, but times have changed, and business is speedier than ever. Today, I'd rather email a simple inquiry than a more costly and involved letter campaign.

Do understand that you usually must connect with prospects several times, and in a number of different ways, before they become your clients. It may take several tries just to connect in the first place. There will be some rejection. Get a tough skin and know that every no moves you that much closer to a YES! Don't be naive, either. Some people will never become clients. So what? Redline them and move down your list. And some equivocal people will string you along with promises that never come through. Keep some hope alive, but don't bank on these fantasies. Most of all, you will find people, and you will make sales, when you do all that is necessary and possess the talent required.

COLD CALLS

Use cold calls to whittle down your leads, make initial contact, generate some interest, and move to the next steps of selling your music. Depending on your research, you may reach the right person directly or have to go through another person. In either case, pick up the phone and call. Be firm, professional, and polite:

This is Jeffrey Fisher. I'm an independent composer, and I'd like to take just a minute of your time to introduce myself and my music composition services to you. Who buys the music for your productions?

Once you get the name, ask to speak with the person directly. If he can't take your call right now, ask to leave a voice message *and* ask what would be the best time to call this person back. Make a note to call back. For the voice message, keep it simple and to the point.

Hello, (name of person), this is Jeffrey Fisher. I'd like to discuss your music needs for your upcoming project (specifics when you know them). My credits include work for PBS and several independent films. I'll call you again at (use day/time you learned was best) so we can talk about your needs in greater detail and how I might help. You can reach me at (phone number). Thank you.

When you reach the person directly, make a quick introduction and then turn the focus of the conversation to them:

Hello, this is Jeffrey Fisher. I really enjoyed your production of (specifics). I noticed that you used some library music for the score. Have you considered using original music?

They may end the conversation quickly with a "we don't have the budget" or some other typical send-off. Or they may be more open. What you need to determine is whether it's worth pursing this more. If the answer is a flat-out no, thank the person and move on. Maybe make a note to contact him or her again in a few months.

When the answer is of the "not right now" variety, ask when would be the right time for a follow-up call. Make a note to call this person again before that future date. There's more on keeping track of prospects and clients later in this chapter.

When the answer is "send me your demo," be careful. Most people are just being polite and use this excuse to get you off the line. Don't fall prey to this tactic. Discuss specifics first and work to get a meeting (if local) where you can present your music in person. If the prospect is not local, you need to use your best judgment as to whether to send a physical demo. Why waste your money on a tire-kicker? You might direct them to your Web site MP3s instead.

Rather than send a demo, why don't I stop by, say Thursday at 3:00, when I can play a few selections and discuss some options for your (name of project here)?

EMAIL INTROS

Email is just another way to generate some leads to possible warm and hot prospects (that you'll convert into paying clients, right?). It is also useful for weeding out the chaff of the truly disinterested. I firmly believe that email (and the Web for that matter) have made it far, far easier to connect with people than ever before. For example, I've found people by reading articles in magazines and sending an email to the address included in the article or visited their Web site and uncovered the proper contact information that way. Even a Google search can make finding people easy.

These email inquiries are not the place for your life story. Their purpose is to find out who is interested and who is not and to inform and motivate those who seem intrigued, moving them further through the sales process. A simple email works along the lines of the telephone examples above. Citing specific information about a person or project is crucial as opposed to a hit or miss approach.

Subject: Article in Post re: music
I really enjoyed the story about your animation company in the latest edition of Post magazine. I was particularly struck by your insight into the role music plays. As a composer with credits from (list a few key clients), I'm always looking for stimulating and challenging projects. Would you entertain further discussion about music for future projects? I'd welcome the opportunity to discuss how I may help.

LETTER FOLLOWED BY "WARM" CALL

Another approach is to snail mail an introductory sales letter, perhaps along with your brochure and business card. Make mention in the letter that you will follow up in a week. Exactly one week later, make a somewhat warmer telephone call and pick up the conversation.

Did you have a chance to review the material I sent to you? I'm very interested in hearing about your upcoming projects and how I might contribute to the emotion and message through original music. Are there any questions I can answer for you?

FACE-TO-FACE

At networking and industry events, you'll often run into a prospect and must quickly switch to sales mode. Ask about them first (even if you already know); then sneak in your elevator pitch.

THE PROSPECT CONTACTS YOU

If you follow the advice in these pages and consistently promote yourself, your music, and your reputation, people will contact you. It's a wonderful feeling when the phone rings or the email arrives with the promise of a new gig. These prospects often have an immediate need and either are actively seeking demo submissions, to narrow down their list of candidates, or are ready to hire you.

Keep the conversation focused on their needs, slipping in some details about yourself when appropriate. Don't oversell yourself. Answer their questions, get them whatever information they need, and then ask about the next step. If they say:

▶ **Send a demo**: Provide a link to your Web site MP3s, get an address, and immediately mail a CD demo along with some standard promotional material. Consider putting together a custom demo (see the demo chapter), based on your conversation with the client, and sending that instead.

▶ **Give us a quote**: Ask for specific details about the project and then drop everything and put the quote together. Email and snail mail it.

▶ **Submit a specific demo**: Here they want you to compete for the gig. Get the details, including if there is a demo fee payable to you, and what the deadline and submission guidelines are.

▶ **Let's meet**: Put together the specifics of your meeting and also ask what they want you to bring to the meeting (demo, custom music, etc.).

▶ **Send a contract or deal memo/Here's a PO**: Whoa! You have the job. Get the specifics and get right on it!

AT A MEETING

This meeting may be the opportunity to see if you and the client are a good fit. Once in a while, the meeting is the final part of the sales process. These meetings may take place by phone, email, or in person. Be prepared; have what you feel the client needs (demo, custom music, etc.). During this initial client contact, make sure you get answers to these questions:

▶ What project(s) require your music services?

▶ Can they afford your fees?

▶ Who has the authority to purchase and approve the music you provide?

Based on these answers, you need to determine whether you can deliver what they need, under deadline, and for the agreed upon fee.

During the meeting, identify the personality type (explained later) and slant your presentation accordingly. Vary your speech pattern and pace to follow your prospect's cue. Listen and take notes. Follow up all meetings whether they result in immediate work or not, with a thank you note of some kind. If you land the gig, congratulations, you have a client. If the projects falls through, make a point to follow up regularly with this prospect.

I'm sorry that we didn't work together on this project. When shall I touch base again? I'd welcome talking to you about a future project in the hopes that we can work together on it.

OTHER METHODS

There are many variations on your promotional game plan that haven't been addressed yet. The *"Promotional Potpourri"* chapter talks further about using publicity, articles, advertising, networking, and more.

Keeping Track of Clients and Prospects

There will be plenty of details with your burgeoning commercial music business. Develop a method for organizing and storing your contact information and various particulars of your dealings with leads, prospects, and clients. Use either a paper or note cards, a word processing program, a PDA, or database software dedicated to the task.

Capture the obvious contact information, for example, name, title, company name, address, telephone numbers, fax, email address, and Web site. Also include details about the projects they do, what kinds of music they use, typical budgets, and other useful insight. Consider keeping a log of your contacts, for example, when you made contact and how, follow-up contact, meetings and discussions, and so forth. Refer to this specific information as you make subsequent contacts. Don't rely on your memory.

Making Sales

Selling is not beneath you. You won't become some high-pressure, pushy, stereotype. You will, however, need to practice talking with your prospects and clients, determine their problems, discover what they want for solutions, and then show them how you and your music will solve their problems. In short, the secret to sales is to find out what people want and give it to them.

Selling requires patience, respect, and often, a little hand-holding. Truly creative people are rather insecure and thus are always looking for recognition. They need validation that what they are doing is good—whatever that means. "Do you like it?" I hear that all the time, putting me in the precarious position of judge, jury, and executioner. Honesty truly is the best policy. Be careful, though.

When in any sales situation, sincerity and genuine interest prevail. Ask questions and then listen. Concentrate on what your prospect is *really* saying. Read between the lines, and you will get the insight you need to both close the sale and do the project that meets their expectations. Avoid being a braggart or name-dropper, but do demonstrate your previous successes. Phrase what you tell so that it reflects the *benefits* your past clients received, not *who* your past clients were.

If your budget is small, perhaps you might consider something several of my clients have taken advantage of. I can write a single theme for you, perhaps only two to three minutes long, and then produce several alternative mixes. You'll get a variety of music, all based around a single thematic concept, and a price that fits your budget. Let me play you an example of what I mean.

Benefits are the secret to sales. From the buyer's perspective, it's simple: "What do I get?" Therefore it's your job to show her and tell him precisely what that is. After benefits comes value. Notice I said value, not price. Are the benefits and results you promise offset by the fees you charge? People don't look for low prices; people want maximum value for their money. It's a subtle shift in perspective, but crucial for you to recognize. If what you offer gives them what they want and need, the sale is easy. If you don't close the sale, it's because you didn't promote benefits and provide maximum value.

Making sales is not some crazy formula. It's simple. Stress the benefits and results of using your products and services. Show the value of your offer and how the expense (whether that's money or time expended) outweighs the advantages. Don't sell your music. Instead solve your client prospect's problems through your commercial music services.

GET PEOPLE TO TELL YOU WHAT THEY REALLY WANT

How do you get at the root of the problem? Ask leading questions. Open-ended, probing questions force your prospects to spill their guts. And they should do most of the talking. If your mouth is open more than 30% of the time, you're talking too much when you should be listening. So shut up and sell!

When in a meeting, you need to focus solely on your client. These questions make sure you don't dominate the conversation. You want to get the information you need to close the sale. Let your prospect tell you what she wants and then tell her how your music fits in. Phrase your questions like the following examples. You may notice a distinct resemblance to the questions asked during spotting sessions.

▶ What is the message of your production?

▶ How do you see the message or problem?

▶ What role should the music play?

▶ What is the purpose of the music?

▶ How do you see the audience responding?

▶ What should the music sound like?

▶ What I understand is that you... (summarize her answers to make sure you are both talking the same language).

▶ If ever you're not sure about something or you're not getting enough information, just ask, "Can you tell me more about that?"

USE ACTIVE LISTENING TECHNIQUES

Hearing is not listening. Active listening is a skill you must master. It takes concentration and focus. Try these tips:

▶ Avoid distractions and time constraints when meeting with prospects and clients. All your attention should be on him or her.

▶ Face the person, lean toward him slightly, and look him straight in the eyes. Make good eye contact, buy don't stare.

▶ Stay relaxed and open. Don't cross your arms or legs.

▶ Watch body language and listen for the *real* message between the lines.

▶ Pay attention. Don't let your mind wander or be distracted. Concentrate on what is being said. Repeat and rephrase each sentence in your head, if that helps.

▶ Don't interrupt your prospect. Let her finish before asking for clarification or answering.

▶ Indicate you are listening and understand what is being said. Nod your head, take some notes, or answer that you understand by uttering a simple "OK."

▶ Don't rush or ramble. Before giving your answer, pause for a few seconds and collect your thoughts. Even if you are excited or nervous, take a deep breath, think about what you're going to say, and then begin.

▶ Summarize what your prospects say in your own words and ask them if your understanding is correct.

▶ Smile and be friendly. Let your enthusiasm shine through.

RECOGNIZE AND DEAL WITH DIFFERING PERSONALITIES

There are essentially six personality types that you'll encounter in the creative world. Virtually everyone falls into one of these categories. And while some may cross over into other types, each person typically exemplifies one main attitude. You must learn to recognize these types quickly and tailor your presentation accordingly.

► **Leader**. Always in control, dominates conversations, makes quick decisions, and follows through all projects from start to finish. These people tend to be *all* business and are only interested in results.

► **Supporter**. Likes being with and relating to people and is often a bit talkative. Usually seeks approval from others before making final decisions. These people are always quite friendly, casual, and relaxed.

► **Optimist**. Always full of energy and creativity. Likes to discuss myriad possibilities, most of which are completely outlandish and impractical. These people can be very energetic and prone to quick, spontaneous decisions. More often, they are the complete antithesis of the leader and never finalize anything.

► **Bean Counter**. Brings highly structured and thorough analysis to every situation. These people look for accurate, logical solutions.

► **Adversary**. Always takes the negative side to things. Can never find the good and tends to nitpick. Completely the opposite of the optimist, adversaries tend to be very conservative and realistic. They are quick to say no and somewhat slower to yes.

► **MOR**. The middle of the road person tends to go with the flow. Never caught making their own decisions, MORs tend to work better in groups where individual thought is not cherished.

This may be oversimplifying human behavior, but in many sales situations there isn't time to fully understand someone. You need to uncover their tendency and use it to your advantage. With the leader, be the consummate music expert; ask about moods, feelings, and such with the supporter; discuss wild ethnic percussion with the optimist; go through the budget and other details with the bean counter; carefully balance the up and down sides with the adversary; and take charge of the MOR. Use these as a guide only. We are all complex human beings after all. And also be prepared for the domineering, friendly director who talks wildly about the bad things happening in someone else's life.

STILL HATE TO SELL?
Being in front of an audience is the number one human fear (death is seventh on the list). Nobody likes to make cold calls, and certainly nobody cares for rejection. If you diligently follow these plans and strategies and develop the proper promotional materials, *people will call you!* That's the whole idea of doing all this preparation. Make sure you promote and market yourself and your music relentlessly. Prospects will seek you out or, at least, know you when you do call. That makes life easier and promotes more sales faster.

Don't worry too much about selling. While I can't say you'll never be in a selling situation, I can say that selling music is not as bad as it sounds. You do good work, don't you? Your demo does demonstrate your talents and abilities, right? You are passionate about your skills, aren't you? If you answered yes to all these questions, you will have no trouble presenting your music and persuading your prospects to give you work. Master these attitudes and skills:

▶ Get comfortable with who you are and what you can do.

▶ Have material ready (demo, brochure, basic quotes, and so forth) in advance.

▶ Practice making your case. Prepare answers to commonly asked questions and rehearse them.

▶ Relax and listen. Your prospects will tell you what they want and need. They either have a problem or want a specific result. You solve that problem, or you provide results through your music. When you look at selling this way, it's easy.

NO TRACK RECORD?

Don't worry if you lack an impressive track record when first embarking on this adventure. Instead of going in with "I've done this and I've done that," *focus your sales presentations on the person in front of you.* Look her straight in the eyes and say, "Tell me about your latest project and how I can help." If she presses for credentials, give her a sample of your work and say, "Here's a record of my skills. I'm currently building relationships with production companies and ad agencies in town and would welcome the opportunity to serve you, too." Perhaps you'll feel inspired and whip something up for your meeting, for example, "After we talked on the phone, I composed a rough sketch of what I thought you wanted for this project. May I play it to you?" Get the idea? Don't worry about your lack of real credentials. Position yourself as the consummate professional ready, willing, and able to help prospects and clients. Soon, you'll have real credentials you can promote.

Vital Telephone Tips

Picking up the phone and calling past clients to remind them of what you have is the single most effective way to generate new sales. When you have something new to sell or you are simply selling your music to people who buy it regularly, use your phone to make contact. I generate 90% of my repeat business through phone calls.

Making cold calls is another necessity toward finding leads to prospects. Break through your fear. You don't have the gig now, right? If you don't call you still won't get the gig. But if you *do* call, there's a chance you might get hired. Take that chance!

Practice what you're going to say, write scripts, and learn to be personable, helpful, and enthusiastic on the phone. Here's another surefire tip: Just before you pick up the receiver, take a deep breath, exhale slowly, inhale again, and smile. Your relaxed, friendly smile comes through during your call. Here are more ways to use your telephone effectively when contacting clients and prospects.

▶ Have a reason to make the call. Are you generating leads, following up email/mail, responding to requests, telling a client about a recent project you finished, and so forth? Prepare a brief outline of the major points of your call.

▶ Make sure you will not be interrupted during the call. Keep distractions at bay.

▶ Use your voice to project confidence and sincerity, and be polite.

▶ Vary your speech pattern and pace to follow your prospect. Quiet, slow talker on the phone? Don't speak loudly or rush your side of the conversation.

▶ Use those active listening skills and take notes. Pretend the person is right in front of you and talk to him or her directly.

▶ Remember that people may try to get you off the line by asking you to send them something. You are here to help them through your music, not just send out demo tapes. Ask about projects coming up and get the conversation started.

▶ If you can't seem to get to whom you need, don't ignore the person you have on the line already. Tell this person how you can help, such as, "Mr. Producer uses original music, doesn't he? I'll bet he pays far too much for it. I can show him specifically how to save money on his next production. Would you see if he's interested in knowing more?"

▶ Make sure you rehearse your technique. You might find it helpful to script your calls or at least the answers to your prospect's most frequently asked questions. Having your notes in front of you can help you get over the anxiety of phone calls. Consider recording a few calls and then listen to them again later. You'll see where you've succeeded and perhaps where you may have failed.

▶ Don't forget your benefits. Put your services and offers in perspective and build some anticipation, like, "There are three ways I can save you some money fast. First…" Next, elaborate on your offer.

▶ Talk only a small part of the time, under 30%. Listening to your clients and prospects is essential. If you give them the chance, they will tell you their problems and concerns. Now it's up to you to use this information to position yourself and show how you can help.

▶ Make sure you use verbal cues while you listen. Say things such as, "I see, I understand, very interesting, really, tell me more," and other phrases that suggest your interest. This is the verbal equivalent of nodding in person.

▶ If the prospect says they don't need your services now, counter with a statement that reflects you're ready when they are. "You have my material. Why don't you keep it with your budget files and the next time a project comes your way, call me and let's talk. Just because we can't work together right now doesn't mean I can't help you in the future."

▶ Just to get you off the phone, some prospects may tell you they are already satisfied with their present music supplier. Don't be discouraged. Ask them how or why they are happy. How has their current music house earned their business? Perhaps you'll discover a niche or service you can provide that they are not getting right now. That gets your foot in the door and can lead to bigger projects.

▶ If the prospect sounds interested or teetering, but you don't feel comfortable springing too much on them, try simply asking, "What's next?" or "What do you need from me right now or next?"

▶ Follow up any contact you initiate by a telephone call with an email or letter. Outline the points discussed during your telephone meeting and provide any other answers or material you promised the person during your call.

▶ Not every call will result in a sale (duh)! Every time you dial, you are moving one step closer to selling your music. Don't stop or give up. Get a tough skin, persist, pick up that phone, and start selling. And should you get discouraged, remember these immortal words from Sir Winston Churchill: "Never give in, never, never, never, never."

VOICE MAIL SECRETS

As you might imagine, I get quite a few phone calls. And many of these end up in my voice mailbox. What is painfully clear to me is how few people know how to leave a cogent message. Use these tips to ensure your calls make sense and get returned.

▶ Prepare what you're going to say before you dial. Think brevity. A voice message is not the forum for your life story.

▶ Don't be vague, either. For example, I won't return calls from people I don't know when they go something like this: "This is Simon. I need to talk to you. Call me."

▶ Speak slowly and clearly; don't rush. Start with your name and the reason for your call. Indicate what you want to happen next, such as "please call me back today with your answer."

▶ Always leave your return number. People often retrieve messages remotely and don't have your number handy. And when you do leave your number, please say it slowly and clearly. I can't believe how fast some people rip through their numbers. Give sufficient time for a person to write it down! You might want to repeat it (along with your name again), too. Sometimes cell phones break up and the number gets garbled.

▶ Remember: Often you're dialing for dollars. Make sure the message counts!

Connecting and Reconnecting with Clients

When you get a client, you want two things to happen. One, you want them to remain your client for a long time and give you all their musical assignments. Two, you want to use them to get more and better clients. It should be obvious that staying in touch with current and past clients is essential. Here are a few methods to employ.

▶ Make sure you alert all your clients to the latest projects you've completed successfully. If you will appear in media (print, radio/TV, Web), let people know about it.

▶ If your *client* gets media coverage of some kind, drop a note that indicates you saw/read/heard it.

▶ Prepare a quarterly email announcement that highlights your activities. Make a round of telephone calls a week or so after sending the email.

▶ Send birthday cards and appropriate holiday greetings.

▶ Occasionally, send friendly emails/letters or make to-just-say-hi telephone calls.

▶ Send publicity reprints or links to appropriate Web sites.

▶ If you find news, tidbits, or something else that you feel would interest a client (even if it is not music related), send it to them to show you always have their interests in mind. Add a note that says, "Thought you'd find this interesting. Keep in touch, Jeffrey."

▶ Hold a client-only seminar, open house, or party of some kind. A private screening of your latest work is a possible idea.

▶ In the event of negative publicity about your business, make sure all clients are informed *before* the negative story appears.

Getting new clients is difficult, at best. Keeping your current clients is equally challenging. Businesses lose customers every day, with a lack of attention on the part of the seller being the major complaint. So build a strong relationship with your clients from the very beginning. Continue to reinforce your commitment to them through carefully controlled promotional efforts. By keeping in contact with and responding to client demands, you will win their loyalty. Personally, I do whatever it takes to keep my clients satisfied. If you *don't* do this, they will walk.

Choosing Your Marketing or Sales Associate

Maybe you don't possess the skills or have the time to oversee all these promotional functions. Or maybe you just want someone else to handle your sales. Here's how to pass on the promoting and selling to another associate, so you can concentrate on music.

▶ Try adding a partner who complements your skills. You compose and record, while your partner promotes, sells, and runs the business end. This is a model that many music houses follow.

▶ Taking on an employee is a big step, so why not consider an independent representative to promote your business instead? This person would promote and sell your music for you in return for either a salary, commission, or both. Commissions can range from 15–25% or more. While you might wince at such a fee, it is fair pay for a decent rainmaker.

▶ Another alternative is to create an informal network. Invite people to recommend you. Supply them with the materials they need to promote you—several copies of your demo and promotional material are best. In return for a commission, they do all the selling. This differs from the single rep above in that you can have several people working for you at the same time. Most independent reps will not like this situation; they don't like competing in smaller markets. However, friends, associates, and others may enjoy helping you while making some money at the same time.

▶ Similarly, make a deal with a production company or ad agency. If they recommend you to one of *their* clients, you give them a discount or a commission when you deliver the tracks.

Make sure you use a simple contract with all your independent reps. It should cover what they do, what you do, what they make, how you determine their fee, etc. You should also add independent contractor language and maybe even a noncompete clause to prevent your reps from selling for other music houses.

FINDING YOUR INDEPENDENT REP

Before hiring an outsider, try handling these functions yourself first. You'll gain valuable insight and learn exactly what it takes to sell your music services. That knowledge will help you choose the right associates who can assist you in reaching your goals. Make sure you read the "Choosing an Advisor" section (in the business chapter) before adding any advisor, especially a sales rep, to your business network. Meanwhile, here are some guidelines for you to follow.

▶ Ask your other business colleagues to recommend someone. Most reps have several (noncompeting) clients they sell for. Some even provide package deals by representing a production company, writer, post-production facility, and a music house all at once.

▶ Ask local professional associations, such as your Chamber of Commerce, for names of possible sales representatives. You really want someone with contacts in the industry, as opposed to a person with general sales experience only.

▶ Your local college can provide you with student interns looking to learn more out in the real world. Contact the cooperative education department.

▶ Take out an ad in the trade or local press:

Sales rep wanted for growing music house. Must be master promoter, publicist, and salesperson. Industry contacts a big plus! Commission only. Contact...

Final Lessons

Learning what you need to promote your music services can sometimes seem overwhelming. It is, though, vitally important to your inevitable success. Though a good chunk of this book helps you organize, start, and continue your promotional efforts, I've written two other books that can augment your education. These practical resources will start working for you the minute you pick them up. And they'll serve as essential references for many years to come.

▶ *Ruthless Self-Promotion in the Music Industry* (Artistpro, 2005)

▶ *Moneymaking Music* (Artistpro, 2003)

Not everyone is a buyer. Understand this advice and save yourself tons of heartache. That's why your contact must perform the crucial screening and separate the cold, cold fish from the ready and willing—and paying—original soundtrack music and jingle clients. Plus, if promotion and sales were so easy, we would all be billionaires. Right?

Industry Insight

Douglas Spotted Eagle
Sundance Media Group, Stockton, UT
dse@sundancemediagroup.com
www.sundancemediagroup.com, www.spottedeagle.com

Recent credits/past projects
Lost Landscapes, The Transcontinental Railroad, French Indian Wars, Hidalgo

Why did you choose this career (and how did you get started)?
The career chose me. I always wanted to be a musician. The harder I tried, the more I failed. So I started working as a systems designer and acoustic designer for a couple of studios and sound companies. Being an engineer turned me into a producer, and then being a producer ended up bringing me full circle, and I started recording myself.

What and how did you land your first project?

I was working at a studio in Lindon, Utah. This is where the Osmonds recorded, and I ended up meeting some musicians that were looking for the "Osmond" sound. So, instead of engineering for them, I ended up producing. That turned into a gig producing some stuff for Marie Osmond, and it went pretty well. At that point, it was hard to screw up her presentation, because of her awesome voice.

What are you working on now and how did you get this current project?

Working on a PBS project, *The Transcontinental Railroad*. My portions of the project came through Brian Keane, one of the most-awarded composers ever in the history of television. It's a four-episode mini-series and has everything from baroque to ethnic, classical contemporary to sound design.

What do you feel makes a good music score (or jingle)?

Anything that evokes emotion is best. Anything that allows the scene to breathe, but helps move it along without standing in the way of the story. The score should be the rails on which the scene is traveling, a guide without too much emphasis on anything. It's punctuation, it's paint, it's the icing, just there to support what lies beneath (or above, depending on what it is).

What gear do you use?

Sony Vegas, ACID, and Sound Forge, Cakewalk, Mackie tools, UAD-1, Waves plug-ins, iZotope plugs, and Audio-Technica mics.

Explain your promotional strategies (what works and why).

I don't promote much, I simply send email to various producers and composers letting them know what I've just completed or what's airing when.

What skills do you feel someone needs to succeed in the area?

You need way more than musical chops. There are a *lot* of creative musicians out there. Being on time, being a good manager, understanding current and cutting trends, being versatile, having a workable personality are all important. The flexibility of a composer is likely one of the most important traits today with so much talent available at a low cost. Producers would rather work with flexible people that are simply good than work with a prima donna that borders on great. When you become super great like Horner, Zimmer, Bestor, or one of those guys, *then* consider becoming a prima donna.

How do you approach projects, technically or creatively?

Depends on what the budget is, the director's or producer's view, time allotments, and passion for the project. Projects I love, I lose money on every time because I throw myself into it. Projects that are cool, I'll do OK on financially, because I know the line between passion and profit. Projects I hate, I'll make lots of money on, because I'll be technically perfect, but not spend a lot of time fussing over the details.

How do you get paid (typical pay for projects, royalties, etc.)?

Flat rate for compositions, usually my contribution is a work-for-hire, so there are rarely royalties involved. Some shows, you'll get royalties if you keep the copyright, but that's pretty rare these days. Directors, producers, and production houses are very savvy. They know to keep the copyright.

What do you wish you'd known then that you know now?

I wish I had had more understanding of copyright law. A Windham Hill artist who came from another label really squeezed me out of a lot of money because of my own stupidity, naiveté, and ignorance. Had I been smarter, I'd be at least $40K richer today on just that one project. I'd also spend a lot more time listening to the masters of the older films, especially those of the late 60s. I'd pay more attention to voicings. Brian Keane has taught me so much about voicings and placement, I wish I'd learned this stuff 25 years ago. Who knows, I might be the Hans Zimmer of ethnic-influenced music. I also wish I'd realized that independence is dumb a lot of the time. Calling a player in for an hour might seem expensive, but generally the quality of musician you'd call in will be cheaper than trying to get it close and then cutting comps in Sony Vegas or other DAW.

What are your plans for the future?

To keep on working, playing, finding new sources, and resources.

Can you comment on using employees, partners, and outsourcing?

Know the people who work in your area. Call them regularly, send them Christmas cards, stay in touch. Help them help you. Let people know what you're doing when it's appropriate. Build a stable of trustworthy and capable people around you. Surround yourself with good musicians; you'll become a better musician as well as getting a rep for being a caring person. Remember that the reason you got into this business is a love of music. Remind others of that love and passion by way of your actions, and it will be contagious. People will realize you're a real person with real feelings and goals, and this helps motivate them to go the extra mile for you.

Is there anything else you'd like to comment on that you feel is important?

Learn technology from the ground up. Don't simply spend your time with one app, learn why it works the way it does. Understand it. Be on top of it. Get training or education everywhere you possibly can.

CHAPTER 8

Inside Secrets to Moneymaking Promotions

"Do what you can with what you have where you are."—Theodore Roosevelt

You will communicate with people—prospects, clients, the media, and more—through both speech and the written word. Learning the secrets greatly improves your chances for success in this field. Everything is a promotional opportunity, so learn to present your music precisely in ways that get people to respond.

When you want to be a success with your music industry career, you must master writing promotional material. From simple email promotions to fan newsletters, from Web pages to full-blown advertisements, drafting persuasive and motivating promotional material is crucial.

Like you, I get a metric ton of promotional and advertising material every single day. Most pieces are sadly disappointing and useless. Why? Because they don't do what they are created to do. And what is that, you may ask? Sell. There is no other reason to produce promotional material, except for the express purpose of motivating someone to buy something.

The approach coupled to the words—copy in the advertising vernacular—is often to blame. I pick up example after example that has no clear benefits, concentrates on the seller (*not* the buyer), is confusing, makes it difficult to buy, and on and on. And since a great deal of promotional material fails to produce any results, we're left with a system that perpetually wastes money and fills the world with hype and egotistical images. Too many amateurs get sullied by the promise of instant business. They seem to say: Take out an ad that says, "We're great, buy our music," and we'll be flooded with business. Guess what? It doesn't work that way. And that is sad, really. There's no shortage of ego or bottomless checkbooks producing the rubbish we see every day.

But not you, right? When you want to motivate the largest number of prospects to buy what you offer and do it by spending the least amount of money, follow these specific guidelines.

Write Right

There is a singular attitude that you must accept before you draft a single letter, email, or Web site page. Focus on your prospects and clients. You can't build everything around you, yourself, and your music. People don't care about you; they care about themselves. Their stance is simple: "What's in it for me?" And it is essential that you provide the answer to that question with every promotional document you create.

Talk directly to the people who would buy your music. Buyers are skeptical, so carefully and completely answer their questions and objections. Focus on what the buyer wants to achieve (not on what you sell). Good promotional writing convinces people to buy because it clearly shows that what you sell is what they really want.

Turn every feature into a benefit. Provide clear benefits and the results of using your music products and services. People don't care about features. They are only interested in benefits and results: *their* benefits and *their* results, *not* yours! For example, a feature is something such as: "We have low prices." That is not nearly as motivating as selling the benefit: "You save money." Everybody likes to save money.

As I said earlier, people usually want only two things: to gain something or to remove some pain. As you prepare your promotional material, frame your emotional and logical appeals using both tactics.

▶ **Gain:** If your music makes a client's production better, if it helps deliver messages more effectively, if it helps sell more products and services, if it helps achieve the results they want to achieve, they'll be happy to sign the check. When you contribute to making their program a success, they achieve all these benefits and more.

▶ **Pain:** "You have a problem (or a need) that I understand. By working with me, we can solve that problem (or fulfill that need) together. Here's precisely how…"

Promotion and selling is about action, about motivating people to take action. You want to create action and urgency. Write in the active voice and use action verbs. Push, prod, motivate, captivate, and ultimately sell what you offer. This is not about image building. It's about telling people how they can benefit from what you sell only when they act right away and buy it.

Ultimately, the action you want is to buy and nothing more. Though it may take several steps before they dig deep into their pockets, load each step with benefits designed solely to motivate action and to move one step closer to buying.

Toward Effective Promotions

Include these essential elements with every promotion you create.

TURN FEATURES INTO BENEFITS

Features are descriptions of things. Benefits highlight what people get and the results they achieve by using your music. Benefits sell; features don't. Always promote your best benefits first; then it's acceptable to follow with some features.

▶ **Feature:** We have low prices. **Benefit**: You save money.

▶ **Feature**: We offer fast turnaround. **Benefit**: You save time.

▶ **Feature**: We are a full-service studio. **Benefit**: You save time *and* money!
And you get exactly what you need to handle every facet of sound for
your project, right here. Right now!

Don't say: "We have state-of-the-art equipment," because the best answer to that statement is "so what?" And that doesn't sell. Two words are all you need to remember to turn any feature into a benefit: so that.

Our studio can produce any sound, real or imagined, so that you get the original music score you need to enhance your production and deliver your message effectively.

Now to really make this paragraph shine, flip it around so the benefit is first.

▶ *Get the original music score you need to deliver your message effectively.*
Enhance your project using our studio to produce any sound, real or imag-
ined.

▶ *Or more simply:*
Get an original music score that enhances your production and delivers
your message more effectively.

Do you hear how a simple rephrasing shifts the focus away from the feature (studio) to both the benefit (enhance) and the result (deliver message more effectively)? Moving the focus away from you and your work to your client prospect's point of view is essential.

You must carefully define your benefits, give them credence, and provide tangible results. Change all "we have" and "it has" descriptions to "you get" this benefit and "you get" these results.

▶ **Bad**: "We compose quality music." Huh? Quality what? How? Why? Prove it!

▶ **Better**: "You get exactly the music you want or your money back!"

Please note that the most wonderful word for any promotion is *you*! Talk to your client prospects one-to-one. Make your promotions sound like a letter to a friend from a friend. And avoid the innocuous "we." Write: *You get this* or *I can help you.*

SELL WHAT THEY BUY

What do people buy? These are the questions they ask. You need credible answers to them all, so for practice, ask yourself the following questions:

▶ Do you possess the musical skills they need?

▶ Are you responsive to their needs before, during, and after each project?

▶ Are you attentive to details and specific requests?

▶ Will you deliver quality music and meet deadlines?

▶ Do your benefits outweigh their cost? That's a value judgment, not a price issue. In other words, are you the best deal?

▶ Can they depend on your music products, services, and company and will you deliver as promised?

▶ Are you ready when *they* need you?

▶ Have you had past success? Are there testimonials and recommendations from others to support that?

▶ Are you friendly, understanding, and easy to work with?

▶ Do they get an overall good feeling in their gut when they meet or speak with you?

DIMINISH THE FEAR FACTOR

Buyers are justifiably scared of making a bad choice. You need to carefully show them there are no risks when they buy from you. Offer a money-back guarantee. Let them try before they buy, such as a free MP3 before buying your whole library CD. Skepticism can be reduced through a track record of success and a solid reputation. Until you reach that pinnacle, devise other means of dealing with people who dread buyer's remorse.

CREATE A COMPELLING OFFER

It's essential to include an offer in your promotions. Offers include hard offers of the "buy this now" variety, or they can include soft offers such as "call for more information" or "visit our Web site." Include a mix of hard and soft offers with every promotion you send out.

Ask yourself what you want the result to be after using a promotion. Make that result the offer. Never—and I mean *never*—send a promotion that whispers: "We're here, call when you want." That's a waste of your prospect's time and your money. Your documents must scream: *Benefit here! Act Now!* Make sure that you include a call to action in every promotional document. That puts you in control of the selling process. Don't rely on their knowing what to do. Explain precisely what you want to happen next, for example the message below:

When you want this result, reply to this email or call (number) now to get started today.

HAVE A DEADLINE WITH CONSEQUENCES

The best offers have deadlines such as "Hurry! This offer expires January 22, 2006." Deadlines motivate people to take action fast. You might remind them of what happens when they don't act right away. They usually miss out on the deal, like the following info:

Stop paying too much for music. Learn how by requesting my free booklet, "How to get low cost music for your projects." It's a $14.95 value, but I'll send you a copy free when you reply to this email. Don't spend another penny on music until you read this money-saving book.

Never rely on the word "free" alone to motivate prospects. The free thing must have value—a defined and explicit benefit. Understand the difference? Which would you rather get? A free demo? Or the secret to saving money? This is rather simple: Sell the sizzle (what's in it for me), not the steak (free demo).

FOLLOW THIS CRUCIAL STRUCTURE

Include these seven major parts with every promotional piece. What's the easiest way to use them all? Write a personal letter to your prospect and either print it on letterhead and mail or email it. This will also work as a Web page.

▶ **Headline** (or subject when it's an email). Use the headline to grab attention and don't waste time or mince words. Make it big and bold and slant it toward either the strongest gain you deliver or the largest pain you take away.

▶ **State the problem.** After the headline, indicate that you understand the problems your clients or prospects face. These problems can be both the gain they want to acquire or the pain they want to do away with. Lay it on thick here and take several approaches so that your clients are almost nodding in agreement as they experience your promotion.

▶ **Sell the solution—you!** Start with something that simply says: "We can help." Propose your solution (which is really *your* music services, of course) in greater detail so it solves the problems outlined earlier.

▶ **Pile on the benefits**. Provide additional benefits to having you as the choice to solve the problems.

▶ **Discuss some of your features**, at this point, but not before.

▶ **Introduce the people** behind what you are selling, such as a brief bio with references to current/past clients and other credentials, especially awards, if you have them.

▶ **Slip in testimonials and endorsements** from media and other satisfied clients to reassure people that you deliver what you promise.

▶ **Make your best offer and ask for the sale**. Make an offer of some kind that motivates action. Try both a hard and a soft approach.

▶ **Place a time limit** and impart a sense of loss if they don't respond.

▶ **Include any necessary follow-up procedures**, such as contact information, how to order, etc.

▶ **Add a postscript** (P.S.) to restate the previous six parts in a concise summary.

KEEP CREDENTIALS IN PERSPECTIVE

People who buy your music don't care what you've done or where you've been unless you put your credentials in context and tell them *exactly and explicitly* how they benefit from your experience and skills. I hate to belabor this point, but all that matters is what you've achieved for others and how your success with one client brings possible success to the next. Facts, like a client list, may impress, but rarely motivate.

By all means *include* your credentials, but don't let them be the main focus of a promotional piece. Use your background to support and complement other more tangible benefits. Being easy to work with, convenient, meeting deadlines, staying on budget, keeping clients (and clients' clients) happy, writing solid music tracks, following instructions, delivering what you promise, charging fairly—these are the credentials that matter most.

MOTIVATING MORSELS

Consider these tactics as they appeal to creative people in the soundtracks and jingle universe. Original music has the following desirable attributes:

▶ Adds uniqueness to projects. Audiovisual producers share a love affair of being creative and of being the first to do something nobody else has done before. Original music adds that special something to their work.

▶ Makes productions stronger by adding emotion and impact.

▶ Allows producers to personalize their production. Most people recognize that when a composer and director share the same vision, the resulting music, indeed the project as a whole, is that much better.

▶ Adds a unique and exciting musical identity to every production.

▶ Helps people remember products, services, and companies, which is precisely why commercials use jingles.

▶ Is flexible and versatile and conforms to a project's exact needs.

▶ Precisely matches screen action, drama, and emotion.

▶ Enhances and supports visual imagery.

▶ Increases the impact of every production.

▶ Makes the message more memorable.

Original music plays a very important role in today's audiovisual presentations. Great music won't save a bad production—it's not a panacea—but it can do what no other soundtrack element can do. Producers want your help, through your original musical contribution, to make a positive difference in how their audience responds. And that means a better, more effective production.

Please understand that most audiovisual producers simply don't care about drum beats, MIDI, equipment lists, and all that stuff (that's just more "me" marketing features). They want a feeling.

They want a certain mood. They want to entertain, amuse, motivate, sadden, persuade, induce, titillate, depress, scare, annoy, educate, and often...SELL! Can your original music fulfill these requests? Do your materials promote these benefits? It should be what you emphasize as you promote and sell your music.

PRESENTATION TIPS

Promotional material often makes the first impression *before* anything else. Make sure it is neat, organized, and well written. Make sure to proofread what you write and revise as necessary. Revision is the real secret to good writing. Watch out for typos, misspellings, and grammatical mistakes. I once received a letter from a composer who used the line: "Where music is at it's (sic) best." I'm sure he meant its, which is possessive, not it's, which is the contraction of it is. Don't you make such an egregious error.

Web pages, letters, brochures, flyers, postcards, and other printed matter need to be simple and uncluttered with clean, readable typefaces. Avoid fancy typefaces that are difficult to decipher. Choose colors that reflect your image. Don't send handwritten letters or labels. The only exception would be a short note or card to an existing client (such as a heartfelt thank you).

Since the world is rather paperless these days, well-designed letterhead will serve for almost all your printed needs—letters, quotes, contract, invoices, etc. Make sure that your letterhead and business cards have complete, up-to-date contact information.

Remember this, though: Stunning design and vibrant colors will never miraculously turn boring words into dazzling promotions. And if your promotions are all about you, nothing will overcome the fact that you are taking the wrong approach.

Stronger Copy Tips

Authors Robert Gunning and Douglas Mueller say that you should write to *express*, not *impress*. That is very good advice. Here's some more good advice:

▶ Talk *to* your prospects, not at them. Use simple, everyday language and write short, action-packed sentences that move from one place to the next. Write as if in conversation with the person.

▶ Cut to the chase. Don't spend too much time on useless background material. State your case up front, make your point, and present your argument. Remember that your job is to motivate further action, not educate or pontificate.

▶ Be specific, realistic, and accurate.

▶ Use action words and choose the simple words to their longer counterparts.

▶ In the battle between intellectual, rational thought and emotion, emotion always wins. Emotional appeals are always stronger and more effective than logical pleas.

▶ People would rather remove a pain first before the potential of gain. Address that with a strong headline: "Stop wasting your money on music that bores your audience. Get original music that excites and motivates."

▶ Avoid hype like the plague. If you can defend your claim, it's not hype. If you can't defend your claim, it's not hype, either—it's lying.

▶ Don't exaggerate, criticize, use clichés, or ridicule. Also, use humor carefully because it can backfire in a politically correct world.

▶ Promotion is about *when*, not *if*. Use it this way: "*When* you want to save money on your next jingle, call me."

Follow these copywriting guidelines and thrive; ignore them and suffer. You must master this skill because it's crucial to your success.

Putting All This to Work

Here are some samples of my promotions that follow the points made in this chapter. These are real documents that have worked and continue to work for me. I use them as letters in emails and on my Web site. Notice the tone talks directly to prospects, makes an offer, and asks for a response. The essentials are here along with some good strategies for making what you do attractive. Use these examples as a guide as you develop your own promotions.

Sample Music Sales Letter/Email/Web Page

Here is an example from my files.

ARE YOU PAYING TOO MUCH FOR ORIGINAL MUSIC?

Today, original music costs between $1200.00–1500.00 per finished minute. That kind of money puts it out of reach for many producers. So you're forced to use library tracks.
But you know that original music makes a difference. Why settle for something that almost fits? Don't compromise your creativity. Get music with impact. Get music that works. Get original music.

I'll score your commercial or corporate project—exactly to your specifications—starting at just $995 per finished minute. Complete. This limited discount offer includes composing, arranging, recording, and delivery. It's an all-in or package deal!

You get the best of both worlds. Exactly the right music, right now. And you get it at a price that makes sense—up to 33% off the average. This is your chance to get original music for small productions, test spots, or anytime you need to lower your budget, not your expectations.

- Original music gives you flexibility and versatility—any length and style (rock, jazz, orchestral, or exotic).

- Original music gives you precisely what you need to match your visuals, create a mood, underscore the action, and enhance your message.

- Original music emphasizes the drama in a situation and creates a more convincing experience for your audience.

You want to deliver your message more effectively, don't you? Using the right music is the key! And at this price you have no excuse not to get the exact original music you want, need, and deserve.

I want us—you and me— to work together making music that works for you. If ever you're not happy with the music I compose for you, I'll refund your money. NO QUESTIONS ASKED! Quality, value, and no risk. I guarantee it.

How can I make this offer? By taking full advantage of today's modern technology. I keep production costs down and pass the savings on to you. You pay for the music, not high-priced studio overhead. You get the music you want, the way you want it, when you want it, and at prices you can afford.

*Just think of it. Original soundtrack music from only **$995** per finished minute. COMPLETE and GUARANTEED.*

Because I want to meet your music needs exactly, here's another offer. If you call me right now, I'll send you five music tracks on CD. You can KEEP and USE this sample music to enhance any of your latest projects. The music is free (a $59.00 value), and you're under no obligation.

It won't have the same impact as music scored specifically for your production, but it just might help you out of a jam when you need some good music fast.

Plus, this offer gives you an idea of the music I can write for you. Other composers send a demo of their past work. I'll send you a sample of my music you can start using TODAY!

Your creative work demands the best of everything. Won't using original music make it that much better? So, stop using library tracks. Get the impact of original music with the same convenience and cost. And get it now.

But hurry, both offers expire on January 1, 2006. Call me today.

I look forward to talking with you,
Jeffrey P. Fisher

P. S.

Why settle for anything less? Get custom soundtrack music that works, sounds great, and is affordable. Let my original music make the difference in your productions. I'll meet your needs exactly. Don't put it off. Call me right now and take advantage of these offers.

Sample Jingles Sales Letter or Email

I've been impressed with the quality of your advertising on Wxxx-FM, specifically your "Hometown Report." Your commitment to community service and general goodwill is refreshing.

However, I am surprised that you haven't included a jingle with your radio spots. The right jingle can go a long way toward enhancing your image. Jingles have the power that keeps your name alive in listeners' minds. I feel strongly that using a jingle would complement and improve your already successful campaign.

It would be a privilege for me to present a custom music package that would give you a new musical identity—and a competitive edge. In fact, I already have an idea in mind.

Could you spare just five minutes of your time to hear the new jingle composed specifically for you? That's right, I can play a finished jingle starring YOUR COMPANY. You'll hear exactly how your custom music package will sound on the radio. And this jingle will separate you from the advertising crowd, especially on Wxxx, where very few advertisers use jingles.

Of course, I will make this presentation without cost or obligation to you. I'll call Thursday morning to set up a time for us to meet. You need do nothing, just bring your ears and open your mind to how the right musical identity can help you improve yours ads, your business, and your profits!

P. S.

Get more from your radio advertising dollars. Jingles make radio ads more effective. Music influences listeners by stimulating their imagination and memory. They remember the melody… remember the tune… and remember your product. In other words: jingles sell. And they work for advertisers, both big and small. That's why you must make a jingle part of your advertising campaign!

Sample Music Promotion Flyer or Email or Web Page

Get the original music you want and save…

Instrumental music scoring for TV, radio, film, video, software, and the Web. Any style. Any genre. Any way. The right music. Right now. At the right price.

$995

Finally. You can have the original music you need and deserve… at a price that makes sense. That's right. You get a complete, original music package composed, recorded, mixed, and delivered fast on CD for that one small fee.

No excuses

You want the best for your productions, don't you? Using the right music helps you deliver your message more effectively. Don't settle for anything less. Get original music that fully meets your specifications. And get it fast. Take advantage of this special offer today.

How do we do it?

Your original music score uses real instruments played by real people, combined with the latest in sound design electronics. This approach keeps your costs down significantly. And we pass those savings on to you. We also limit your rights to the music and do away with time-wasting production meetings. Just tell us what you want by phone or e-mail and we'll compose it for you.

How do you get started?

It's oh-so-easy to order your original music.

- Pick up the phone and dial (630) 378-4109 or email jpf@jeffreypfisher. com and let's discuss your needs.

- Visit our Web site, www.jeffreypfisher.com/995 to hear samples and to order your original music today. You can even pay for your music online using your credit card.

What's the catch?

- Music tracks can be *any* length, :29, :59, up to 1:59 for the same low, low fee.

- Instrumental tracks only (sorry, no voices at this rate).

- No travel hassles. We work together via telephone and email meetings only. You describe the music you need, and we deliver it. It's that simple.

- Sessions are closed. To save time—and your money—we can't have you producing the music sessions. Give detailed direction and let us work our musical magic. However, we can deliver works-in-progress via email before completing the final mix.

- Nonexclusive use. We keep all rights to the music and can sell it to somebody else in the future. Do you need a buyout? Multiply the offer by ten ($9950), and the music we compose is all yours...forever!

Don't have $995...but still need good music?
Use our two-volume Melomania *buyout, royalty-free music library for only $99 instead. You get 64 tracks of today's hottest styles specifically created for audiovisual and multimedia projects. Hear samples from the over two-hours of music available to you exclusively at **www.jeffreypfisher.com/melo.html***
Don't compromise your creativity. Get up to two minutes of original music for only $995. Complete. Don't delay. This offer won't last forever.

Sample FAQ

One effective promotional tactic is to use the question and answer format. Again, lead with a headline, state the problems facing your clients and prospects, show how you can solve these problems (through what you sell), address every sales objection, and last, provide instructions on how the person can get what you offer. This format is versatile since it can be a letter, a brochure, and a Web page.

Get Music You Can Use FREE for 15 days!
Do you need music to do the following:

- *evoke* a mood or feeling?

- *create* a convincing atmosphere of time and place?

- *inspire* and motivate?

- *underline* elements of character and situation?

- *supply* a neutral background filler and help bridge scenes?

- *build* a sense of continuity?

- *enhance* dramatic elements?

- *complement* and support your message?

We can help!
Introducing the **Melomania** *music library*
Sound is one-half of every audiovisual presentation. And music plays a very important role in every soundtrack. You already know that using music effectively makes your productions stronger. Great music won't save a bad production, but it can do what no other soundtrack element can do. That's why we created the Melomania *music library. Your creative work demands the best of everything. Don't compromise. Now you* can *get the music you need!*
What is **Melomania**?
It's a new two-volume, two-hour buyout music library of today's hottest styles, specifically created for your audiovisual and multimedia projects. You get 64 music tracks, all 100% royalty-free!
What does royalty-free, buyout mean?
When you purchase Melomania, *you get a nonexclusive, single-site, lifetime license to use any of the music on the CD within your own audiovisual productions. That means you can use the music for any purpose (radio, TV, training and promotional videos, computer multimedia presentations, animation, trade shows, and more) without paying* any *additional fees. No royalty worries! No copyright infringement issues! The music is yours to use as you see fit.*

What makes Melomania different?

Too many other music libraries fail because they try to be complete songs that stand on their own. While this pleases the composer, the resulting music is often overpowering and overbearing. It just gets in the way instead of playing a supporting role. Melomania delivers music that works to reinforce your message, not dominate it. That doesn't mean the music is boring; it just means Melomania music works with other elements and never tries to be a hit song. We've kept most tracks straightforward and free from huge leaps in tempo, walls of sound, or other annoying passages that compete for attention. While most of the tracks can stand on their own, Melomania's real strength lies in how well the music sits inside a project, leaving space for voice-overs, dialogue, sound effects, and visual imagery.

What kind of music is on the Melomania CDs?

The 64 tracks provide a strong mix of genre-specific music and styles. Most tracks are purposefully understated so they help support and reinforce your message. You get theme music, underscore, world flavors, rock, pop, hip-hop, ambient, ethnic, orchestral, and more. Many tracks are on the leading edge of music. Several offer unique twists on memorable styles. And you also get a versatile collection of sparse tracks full of mood to hold under narration, dialogue, sound bites, and interviews. Look at what you get:

Melomania *Volume One*

Nouveau Retro (4:22) Old and new combine into a tight, up-tempo statement.

The remaining descriptions for volume one music cuts follow.

Melomania *Volume Two*

Rain Forest Boogey (2:38) Jungle sound and hip-hop beats abound.

The remaining descriptions for volume two music cuts follow.

How much does Melomania cost?

This two-CD package—64 tracks and over two hours of music— is yours for only $159, including priority shipping and handling. That's less than $2.49 a track! To sweeten the deal, you can preview Melomania FREE for 15 days!

How does my 15-day free trial work?

Order Melomania today by calling (630) 378-4109. We'll ship your package by priority mail. Once it arrives, try the music for 15 days. If you like what you hear and agree that this is the freshest, most versatile, and ultimately most usable music volume, pay the $159 invoice after the 15-day trial period ends. It's that easy. However, should you feel Melomania doesn't meet your music needs, return the entire package to us and owe nothing. You have absolutely nothing to lose!

Why choose Melomania?

You want to use music that inspires you. And you don't need to waste time looking for it. You want music with feeling. You want music to entertain, amuse, motivate, sadden, persuade, titillate, depress, scare, annoy, educate, and even sell! Because when images, sound, and music all work together, you can deliver your message more convincingly. The Melomania music library gives you a versatile tool to help realize your vision and make a difference in how your audience responds.

What else is unique?

Unlike the other libraries that just give you an alternate mix or different timing, you can get any Melomania music track customized to your exact specifications. We call it Flexitrack, and no other library offers this innovation. You've found the ideal track, but you need it tweaked to work perfectly.

Need the sax line or guitar solo deleted? No problem. Want another mix with just the drums and bass? Done. Need the tempo and timing adjusted slightly? Just ask. We can usually make these changes and deliver a custom CD to you in 48 hours. Our Flexitrack option gives you unprecedented control over your final music at very reasonable prices.

Do you offer other services?

Alternately, you can work directly with us to create truly original custom music for your projects. The rates for these services are surprisingly affordable and are based on your project specifications. You can get original music that works and sounds great at a price that's easy on your production budget. Describe what you need, and we'll get right back in touch with a firm quote.

How was Melomania produced?

Melomania artfully combines real musicians—many the finest players from around the globe—playing real instruments with today's electronic technology. Only the most sophisticated digital recording techniques were used to create, arrange, record, mix, and master the music tracks. Jeffrey P. Fisher, whose original commercial music work can be heard on dozens of corporate, cable, and commercial productions, composed and produced all the Melomania music tracks.

Still not sure if Melomania is right for you?

Remember: You can preview Melomania FREE for 15 days!

What's next?

Order Melomania for your 15-day free trial today by calling (630) 378-4109 or sending e-mail to jpf@jeffreypfisher.com. Make sure to include your complete contact information (name, address, and phone number). We'll send your package via priority mail, and you should get it in 2–3 business days after that. Remember you have 15 days to listen before the invoice is due!

Anything else?

Take advantage of this special offer instead. Order Melomania today and get a bonus CD of 10 cuts FREE! That's right, you get a third CD with even more music you can use to start enhancing your audiovisual productions. This $39 value is yours absolutely free with your paid advance order.

Whether you choose the 15-day preview or pay up front and get the bonus CD, you can be assured of getting the freshest music, ready to make your audiovisual productions sizzle. Get Melomania today!

Sample Biography

Jeffrey P. Fisher works from his project studio providing music, sound, writing, video, training, and media production services for corporate, cable, and commercial clients. He writes about music, sound, and video for print and the Web, including nine books:

- *Cash Tracks: Compose, Produce, and Sell Your Original Soundtrack Music and Jingles* (Artistpro, 2005)

- *The Voice Actor's Guide to Home Recording* (with Harlan Hogan, Artistpro, 2005)

- *Instant Surround Sound* (CMPBooks, 2005)

- *Instant Vegas 5* (with Douglas Spotted Eagle, CMPBooks, 2004)

- *Instant Sound Forge* (CMPBooks, 2004)

- *Moneymaking Music* (Artistpro, 2003)

- *Profiting from Your Music and Sound Project Studio* (Allworth Press, 2001)

- *Ruthless Self-Promotion in the Music Industry* (Mixbooks, 1999)

- *How to Make Money Scoring Soundtracks and Jingles* (Mixbooks, 1997)

Jeffrey's library music CD, Dark New Age *(Fresh Music, 2004), along with his* Atmospherics *CD and two-volume, buyout music library,* Melomania, *showcase his musical vision. He also teaches audio and video production and post-production at the College of DuPage Motion Picture/Television department in Glen Ellyn, IL. And he co-hosts the Acid, Sound Forge, and Vegas forums on Digital Media Net (www.dmnforums.com). For more information, visit his Web site at www.jeffreypfisher. com or contact him at jpf@jeffreypfisher.com.*

Sample Postcard or Email or Web Page

Paying too much for original music?
Your creative work deserves original music that works, sound great, and is affordable. Why lower your expectations just to lower your budget?
Let us score your next commercial or corporate project—exactly to your needs—starting at only $995.00 per finished minute. COMPLETE!
Deliver your message more effectively by getting the exact music you need and deserve. For less. Don't put it off. Call or contact us right now for music that works, sounds great, and is affordable.
This special offer expires on April 1, 2006. No fooling!

Sample Small Ad or Web Banner

Radio and TV ads not working? Get a jingle and make your commercials more effective AND profitable. Prices starts at $995. Call . . .

Sample Thank-You Note

Thank you for your kind words about my article you saw in Electronic Musician. *It makes me very happy to know that you found it useful.*

I was happy to duplicate your radio commercial CDs for you. And should something like this come up again (or any other audio or music needs), please do not hesitate to call. I'm looking forward to helping you on an upcoming project. Thanks again!

Sample to Use When You Lose the Gig

I was sorry to hear yesterday that our proposal was declined. Thank you for taking a minute from your day to leave a message for me.

Please understand that I still hope we can do business together soon. I've had many successful relationships with other production companies in the past. I hope that soon we can work together as well.

Until then, I will keep you up to date with my activities and call periodically to see how I might help you. And I would be grateful if you would keep me informed about all the activities and successes at your company, too.

Industry Insight

Brian Tarquin
Jungle Room Studios, NY
bohemiandiscs@msn.com

Recent credits/past projects:
Jungle Room Studios in New York is home to composer, guitarist, and electronic musician Brian Tarquin. He's a busy professional who scores for *All My Children* (and has won two Emmy awards for his music) and writes for both sample and music libraries. His music has been on *Good Morning America, Bernie Mack, Friends, X-Files, Top Model, Making the Video, Tough Enough, WWE, E Entertainment*, and various reality shows, along with a Volvo car commercial and the theme music for MTV's *Road Rules*. His sample CDs include *Guitar Studio* and *Guitar Studio 2* for Big Fish Audio (www.bigfishaudio.com). His music library work includes full-length CDs for Megatrax, Sonoton, FirstCom, Zomba, and ABC TV's Fifth Floor Music. Teaming up with collaborator Chris Ingram in Asphalt Jungle, Tarquin has released his own recordings: *Electro Ave., Enjoy This Trip*, and due out in 2006, *Junglization*.

Why did you choose this career (and how did you get started)?
I started as an assistant engineer at a jingle house in Manhattan after attending the Center for Media Arts in Manhattan. I thought that going toward the production side would be my backdoor into the music industry. I quickly found out about music libraries and hooked up with a small start-up music library, Radical Entertainment. I then worked as an engineer for Powerhouse Recording in L.A. While there, I teamed up with the then-tiny Mastersource library and approached them

161

with some of my songs. I started doing aggressive power trio recordings for the sports-oriented programs and ended up getting my music placed on both the 1992 and 1994 Olympics.

At the same time, I started in radio promotions for indie rock label Restless Records and later went to Virgin in Beverly Hills, where I quickly learned the whole nine yards—business, finance, recoupment, etc.—about the record industry. After that, I signed to my first label MCA Jazz Inspiration out of Toronto. I was really into Acid Jazz at the time, so *Ghost Dance* (1995) was the result. I moved to Instinct Records in 1996 and did three Acid Jazz records with them: *Last Kiss Goodbye*, *Soft Touch*, and *High Life*. One of my songs on their compilation CD, *Best of Acid Jazz 2*, went to the top 20 on *Billboard*. Around 1997, I started Asphalt Jungle with my partner Chris Ingram and found that we were getting so many requests for the music that we ended up doing two theme songs for MTV's *Road Rules*.

During this same period, I did CDs for several music libraries, such as FirstCom and Sonoton, but I've really found a home at Megatrax, where I'm basically doing *Asphalt Jungle* in a way that appeals more to video producers. There are other avenues for musicians besides the record deal. Music libraries are a great place for your music. You just compose, and after your initial sale to the library, they take over and promote and sell your music over and over again. You just write, and they sell! It's a great way to get some up-front music money and ongoing royalties.

I started watermarking my music in the 90s using Verance (www.verance.com). Watermarking is an inaudible print on the master song that is detected by Verance. They monitor all TV playback 24/7, and their database then tracks everything. I'm signed with SESAC as my PRO, and they pay for the watermarking reports and then pay me the royalties due based on those reports. It's the local and small cable channel stuff that often falls through the cracks. These outlets tend not to file cue sheets like the networks do, and therefore the only way to "catch" them is via watermarking technology. When I switched to Verance with my Megatrax recordings, I went from a few-page summary of plays to sometimes as much as a 200-page report. Now some are really small hits, a few pennies, but it really can add up fast. The best part is that the watermarking process itself is free to the composer. Megatrax and SESAC pay for the reports from Verance. It's good business, really, as the library gets the publisher portion anyway while I keep my writer's share. They are really investing in their own bottom line, and I benefit from an essentially transparent technology.

What are you working on now and how did you get this current project?
The *All My Children* gig came from my Instinct Records recordings. Some of the daytime dramas started using my Acid Jazz music for scenes in bars and restaurants. I even appeared on *General Hospital* actually playing guitar in the background. After a while, *All My Children* realized they were using so much of my music that they asked me to be the composer for the show. It started by having me do an album of songs just for them and grew from there.

For many TV shows, you just compose a package of music that they use over and over. You also provide alternate mixes/timings and sometimes stems, too. They take what you've done and place it in the show. This is really the approach for reality TV, but network drama and sitcoms also do this.

I compose, record, and deliver an underscore album a week to *All My Children*. It's really a great gig because I get to do a lot of cool stuff. Essentially, I deliver a library of music cues based on emotions and mood, such as tense, pensive—a real variety of elements. Often, they'll ask me to write a theme for a scene, storyline, or even specific characters. All the music I compose is based on these kinds of directions. I don't have to write locked to picture—there isn't time. I'm free to write songs that the show can slip in as needed. Each weekly session averages around 10 songs.

TV shows like using the same music cue, but they do prefer variations on that theme. I'll put a lot more elements into a single song and then mute tracks and such for these alternative mixes. There might be piano, strings, pads, and beats in the main theme, but I might give them a piano-only version, a pad/strings version, and so forth [the master cue approach—JPF]. I also deliver lots of breakdowns comprising shorter timings, 60-seconds, 10-second stingers/bumpers, and so forth. *All My Children* doesn't really want stems, so I do the remixing for them myself. I mostly deliver the music on audio CDs and only once in a while as a ProTools session data file.

What do you feel makes a good music score (or jingle)?

It depends on a number of factors. For me, it's all about emotion. I want my music to draw the audience into what's really happening in a scene. I find writing full-blown strings works better than just a pad. I also feel that modern electronics juxtaposed with a more traditional score works very well. For example, *All My Children* loves the acoustic guitar with piano and some strings (and a big-ass groove behind it to keep them happy). Some of the best music scores right now are on action sports TV. I also thought that the score for *Fight Club* was very good. It used a lot of different electronics, but also used strings and other traditional orchestral elements.

TV dialogue rules, so I often resort to filters and other mixing tricks, coupled to instrumental choices and arrangements with breakdowns to stay mindful of the dialogue. You can't let what you compose get in the way with extreme solos and so forth, but you do still want to be interesting and connect with the scene. Choosing a good sound palette, and sticking with it, is another technique that's very effective and that producers like.

What gear do you use?

I'm a gear guy, no doubt [Tarquin sent in a three-page list of everything he uses!—JPF], but here's a brief overview.

▶ ProTools with the Digi002 running on a Mac G5.

▶ Akai MPC 4000. I love hardware, so this is my primary go-to device.

- With guitar as my main instrument, I have guitars and amps too numerous to mention, both vintage and modern.

- I use a ton of plug-ins, effects and soft-synths alike. The Artura Minimoog 5, Yamaha CS-80, and Presonious strings are particular faves right now. The East-West StormBreakz are really impressive, and the Plugsound drums work well for me. I also use the new Big Fish Audio London solo strings and symphonic percussion.

- I recently tried Reason as a lark and find it a cool, self-contained product, too.

Explain your promotional strategies (what works and why).
I do a lot of promotion for the Asphalt Jungle albums. They are indie records, not at all mainstream, which forces me to find magazines that are still cool and credible and reach our audience through them. That may be via an ad, feature article, or even a review. You can't ever rest. It's important to always be going after new avenues to promote. While the record label does some promotion, I feel it is really in my best interest to do my own thing, too.

The music libraries get a little funky if you write for others, so I stay with Megatrax, and they do a fair amount of plugging to get my music used for TV shows. It's not a bad way for a new composer to start out. Writing for music libraries can let you build a reel, gain some experience, and make some money, too. If you do it right, it can lead to bigger and better gigs for you.

For film and TV shows, I find the *Hollywood Reporter* invaluable. It shows you all that's going on in film/TV. You will see all the news shows, and who's working on them. I work hard to get each new album out to the people who are looking for music. Also, I look for specific shows and production companies that do certain kinds of shows where I feel my music will fit in nicely. I've definitely found that having albums and pitching the licensing of those songs is the best tactic for me. Most of these little shows don't have composers, and they license tracks instead. I push my records in that direction by contacting music supervisors. They love using the record and may ask for more. Having the Asphalt Jungle CDs can and *does* lead to other avenues. You have to understand that most music supervisors are freelance, and it's not uncommon for them to be doing 3–5 other shows at the same time. You get in right with one, and you have other opportunities. These guys are always looking for new music—it should be your music—so making friends here can really pay off.

My advice is to target carefully. Watch the shows and see what fits. Find the music supervisor for the show using the Music Registry guide (www.musicregistry.com), make tons of phone calls, and get your music into the right hands. This is not like being a doctor. There is no real career path, and nobody tells you anything in this business. You learn as you go along. As you do more and meet more people and gain experience, then you realize how things work.

What skills do you feel someone needs to succeed in the area?

I know it is hard to believe, but nevertheless true. You need 85% business skills and only 15% music skills. Buyers will take for granted that you can write, compose, and put out a decent project. With today's technology, you can do some amazing stuff in your bedroom. The real challenge is finding the work and getting in front of the right people. You have to be rather aggressive repping yourself to the film/TV crowd. You can't be lazy. You have to really build up relationships because so many shows need music, but it is up to you to take your music *to* them. While it may seem intimidating at first, get past your fear. Be aggressive. Pick up the phone, make the contact, and start building those relationships today.

How do you approach projects, technically or creatively?

I do a lot of research because new sounds inspire me. There are some terrific underground record stores in Manhattan, and I'm forever perusing the bins for 12" remixes. I take them back to my studio to listen and check them out for sounds. What's being used on these records? And how can I emulate them? I spend a lot of time getting drum sounds, finding the right samples, and tweaking them in ways that help me create new music. Since I'm not writing to SMPTE and mostly just handing in a library package of music for the show to use, I'm far freer to experiment with new sounds, arrangements, and such. That alone is a real boost to my creativity. I write the way I feel and make my own song. I may start with a chord progression or may find a groove, tempo, or sound and build a song around that.

How do you get paid (typical pay for projects, royalties, etc.)?

There is both front- and back-end money. For *All My Children*, I get paid for the music and also earn Musician's Union fees because I play on all the recordings. I also keep my writer's share, which lets me earn performance royalties for the music when it plays on ABC. Currently, that's about $200 a minute for underscore (primetime would be about $500/minute). There aren't a lot of reruns on daytime TV, but they reuse tracks a lot. And, as I mentioned earlier, watermarking and SESAC together bring in a steady flow of performance royalties from my music library work. Megatrax pays a flat-fee buyout for the CDs I do for them, and I keep the writer's share, of course. Finally, my two sample libraries for Big Fish Audio pay royalties on sales.

What do you wish you'd known then that you know now?

1.) I wish that this industry had been explained to me all in one place. Knowing how to piece together a career, especially the composer's rights situation, would have helped tremendously.

2) Watermark everything! You should get paid when your music plays on TV. If you do libraries and music for shows, make sure you get paid for plays in places that aren't so cue sheet compliant. Also, in my opinion, SESAC is the best PRO for TV guys like me. The pay is better, and they really go after those pennies, which adds up fast. And if I ever have a problem, they've worked hard for me to make adjustments, which I like a lot.

What are your plans for the future?

I plan to keep busy with all that I do. I've taken a little hiatus because of a new baby, but I'm itching to get back at it!

Is there anything else you'd like to comment on that you feel is important?

You have to be thick skinned and take criticism well. People will offer their candid opinions, and you have to deal with that. Hang in there and keep going. So much of this business has to do with timing and relationships. Don't give up.

CHAPTER 9

Promotional Potpourri

"The shortest and best way to make your fortune is to let people see clearly that it is in their interests to promote yours." —Jean de La Bruyère

When it comes to promoting your music industry career, you'd better be ruthless. Do whatever it takes to get your message across to people who would buy the music you have to sell. This chapter supplies additional insight into this crucial aspect of your career.

Get Publicity

To make your commercial music business successful and profitable, you must master publicity. And that means taking steps to present your image, people, music, current/past success, and products and services to the world, using free media exposure. Publicity helps position you as a leader and recognized expert in your particular slice of the soundtrack and jingle world. Establishing, promoting, and leveraging publicity works to build your reputation, and that, in turn, builds your business. It's not an ego thing, either. Publicity is about generating leads to prospects and making more money.

What's especially beneficial about publicity is how it comes from a third party. That adds powerful credibility to you what you do. A media announcement, review, or article/story is a tacit endorsement of you and your music. More people will believe what the media says about you over anything you or your promotional material states.

Publicity is the soft-sell facet of promotion. It is a means to say what you've been up to and the results you've achieved and to imply that you can do the same for others. You have a responsibility to help your clients in any way possible. And that means giving them advice and solving their problems. Also, publicity is the ideal platform to publicly thank your clients for their business. Use your local, national, and World Wide Web media appearances to show how you can and already *do* help clients.

When it comes to promotion, the only road to success is to recognize what the media really want: factual news, problems, and solutions. That's the real meat for most media. To earn media coverage, you either expose a problem or offer a solution to an existing problem. Follow this simple equation: *Provide value: earn a plug.* The amount of promotional currency (the plug) you get is directly proportional to the value you provide. For example, write a short case study that demonstrates how you overcame a client problem and the lessons you learned. This article provides value in an informative format the media love. This is not shameless promotion, but rather knowledge the media use to help their readers. In exchange for that valuable essay, the media outlet lets you promote (or plug) your business.

NEWS RELEASE

Send news releases regularly to the media outlets that serve the people you need to reach. Issue news about recently completed projects, new products or services, staff changes, equipment purchases, and so forth. Also, send news releases that piggyback on national, state, and local coverage of your topic. In other words, you want to be known as an expert the media can call on for quotes when stories come up with which you have relevance, experience, and opinions.

Factual news leans toward the announcement variety. Follow the journalistic format of who, what, when, where, why, and how. Keep out fluff and blatant promotion. Including quotes makes the story feel more like an interview.

If you mail the release, double-space the information and print it on your letterhead. Add "For Immediate Release" at the page top along with a headline. When emailing, put "News Release: Headline" in the subject field. After the body of the release, add # # #, which is the traditional way to end a news release. Don't forget to include contact information and a short biography at the end of the release. Here is a short example of a news release.

Subject: News Release: Fisher Scores for XYZ
For Immediate Release
Fisher Scores for XYZ
Jeffrey P. Fisher recently completed the musical score for The Capital Trip. *Produced by XYZ for Tours, Inc., the video promotes class trips to our nation's capital to area junior high school students. Composed, produced, and recorded at Fisher Creative Group's Chicago-area project studio, the score centers around two main themes.*
"First there is a light and upbeat rock track," Fisher explains, "featuring bass, drums, guitar, and keyboards. The other piece has a more serious tone with a heavy military, almost drum and bugle corp, influence." He also confessed that this was his favorite kind of project. "I really enjoy doing scores like this. They're challenging and fun. And when you get to work with a straightforward client like XYZ, it makes the experience even better."

There's no guarantee that your news release will be published, but that shouldn't stop you from trying. Building a good relationship with the media you approach—treat them as a good client—is an important contributor to publicity success.

ARTICLES

Media stories about you and features written by you lend tremendous credibility to your efforts. Getting featured in an article or writing a more extensive article yourself is another publicity angle to explore. Convincing the media to feature a story about you isn't easy. Inquiring about articles you want to author also takes some finesse. I can't emphasize enough that the media are not out to promote you. They want problems/solutions. Frame your pitches around what the media audience gets, not the plugs you hope to receive.

Do some research to see what the media have done in the past. They don't want more of the same. You need to bring them something new or a fresh twist on a proven idea. Whether you are pitching a story idea about yourself or asking to write an article, start with a query. Find the editor or producer (radio/TV) who handles the general topic you will pitch. Consider approaching an author or journalist directly, but only when you know this person has had some success with the media outlet in question.

Put together a brief synopsis of your idea. Describe your idea, what is important about it, why it's important to the media source's audience, and why you are qualified to write it. Follow this inquiry with a brief biography and list of credentials. Either call or email this query to the editor and follow up judiciously.

Subject: Article Query: Compose Your Own Music Score
Music can greatly enhance almost any presentation. Since using copyrighted material is a no-no, where do presenters turn for the music they need? They can hire a composer, but that usually costs too much. They can buy library production music, but finding just the right cut can be time consuming. They can compose their own music, but...what? How can a nonmusician write his or her own music? One word: Acid.
Sony's Acid essentially lets anyone combine previously recorded sound loop snippets to create his own original royalty-free music. The software makes it a snap to pick sounds, paint them on a grid, and play. Acid matches everything up perfectly in time. Best of all, you can choose from a huge inventory of music loops in a variety of styles—solo guitar, orchestral, rock, hip-hop, techno, ethnic/world, and everything in between.
As a professional musician who composes soundtracks and jingles (and who wrote the definitive book on the subject, CASH TRACKS: Compose, Produce, and Sell Your Original Soundtrack Music and Jingles)*, I'd welcome showing your readers how easily they can use this amazing software product to create original soundtracks to accompany their work. How does this sound?*
Should you have questions or need additional information, please call (contact information followed by a brief biography with credits).

You may get paid for writing the article. While you could take the check, consider swapping it for ad space. Only do this if an ad in the publication would reach your market. Ask for twice as much value in ad space as you would get paid. Then put together a convincing advertisement and run it in issues other than the one your article appears in. This gives you more bang for your promotional buck. Plus, whether an article or a book, being a published author brings with it a bankable cachet.

REPORTS, BOOKLETS, AND NEWSLETTERS

Consider taking article writing to the next step by additionally publishing them yourself. You can either print and mail them to clients or post them to your Web site. Self-publishing won't have the same impact as the third-party endorsements from the media, but it will build your expert status and reputation. Pick a soundtrack or jingle music-related topic that you know and write about it. Find dozens of examples on my Web site (www.jeffreypfisher.com/free.html). A series of articles can transform into a short booklet that you can offer as a premium or even sell.

Package some of the same information you send as news releases into a quarterly newsletter. Again, either print or email it to your list of prospects and clients. Talk about your latest projects, profile client case studies, provide valuable tips, tricks, techniques, and other information, and maybe offer a special discount. Carefully balance pure information with subtle (and not so subtle) promotion. It takes some commitment to keep this up, but it really is a low-cost, efficient, and potentially remunerative promotion.

By the way, I've published my free Moneymaking Music Tip of the Week *enewsletter since 1997 and can personally attest to the rewards a regular promotion such as this can deliver. It's the primary way I keep in touch with readers, clients, the media, and more. Subscribe to it yourself and see what I mean. Send an email to mmmtow-subscribe@yahoogroups.com. Visit the archives on my Web site (www.jeffreypfisher.com).*

Articles or a newsletter subscription make a highly effective offer or premium when promoting what you do. These incentives showcase your expert knowledge in a valuable package.

SPEAKING AND SEMINARS

Delivering speeches, training sessions, and full-blown seminars is a terrific way to reach your prospects and clients and to further develop your reputation. Start small at a local Chamber of Commerce or industry meeting. Work your way up to regional and national trade shows or other industry events. In the past year, I've taught in a dozen cities around the country, including at major shows such as CES, NAB, Government Expo, and more. These engagements help promote you as a leader in your field.

A little research will reveal the kinds of sessions available. Contact the people who organize the events, such as training companies or event planners. Pitch them on a session led by you using the same techniques for pitching story ideas to the media (see above). For local appearances, get involved with organizations that serve your community.

ON THE AIR

While it's doubtful you will use radio, broadcast TV, or cable to advertise and promote your music, there is a related technique you must employ. When your music appears on readily available media, such as a radio jingle, TV theme/score, or similar outlets, drop an email or postcard to your clients and prospects. Let them know when, where, and for whom you contributed your music. Hearing your music from another third-party project gives you more credibility than hearing your music demo—even if it's the *same* music. You easily reap most of the benefits of broadcast media without buying advertising time.

> *NOW HEAR THIS! Are you still wondering whether Jeffrey P. Fisher's music can help you? Maybe this will convince you: Listen for Al's Body Shop jingle on Wxxx radio and other stations in this area. Al claims his sales have increased 8% since starting his new radio advertising campaign. We like to think our jingle has something to do with that. Let us do the same for you. Call now to get started helping you or your clients use music more effectively.*

Let's close this section with the insightful comments of Brendan Behan: "All publicity is good, except an obituary notice."

Words on Word-of-Mouth

If you asked 100 people in the music industry what the best promotion is, 90% would say word-of-mouth. If you asked that 90% what that exactly means, only a handful could tell you. The elusive word-of-mouth promotional strategy implies that you do nothing and people just naturally seek you out. This is, of course, ludicrous. Successful word-of-mouth needs constant coaxing on your part.

First and foremost, you must constantly deliver quality music and outstanding service. Nothing creates repeat and new business better than a job well done in the first place. Do your best work for those who buy, and they'll become your best sales representatives. They will go out of their way to tell others about what you did for them.

What you want to do is use your success with one client as a springboard to others. Work hard to get that first major success; then you can leverage it to get more clients and subsequently use them to get still more business, *ad infinitum.*

Second, make sure you tell everybody about your successes. Using both publicity and direct contact via telephone, email everyone and remind people and the industry of all that you do. Also, encourage people to pass on your information to *their* contacts.

Third, work to get referrals from satisfied clients and then pursue them aggressively. And fourth, display your contact information prominently on everything you create, making it easy for people to find and get in touch with you.

Real, effective word-of-mouth needs nurturing to work properly. Your effectiveness will come partly from reputation and partly from perspiration. Earning a reputation helps you perpetuate your word of mouth. People who are satisfied with what you did in the past will likely purchase from you again. With that rep in hand, it's time to push it a little harder by encouraging satisfied customers to spread the word for you. Here's how to get your word-of-mouth work working:

▶ Decide what it is you need to promote. Get specific. What gig(s) do you want more of right now?

▶ Make a detailed list of all the people you know. Include current/past clients, prospects who never bought anything, relatives, media contacts, business associates, and so forth. Put anybody who knows your work and reputation on this list.

▶ Develop a promotional package that highlights what you need to promote. Include all the appropriate and suitable materials, such as brochure, business card, and demo CD.

▶ Send this promotional material to each and every person on your list. Make sure in the cover letter you stress that you are not asking for their business. Instead, you want them to pass this information on to someone they know who would be a candidate for your work and benefit from working with you. Make sure you thank them for helping you spread the word.

Of course, you can bypass this step and simply ask your clients for referrals to other people, too. Take the contact information they give you and use it an entrée to the prospect.

▶ Additionally, contemplate offering incentives to those who help. Either give them a discount toward a future purchase or kick back a commission for a sale that comes as a direct result of their recommendation. Use your best judgment here. Some people like to help other people and will perceive the discount/cash as an insult. Perhaps, send a warm thank-you card and a small gift or treat for an extravagant meal.

Advertising

Advertising is a wholly passive promotional tool. You throw your message out into the world and hope it sticks. Frankly, I hasten to mention this promotional tactic because ads are expensive and rarely pay off in this business. Why people continue to waste their precious capital resources on advertising is beyond me. Instead, seek free publicity and connect directly with people. These promotions generate far greater returns than the money plopped down on an ad.

With those warnings in mind, it can still be effective to advertise in the trade publications and on Web sites that hit your target market. Employ several small ads rather than a single hit with one big ad. Repetition of your message is what makes advertising work. You want your ad in front of people so that when they need music, they contact you first. The same kinds of strategies and offers you use in all your promotional material work, too. Ads are best used to generate leads, not to sell directly. In the soundtrack and jingle world, people need more information to make a decision. They won't click a Web banner and buy your music (unless it is a music library, perhaps).

Well-conceived ads include these essentials:

▶ Audience identifier. Who is this for? You can skip the audience identifier if the ad will appear in a targeted place, such as on a Web site that appeals to video producers.

▶ Main benefit. The gain they get; the pain you remove.

▶ Offer. What they get when they respond.

▶ Necessary details, such as contact information: "Call (number) now!"

▶ All that's left is to create an eye-catching design.

Let's use the example of a Web banner. Start by writing down what you want your ad to say:

Audiovisual producers can save money with their next original music purchase by getting a free consultation with composer Jeffrey P. Fisher. If they contact him, Jeffrey will provide the details on how to save money and still get original music that works, sounds great, and is affordable.

That has the information, but now reduce the needless details. Don't use abbreviations. Whittle down the words to the barest minimum needed to present your benefit and make your offer. Don't sacrifice words for clarity, though.

Save money on original music. FREE music planning kit. Click here.

Make sure you track all your advertising. When people contact you (or use Web site statistics), ask them how and where they heard of you. Keep a record of their responses, so you can see where your money, time, and energy are best spent.

POSTCARD REDUX

What makes for a strong small ad also makes an ideal postcard. They are inexpensive to produce and mail, plus they remain an effective promotional tool. Limit the postcard mailing to a single idea or offer. Don't try to cram every last detail into this small space. Grab attention, state your benefits, and urge readers to take action now.

Better Network = Bigger Net Worth

It's a well-known saying that "a wise man knows everything; a shrewd one, everybody." If you wish to compose, produce, and sell your original soundtrack music and jingles, *who* you know is by far the right path to success. Although these industry contacts may be few and far between in the beginning, devote quality time and effort toward cultivating these relationships.

Networking essentially means that you help people first and give them something of value they can use. At that point, you are in a prime position to get something in return—some form of promotion, even new business. Networking allows you to gather useful information (and share what you know) and make valuable contacts with people who can help you. Networking is both give and take. You want to help the other person as much as he wants to help you.

The key to building a network of contacts requires that you become part of a scene. For example, to be a successful soundtrack composer, you must associate with people who need music for their audiovisual presentations. Joining and participating with them will help you in the long run. Your research should reveal many networking opportunities, such as industry meetings and events, trade shows, and similar occasions.

Also, don't forget family, business contacts, religious affiliations, alumni organizations, schools, civic groups, professional groups, and unions—let *everyone* know you are in business and make sure they know what you do and what kinds of clients you are looking for.

Other promotional tips already discussed apply. Here are a few more tips:

▶ Be confident.

▶ Don't wait for someone to speak to you, strike up your own conversations. It may surprise you when the most mundane of circumstance results in a lucrative project.

▶ Ask about their background and needs first before telling your story.

▶ Don't be shy about letting people know what you do. Use your elevator pitch.

▶ Practice active listening skills and add in some humor, kindness, and genuine interest.

▶ Make eye contact and use both verbal ("That's interesting, tell me more, etc.") and nonverbal cues (nods, smiles, laughs, etc.).

▶ Have business cards handy. Trade contact information with your colleague.

▶ Don't hand out demos at networking opportunities. I strongly feel that sending your CD (or Web link) after the event makes for the ideal follow-up. It's a reason to reconnect with the person(s) you met.

▶ Follow up all business leads with calls, letters, or emails. Allude to your meeting when contacting this lead.

INDUSTRY EVENTS

Trade shows and their ilk are a terrific opportunity to build your business. Not only can you see the latest, greatest gear, but you have an opportunity to promote your own wares. The savvy self-promoter sells across the booth. How? Approach companies that are exhibiting and offer your services. Also make contact with as many people as you can by going to booths, demonstrations, training sessions, parties, and so on. Use the time to build your network and put together mutually beneficial projects at the show.

ROLL UP YOUR SLEEVES

You're never too big to help out with the little things that matter. At a recent training event on the road, the sponsors had borrowed the offices of another company. The event served some pizza and libations, lasting about three hours. When it was all done, and I was preparing to leave, I noticed the sponsors themselves cleaning up the room. When queried, they told me that they felt they should return the room as it was in before we started. Now these weren't grunts. They were top dogs at a large, successful company, scrubbing the room with cleaners, brooms, vacuums, and garbage bags. They probably could have left it all for a cleaning crew, but they didn't. The moral? Maintaining solid business relationships sometimes means going above and beyond. And sometimes it means crawling around in the dirt, managing the minutia. Don't be unwilling to roll up your sleeves when appropriate, because often the simple steps you take in business reward you many times over down the line.

OPEN HOUSE/PRIVATE SCREENING/PARTY

Throw a party and invite clients, prospects, fans, family, media, and other influential people from your music world. Bring them to your studio or secure another venue. Perhaps this will be a product release party, such as when the game you scored is released or a special screening of your latest work. Have plenty of promotional materials to give away, maybe even door prizes. Serve some munchies and libations. And show off what you can do.

THE WAS (THAT WAS)

David Was used Sony Acid to create the music used for the 2002 Academy Awards show. The makers of Acid promoted this fact quite heavily. I, being a strong proponent of the software, was keenly interested in the story. Little did I know that our paths would cross a few years later. In 2005, I was asked to speak on a variety of audio topics at the Post/Production Conference at the National Association of Broadcasters (NAB) convention. One session involved organizing a Sony Acid Power Users session with the possibility of having David at the helm. I had never met David before, but I knew of his work. We exchanged emails (through a third party) and talked extensively about commercial music, technology, and life. I found him to be an erudite and generous person with terrific ideas about music. Although the NAB session didn't materialize, I did ask David if he would contribute to this book. He graciously agreed, and you can read my interview with him elsewhere in these pages.

My point is this: Networking and serendipity often play a greater role in putting you together with the people you need to know. Don't neglect the power of this primary promotional strategy. You have to let people know you are looking for specific projects and specific people. You have to be equally prepared and willing to help those who inquire the same from you. We're all in this together, and ultimately we can all help each other through this crazy world.

Web Ways

The Internet is a low-cost but high-involvement medium. You'll get from it what you put into it. It will take your time and energy to maintain a cool Web site and continually monitor other activities. Today, virtually everyone in the music industry can benefit from a Web site. With most music bought online, the Web is the place to be. Set up your Web site as your personal Web community and storefront where everybody comes to get information, learn about you, and buy from you. Your site should carry all the information prospects need to make buying decisions. There should be information specifically for the media. If it applies, there should be a section devoted to your vendor and other supplier needs. Your Net presence should appeal to your clients and provide value-added products and services that keep them loyal.

FIND WEB SPACE

You need a place to host your Web site. Chances are that your Internet service provider (ISP) supplies server space as part of your regular Internet connection fee. The downside to an ISP site is that it's bound to have a weird URL name. Instead, rent space from a company providing hosting services. I recommend Addr.com (www.addr.com), having used them for five years or so with few issues. Audio and video clips can eat up a lot of server space quite quickly. Make sure you have enough space to meet your needs.

GET A VIRTUAL DOMAIN

With your space set, go to Network Solutions and register your own domain. Choose your name wisely; use your personal or business name or both. Domains at Network Solutions cost about $35 a year or less. For an additional fee, you can have your "virtual domain" routed to any weird Web address you have. This way, people type in www.jeffreypfisher.com and are automatically taken to the right Web site no matter where it actually hosts. After that, navigation links on your site take over.

The real advantage of a virtual domain is that you can route it anywhere. If your hosting service or ISP goes belly up, your Web site can be hosted elsewhere in a day or so. Securing a domain from a heavy-hitter such as Network Solutions means your domain should be around for many years to come.

SET UP AN EMAIL ADDRESS

Along with the domain, set up at least one email address. Go with yourname@yourdomain.com or info@yourdomain.com. Don't be cute or cryptic. Choose a name that reflects your business image and personality.

PUT TOGETHER A BASIC WEB SITE

Think of your site as a store, of sorts, that sells you and your music. Surf the Web and research how other composers are using the Internet. Use what you learn, good and bad, to pull your promotional site together. Your Web presence should be a reflection of your business image. Keep your pages updated with your latest projects, new demos, and other fresh content.

Concentrate on the *content* of your pages and leave the technical side to a professional to help you design and program your pages. Ask your hosting service for leads to Webmasters. Sometimes templates are included with your fee. Whether you choose to design and program yourself or hire a Web designer, plan your site carefully before you begin. Include these basic elements:

▶ An introductory page that provides an overview of you and your music

▶ Details about the services you offer

▶ A bio, list of credits, awards, and other credentials

▶ Testimonials and recommendations from past clients

▶ A FAQ about your music composition services (costs, rights, etc.)

▶ Reprints or links to publicity about you and your work

▶ MP3 music demos

► FTP area (see below)

► Anything else that's specific to your situation. For example, I sell my music library and books. I also have several helpful articles for clients that add value to my Web site and build my reputation.

CREDIT CARD CUES

If you sell products online, you must accept credit cards. CCNow (www.ccnow.com) provides custom, secure online ordering tools for processing product sales. You can also use PayPal (www.paypal.com) for either products or services.

GET PEOPLE TO YOUR SITE

Obviously, you need to generate traffic to your Web site to reap the most benefits. The Web is one gargantuan promotional opportunity. Between email, forums, chat rooms, email groups, and the Web itself, there are endless ways to bring your message to tightly focused audiences and find specific people with particular interests. The Web can be soft-sell *and* hard-sell. You can build your reputation as you would with traditional media. You can host your own storefront where people access your online brochure and hear your latest musical creations. There is a dizzying array of possibilities. And you'd better take advantage of them all!

To a certain extent, consider the Web as just another media outlet and follow the publicity advice mentioned earlier in this chapter. Also, consider the Web as another way to connect with people just like an industry event, so follow the earlier networking tips, too. Join relevant chat rooms, newsgroups, forums, email lists, and Web sites and, most of all, participate. Promote your site online and offline. Send news releases, post to applicable newsgroups and mailing lists, send direct mail and email to clients and prospects, add your information to business cards, letterhead, brochures, and ads. Also, provide an email signature that explains what you do and directs people to your Web site location. Have reasons for visitors to keep coming back to your Web pages. Don't just make your site one long advertisement. Provide value by supplying information, samples, useful tips, link, and more.

FTP

Often, clients will want to send you, and likewise you may need to send them, large digital files, such as video files and music works-in-progress. While you can usually squeeze 1MB files or smaller into an email, as file sizes grow, the possibility of delivering them successfully via email dwindles. Many email programs and Internet service providers (ISPs) reject large email attachments. Similarly, the recipient may not have enough space in his mailbox for the files.

The best solution is to have a File Transfer Protocol (FTP) area on your Web site that can be used to upload/download these gargantuan files. Consider password protecting this area and issuing passwords carefully. FTP is perfect for the 1– 200+ MB files you may encounter. Of course, you need a high-speed Internet connection for moving this amount of data regularly. Beyond a couple hundred megabytes, though, I find messenger and overnight delivery of CDs/DVDs still the better choice.

FTP is very convenient, and you don't sacrifice quality for file size, either. Harlan Hogan does voiceover work for me. I email him the script, and he records it in his home studio and then uploads the full-quality WAV file to his FTP site. Then he sends me a password that lets me log in and download the file at my leisure.

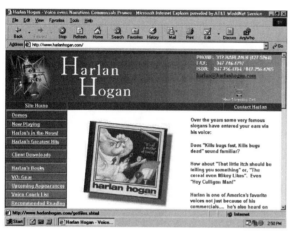

VO pro Harlan Hogan has a password-protected FTP area for clients to download his voice recordings.

Email Tips

Use the subject line to give a real indication of what your message is about. It should carry a benefit or allude to a project or other client connection. Don't be obtuse or gimmicky. Think about what you are going to write *before* you start typing. Take the time to organize your thoughts. Be sure your writing serves its fundamental purpose: to communicate ideas and information. Use simple, every-day language and write short, action-packed sentences that progress in a logical way. Proofread, revise, and check your spelling before releasing your prose to the world.

Keep the message brief and get to the point. Talk warmly, but usually be more succinct than a regular letter or Web site. If you're asking a question, do it right away. Don't bury your inquiry at the bottom of a lengthy life story. Make sure you say what you want to happen next, too. Don't give the recipient an easy way to trash your message. Ask for a specific response. Also, use an email signature to do a little selling for you (include a link to your Web site).

It's a good idea to develop some standard replies to cover your most asked frequently questions. I have several generic email messages that contain general correspondence, promotional pieces, proposals, thank-you notes, and more. It takes time to gather this material, but in the long run you save time. Once you develop these basic responses, use them repeatedly. Make sure you personalize each piece by simply slipping in a custom sentence or two.

Make sure you call out previous queries.

>>*can you deliver by June?*
Of course, no problem. If I can get final approval the last week in May, I will deliver the final mix by June 1.

Don't send spam, but do send promotions to people who have already identified themselves as wanting to hear from you. Be careful what you write in the subject line. If it looks like advertising or other junk email, your message might get deleted before being read. Try personalizing your approach instead.

Enthusiasm Rules!

There is one simple skill you should master that can often have a surprisingly positive effect on your music career. What is it? Enthusiasm. Have you ever noticed someone extremely happy? Their whole demeanor changes. They smile, laugh, become more animated, and generally gush warmth into a room. They'll frequently be unable to sit still, will talk with their hands (and arms!), and make other wild expressions and gestures. Their speech is higher in pitch and frequently more rapid. It's almost comical to experience someone when they reach this mood. Yet still, you can't help but be impressed and swept away by their joyous mood.

Enthusiasm is contagious. When you're excited about something, those around you get excited about it, too. Your passion rarely goes unnoticed. People quickly see that you're not only serious about what you do, but you have a fire raging inside that won't be easily extinguished. Happy people make others around them feel good about themselves, too. And that's the key to this skill. You need to elevate your good mood when you come into contact with people. When you make others feel good about themselves, they'll reward you.

So have fun. Few free promotional techniques work better or are remembered more. Love your work and let that love, commitment, and enthusiasm shine through everything you do. Many clients have told me that the way I get excited about their projects energizes them. I'm extremely passionate about my work, and I only want to give clients my absolute best. They *feel* my enthusiasm, and that works to abate their fears (am I right for the gig?). I feel that I get hired more often because of my enthusiasm rather than my *curricula vitae*.

You can't get by with some phony and faint expression of interest, either. People can sense a poser. Your enthusiasm must be genuine. You are passionate about what you do, right? You do believe in your music? You do want others to share in your joy? If you answered yes, it's time to cultivate your eagerness, showcase your zeal, and use that fire in your belly to impact people.

Enthusiasm is by far the easiest way to get more people on your side and a sound strategy that you can take to the bank.

'Tis the Season

Holiday gifts are a tradition for many businesses. Unfortunately, too many people think narrowly about the gift. "Send 'em a tub of popcorn," usually with a computer-generated note card. Hold on a minute. What is the purpose of this business gift? I suspect there are two: (1) To thank your best clients for their business and remind them of how much you appreciate their support; and (2) to encourage your clients to buy from you again (and again and again). So, what makes the ideal business gift?

Give them a discount coupon for your music services. This can be either a percentage or a dollar amount toward their next purchase from you. Make this coupon somewhat fancy. A Certificate of Appreciation motif is a good start. Use it to thank your customers for their business and tell them how you are rewarding them with this special customer discount. This strategy meets both of the criteria above. You thank *and* reward your clients at the same time. Plus, your coupon is good only for your business, so you automatically encourage them to buy from you again. That can't be bad, right?

For your top clients, those who have spent the most money with you during the past year, sit down at your computer and write a short letter that offers your sincere thanks for their support throughout the past year. Though the bulk of the letter can be generic, be sure to throw in items specific to each customer to remind them of how much you care about their success. Include this highly personal letter with your discount certificate and send it at holiday time. Consider sending this right after Thanksgiving before the typical *anschluss* of holiday cheer permeates and your little token of appreciation gets buried under the clutter.

For other customers, send a simple secular holiday greeting card with a personal note. Even just a sentence or two scribbled on a greeting card thanking them and wishing them future success will go a long way toward building loyal customers and your business. Of course, you can include the discount coupon in this mailing as well.

Client Concerns

Build strong relationships and make clients, not sales. While it's always tempting to go after quick bucks, the real money is made by cultivating healthy, long-standing relationships with clients. Project the right image so your clients see you as a helpful, knowledgeable, dependable, and creative musical professional. Here are more tips to help you keep in touch with clients, keep them happy, and keep them yours.

▶ Be neat and thorough. There is nothing worse than hastily scribbled notes, typos, missing pieces, wrong files, or other oversights. Do your best work all the time. Never hand in shoddy work and never apologize for your work before playing it. Say that this is the best work you've done so far.

▶ Don't forget the telephone. There is nothing wrong with picking up the phone and simply saying "Hi" and asking about the work they are doing. Don't try to get work for yourself, just touch bases and make another contact. Be genuinely friendly and helpful. Clients remember these little tokens; use them to your advantage.

▶ Dress appropriately for meetings, slightly more formally than casually. Think of it as a job interview and choose an appropriate wardrobe. Don't ever show up in jeans and a T-shirt!

▶ Be on time to all meetings. If you are running late, call ahead and explain your delay. Be prepared for these meetings and have the information you need readily at hand. If you can't get them an answer right away, explain why.

▶ Return all their phone calls promptly and deliver quotes and contracts within a day. Even if you don't get the person who called, make sure you leave a message to show that you indeed tried. Often I'll send an email to those I miss. When they get back to their office, my message is sitting there waiting for them.

▶ Always meet your deadlines and do exactly what you say you are going to do. If you tell someone you'll call Friday morning, do just that. Should you have to choose between incomplete work and missing a deadline, miss the deadline. Call the client and fully explain the troubles you're having and work to a mutually beneficial solution.

▶ Give your clients more than they ever expected. It could be something simple, like doing an alternate mix of a score or jingle, making a few extra copies on CD, shipping files by courier or overnight instead of regular shipping, etc. When you work on a project, think of ways you can go the extra mile. Don't charge for it, just do it to show you are working hard to make them happy with your service. And make sure your client knows what you've done. Be subtle such as, "I took the liberty of creating a mix without the lead guitar, just in case you need some filler under the narration."

▶ Here's something I've done a few times. Clients invariably call up and ask for a simple job, such as a new mix or extra copies. I go ahead and do the job and then send them an invoice outlining the regular charge. At the bottom, I write "NO CHARGE." The client sees what it would have cost them for the work but appreciates the in-kind, extra special treatment.

▶ This one's not so unique, but it works anyway. After a major project, send small gifts to the principals involved. Something project- or music-related is best. The problem with sending food is that it is eaten and forgotten. Sending a book, CD, or other gift has staying power. They see it and are reminded of you. And that's the situation you want.

▶ Make sure you mention your clients in promotions. Also, send them copies of your publicity, articles, booklets, new demos, etc. Think of the many ways you can contact them and make a list. Divide the list up and start doing these things regularly as the year progresses. At the end of the year, make a new to-do list and start fresh.

▶ Don't dominate conversations. Listen to the full story and then answer in the complete manner that shows you understand the problem and that you care about solving it satisfactorily. Use all client contacts to gather the information you need to close more sales with future prospects.

▶ Don't be afraid to ask for more information. If you don't understand something, ask for clarification. It's better to be thorough than to be ignorant—or worse, make a costly mistake.

▶ Be warm, kind, interested, enthusiastic, and genuine. Make sure your client knows you care. And don't put up some fake façade. Be yourself in a straightforward manner. People reflect what they see in you. If you are passionate about your music, you will excite your clients and prospects.

GET AND USE CLIENT TESTIMONIALS

Inducing clients to say great things about you and your music is essential. A few words from a well-respected industry leader can work wonders. Use these quotations in your promotions. But how do you secure these endorsements. Simple, really, just ask.

After you've achieved something significant for a client, ask if she wouldn't mind putting her comments down on paper or in an email. Some clients will send you nice comments without being prodded. Be appreciative of these thoughtful individuals. Always ask for permission to use what is said in your promotional literature, though. You may use the entire letter at times; other times pull quotes and put them on your Web site, in a brochure, and so on. This is yet another third-party validation of your work that can quickly diminish the fears of other prospects teetering on whether to hire you ore not.

Conducting an informal survey is another way to gather useful quotes. You will learn more from what they tell you. Clients will happily tell you what's right with what you are doing, so you can keep on doing it. And they'll tell you what's wrong with your approach, so you can improve that, too.

RESOLVE CLIENT CONFLICTS

It can happen to the best of us. No matter how hard you try, something goes wrong. And your client is unhappy about your work. Don't panic. And don't shrug it off. Confront the problem head-on and attempt to resolve it. Don't pass the buck, either. No matter what happens, don't shift the blame to someone or something else. Always assume *full* responsibility.

The best approach is to ask the client what the problem is. Then sit back and listen. Often, the client just needs to vent some anger. While I don't think you should stand for any abuse, you should listen to their side of the story. When it's your turn, try to answer the points brought up by your client. Summarize the client's position to make sure you fully understand what it is they want. If there is something you can do right now to fix things, *do it*. If they must wait for the resolution of their problem, assure them that you will drop everything and work to their satisfaction. Explain what you will do resolve the issue and by when you expect to have it resolved. Take action right away. Follow up to make sure your client is satisfied.

Pump Up the (Business) Volume

Whether your music business is growing exponentially or grinding to a halt, you should never stop promoting or working hard to land new clients. Follow these simple ideas and keep a steady stream of business coming your way.

WORK YOUR STRENGTHS

Concentrate on the projects and clients that bring in the most money. Let the rest go. If you are making decent cash pursuing certain work and wasting too much time on pet projects that bring in peanuts, it is probably time to reevaluate your priorities. Swallow hard and commit to pursuing only the real moneymakers, and quit chasing rainbows.

ASK FOR MORE

The best time to ask for additional work is right after you've finished a successful project for a client. If people are happy and satisfied with what you did, parlay that euphoria into more work. Simply inquire about the next project. Don't be coy about proposing a project yourself. If you can't get work from that client right away, at the very least ask for referrals to others who need your services. Follow up these recommendations promptly.

LAUNCH NEW PROMOTIONS

Don't forget to look ahead. Promotion is often neglected when you get busy or when things seem to be falling apart. I urge you not to be complacent. Always be promoting a little, especially when you're swamped, to secure future work. Spend a little time each day letting people know about you and your music and how what you sell can help make their lives better.

Call past clients and see if they have any new projects coming up. Make some cold calls to possible prospects. Write a news release about your latest accomplishments and send it to the media that reach your target market. Put together a simple postcard or email about your services and send it to your contact list. Look for networking opportunities and go where the work is. Make some inroads toward landing new gigs when your current workload finishes up. You'll sleep better knowing that today's good fortune won't dry up through sloth. Get busy...and stay busy!

FIND BETTER CLIENTS

If you are wasting time on nickel-and-dime gigs, it's well worth the extra effort to find those clients with bigger budgets. Find those deep pockets and pitch your most persuasive argument so they hire you. A few projects from better clients can keep you busy for weeks and paid handsomely.

HIT THOSE OLD LEADS ONE MORE TIME

You probably have contact information for people who inquired about what you sell but never bought anything. Don't give up on these people too soon. One reader of my *Moneymaking Music Tip of the Week* email newsletter shared this invaluable advice: "Recently I went through my year-old list of leads to which I had sent out promotional kits. Before removing them from my list permanently, I phoned each of the contacts one last time. Nearly all of the contacts were no longer with the companies. However, most of the "new" hires requested updated promotional materials and demos. They hadn't known about my services." Don't let these people slip through the cracks.

PITCH NEW WORK TO ANCHOR CLIENTS

Don't neglect the 20% of your established client base that provides 80% of your revenue. Treat them well, and they'll reward you with their continued patronage and loyalty. Everyone in this business has a few really good clients who account for a significant percentage of their total sales. These people usually buy regularly, often without any effort on your part. Today is the perfect time to connect again with those people who are already sold on you. Reselling a satisfied client is far easier than starting from scratch.

I suggest you take a new tactic with this group. Start pitching new or additional services to them and see what happens. I find that simply picking up the phone and either inquiring about new projects or pitching my own ideas invariably results in an assignment. You can't expect people to call *you* all the time. Often, you just need to plant the seed of suggestion in someone's mind first. Who are you going to contact today?

ASK FOR REFERRALS

One overlooked way to drum up new business is from within the *same* company. For example, you may work for one department of a larger company or one account team at an ad agency. Other departments or creative teams within that same company may also need your services. However, these people may not know about you (and how you've helped their colleagues). When you've finished a project for one department, ask your current client about other people who may need similar help. Either ask permission to use their name when you call the other department or have the current client call on your behalf.

SET UP MORE IN-PERSON SALES SITUATIONS

The personal touch really works in today's often sterile, anonymous world. No letter, email, flyer, or Web site will ever replace standing face-to-face with someone and making your pitch. Building rapport, addressing every objection, and winning people over with your charm, enthusiasm, and music prowess work far better in the flesh.

This works especially well if you have had only email and telephone contact with a prospect that's still wavering on your proposal. Set a meeting on their turf, and you can often close the sale right away or get the negative response. Although the latter is disappointing, getting a no sooner is better than being strung along for days and weeks.

IMPROVISATION

Many of us improvise when playing our music. However, the same thought process can apply when running your music career. Sometimes, you just have to make it up as you go along. However, most will agree that to be a good music improviser, you need solid music skills. The same applies to your career. You need strong business skills and a track record of success before you can start improvising. Because when you know the rules and what works, you can break them to your advantage. You'll know what to do when it matters the most. Call it experience. Call it intuition. Improvisation means being flexible and creative and using your knowledge to go with the flow. It doesn't always pay to be tied to traditional ways of doing things. Stretch yourself a little and see where it takes you. You may be pleasantly surprised.

Promotion's Final $0.02

Your past work will get you more work because success breeds more success. People want security. If they have confidence that you can indeed do the job, they will buy. Of course, your music, services, and prices all affect sales. However, you must instill confidence in your clients and prospects because otherwise these sales objections will not matter. Have the confidence that you can write the exact music your clients want. It's vital that you back up every claim you make with tangible evidence. People buy from businesses with which they are familiar. Familiarity breeds confidence, and confidence means sales. Therefore, you must concentrate on becoming the familiar professional upon whom your clients depend.

Keep watching for opportunities because change is inevitable. Pay attention, stay informed, and use information you discover to improve your situation. There may be voids in the market that your music services can fill. Do you see them?

There is an old business adage that says you must spend money to make money. I heartily disagree. You must spend money *promoting* to make money! It's not an expense, either. Promotion is an investment in your future success.

Industry Insight

Ronen Landa
New York City
ronen@ronenlanda.com, www.ronenlanda.com

Recent credits/past projects:
Original score, "The Dreams of Sparrows" (the first Iraqi-made documentary in the post-Saddam era), and a host of other projects (docs, shorts, commercials, etc.).

Why did you choose this career (and how did you get started)?
I decided to become a film composer when I discovered the music of Ennio Morricone (originally by hearing John Zorn's covers, and then listening to the originals). In college, I thought the only way I could pursue more adventurous music was in a stiff academic setting, and that disappointed me tremendously. The realization that I could do so while working with film changed my entire professional outlook instantly.

What was and how did you land your first project?
I had a friend in college who was making short films. He is a composer as well, but I harassed him and didn't let up until he let me score one. He even paid me for it!

What are you working on now and how did you get this current project?
Currently, I am working on another feature documentary, and there are several more docs in the pipeline. I met the director I am working with now while promoting "The Dreams of Sparrows" at the South by Southwest festival in Austin.

What do you feel makes a good music score (or jingle)?
Score can be two things: It can be a "wallpaper" background, or it can be an active participant in the storytelling. Film music can be good and competently composed either way, but I much prefer

to work on projects that call for the music to play a role in the story or to enhance the audience's emotional connection to that story.

What gear do you use?

I often sketch my ideas with pencil, paper, and piano keyboard or guitar. I take those ideas to the Mac (Digital Performer, soft synths, and soft samplers) to flesh them out with respect to orchestration.

Explain your promotional strategies (what works and why).

The best promotional strategy is networking. People generally hire me because they like me. I know that's frustrating to hear when you've spent years honing your musical skills, but it's just honest. The people who are hiring often don't know much about music, so demos will only take them so far in the hiring process. I've sent out tons of demos that have received no response, but if I've met the person to whom I'm sending it or was referred to them by another filmmaker or friend, my success rate is much higher.

What skills do you feel someone needs to succeed in the area?

Despite what I said above, you do need musical skills. Unless you are a hell of a con artist (and there are some out there, I understand), you need to project a great deal of confidence. Filmmakers want to hire someone confident and someone who makes them feel at ease, because music is one area where many filmmakers feel unsure. Your confidence is built on your musical skills. Beyond that, having your production chops together is an important corollary; you need to know how to make your music sound professional.

How do you approach projects, technically or creatively?

It's important to have detailed discussions with the filmmakers regarding a creative direction, budget, and timeframe because this information will affect the approach a great deal. Before I start composing, I like to think about the identity of the score: What makes this film unique? How can I express that musically? Are there any sonic ideas that will give this score a distinct character? I prefer to avoid aping a piece or style directly. I may use that as inspiration, but I always add my own twist. Once I settle on the film's sonic/musical identity, I score a scene that will present one of the main themes and then score several scenes using variations on that theme.

How do you get paid (typical pay for projects, royalties, etc.)?

I've scored feature films for less up-front money than I've received for a commercial demo! If you feel that investing in a specific relationship or a specific project is worth your time, you ought to do it. It will pay off eventually. On the other hand, never underestimate your worth. If a potential employer is asking you to work for free, they do not (and will not) value your services. Tread carefully.

Can you comment on financial strategies you use/used to start/run this career/business?
When starting my career, I needed income from nonmusical sources to pay for food, rent, equipment, etc. I chose to tutor children, which was perfect for me because hourly rates are high, and hours spent working are few. That choice freed up time to work on music and promotion. I also recommend having a rounded financial life—if you blow your cash on gear, you'll have a great studio, but you might not have money to pay for your kids' college tuition. So take the time to balance your professional and personal investments. There is no one formula, but try to find a formula to which you can adhere as strictly as possible.

Can you comment on using employees, partners, and outsourcing?
I was recently away on a personal trip when a commercial client needed some changes made fast. If I didn't have someone in New York to call and take care of the work, my relationship with the client would have been decimated. Develop a network of people who can lend a hand, along with your network of clients. That should include people with diverse professional strengths. Treat the people you hire the way you want to be treated when you are hired, and they'll likely return the favor when they need your expertise. Each of us is only one person, so never feel like you have to do everything alone.

What do you wish you'd known then that you know now?
I recently read in a book ("*Million Dollar Consulting*" by Alan Weiss) that customers not only get what they pay for, but they perceive that they get what they pay for. Mull on that—it's had tremendous implications for my business model.

What are your plans for the future?
As a young film composer, I feel very blessed to have already had the opportunity to work on some amazing projects. I love working with film, and I also hope to continue pursuing concert music as an adjunct. The best thing about film music is that if you keep an open mind and an open ear, you will never stop learning!

Is there anything else you'd like to comment on that you feel is important?
Learn the details of the music business: royalties, contracts, and so on. Have a lawyer review your contracts, because they understand how your contract will be interpreted in case of a dispute. Unfortunately, music and the music business are not the same thing—develop your knowledge and skills in both as vigorously as you can.

CHAPTER 10

Taking Care of Business

"The greatest mistake you can make in life is to be continually fearing you will make one."—Elbert Hubbard

This is the reality-check chapter that most musicians hate. Unfortunately, you can't be in business without knowing these essentials. What I'm about to tell you is what I do and what has worked for me. I'm neither an accountant nor a lawyer. The following ideas, systems, contracts, and legal stuff are what I've developed to operate my business for over two decades. It is pertinent to my particular situation (and my local laws as well). Use this information *only* as a guideline or an outline to follow when you sit down to talk with your business advisers.

By definition, I don't consider myself an entrepreneur. An entrepreneur is someone who loves the *business* side of being in business. I prefer the term *propreneur*, coined by authors Paul and Sarah Edwards. A propreneur is a professional person who provides a service and is more interested in *providing the service* than in running the business itself. Running a business requires certain discipline, but don't let the details discourage you. Always remember that you are a professional composer who just happens to be in business.

Start Right

Before you take another step, visit your local governing body, usually a municipality of some form. Try the clerk's office and ask for information about starting a business in your town. Consider checking out your state's commerce department for additional details. Either of these resources may even have a start-up kit of some kind that will save you hours of time and possible headaches. These two steps will tell you everything you need to know to legally start and operate a business where you live. And although some of these necessary legal matters may carry a fee, the money you pay is far less than the penalties you would incur by doing something illegal. Ignorance is *not* an acceptable legal defense.

LEGAL STRUCTURE

This is a complicated issue and one that can't be sufficiently dealt with in this book alone. Since the choice of business form has both tax and liability issues, you should consult with a lawyer and a tax adviser before forming your business structure. Here are the five forms your business can take.

▶ **Sole Proprietorship.** It takes very little effort to start a business under this banner. You essentially declare yourself in business, and outside of some legal matters detailed below, you are good to go. This is a popular form for many people because of its simplicity. You handle the finances for the business as an adjunct to your personal taxes. The primary disadvantage is that you have unlimited personal liability and responsibility.

▶ **Partnership.** Partnerships are similar to sole-proprietorships because each partner reports business income along with his personal taxes. The partners involved agree to certain terms, such as who does what, how much each makes, what each partner brings to the business, who owns equipment, copyrights, and so much more. Partnerships are akin to marriage, but make sure that you have some form of contract or agreement. Fees for starting a partnership are higher because an attorney should be consulted to create this agreement. Having more than one person working on the business can be beneficial. However, there is often a somewhat hazy line of authority. Again, a partnership agreement should take care of most roadblocks.

▶ **Corporation.** A corporation functions as a unique entity. It pays taxes and files certain reports as if it were a taxpayer. Even the owner of the corporation is considered an employee. The corporation pays everyone involved, and whatever is left is corporate profit. The corporate form of business is the most costly to start and maintain as attorney, registration, and ongoing fees can be considerable. Unlike sole-proprietors/partners, a corporation's owner(s) are protected from some liability. There are also some tax, money-raising, and other advantages to this business form.

▶ **S-Corporation.** The essential difference with the S corporation is that its business profits flow through to the owner(s) who records the profits on his personal tax returns.

▶ **Limited Liability Company (LLC).** This is an unusual hybrid of both the corporate and partnership business forms.

One advantage of the corporate forms is the presumption that it protects the employees from personal liability. Where a sole proprietor or partnership can be sued with damages awarded from *personal* assets, a corporation protects the people who own it. However, a closely held corporation, such as having only one principal employee, may not be so protected. Hence, this liability issue—the primary reason many people form corporations—is somewhat blurry.

NAME GAME

Selecting the name for your music business is an important strategic decision. Since you alone are such a big part of your career, I suggest going with your own name. If that won't do, choose a name that will endure and one that says what you do. For example, Amalgamated, Inc., is too vague, while Commercial Music Producers is better. Though my company, Fisher Creative Group, is the umbrella for the variety of activities that I pursue, my legal name alone suffices for music activities.

Most states require that you file a fictitious name statement or DBA (Doing Business As if you operate a business bearing a name other than your own. Check with your local municipality, county, or secretary of state for more details about DBA. Typically, you pay a small fee and must publish your DBA in the legal notices of a local paper. After that, you can continue to use the name.

BUSINESS LICENSE

Your local governing body may also require a business license. Again, talk to the clerk's office or equivalent for the proper procedures. Be very specific about the business you will run, as most license fees are tiered based on business descriptions.

TAX ID

You may need to secure a tax ID for your business. If you are a sole proprietor, your Social Security Number is all that's required. Partnerships require an ID that identifies the partnership, but the principals use their SS#s for reporting income. Corporations need a separate, unique tax ID, though. You will secure this when setting up your corporation.

SALES TAX ID

Similarly, states with a sales tax may require a separate sales tax ID number. If you sell products, you may be liable for collecting sales taxes and remitting the money to the state. Contact your state's department of commerce and industry for details.

TAX ISSUES

You need to fully understand *all* the tax ramifications of being in business. It is such an important aspect of business in the U.S. that there's more information on it in the next chapter.

ZONING/RENTING

Should you plan to run your commercial music business from your home or apartment, you need to see if there are laws that stand in your way. While the home-based business is not quite the radical idea it once was, some antiquated laws still remain. Most municipalities have some constraints on home-based business operations. For example, you can't disturb your neighbors, have trucks making deliveries, and allow clients at all hours. If you rent, your landlord may have certain restrictions. Your lease may even expressly prohibit you from running a business from your apartment.

Find out what the real deal is and make sure you comply. You may discover that you can't do what you want to do in your current situation. You may be forced to rent an outside office or even move elsewhere.

EMPLOYEES

If you decide to take on employees, your state may have regulations that pertain to them. Don't hire a single person until you find out and understand what's required. There are also tax issues related to employees that will require your attention.

MONEY MATTERS

► **Bookkeeping**. Devise a bookkeeping system to handle your income, expenses, and taxes. This is the subject of the next chapter.

► **Start-up costs**. These are the initial funds needed to open the doors. This would include purchases, such as gear, furniture, professional services, business forms, deposits, licenses, and so forth. Hopefully, you won't need a huge infusion of cash to get started unless you are starting entirely from scratch. Chances are you already have some things in place and you just need some start-up money to take care of some legal and promotional matters.

► **Know your overhead**. Find out what it is going to cost to stay in business. Called overhead, these are the ongoing costs incurred whether you bring in income or not. Typical overhead expenses might include rent, utilities, promotional expenses, professional dues, supplies, insurance, loan payments, etc. Don't neglect the *real* costs of doing business. Don't forget about taxes, healthcare, retirement, and all the myriad business details that you must control. It can seem overwhelming at times, but your mastery of these basic skills is crucial. Watch your everyday expenses, too. You must be careful not to overspend.

► **Price competitively**. Don't be the cheapest composer in town. This is the single biggest mistake made by fledgling businesses. It can get your foot in the door, but it can backfire as well. Again, there's more on this issue in another chapter.

▶ **Be financially prepared** for a few months of slow progress before you get your first important client. Your promotions need time to take effect.

PROTECT YOURSELF
There are several types of insurance, including health and property, that make sense for your business. More detail on this in the sidebar.

Get Free Help

There are some terrific resources available to you, and I urge you to take advantage of them. Particularly, women and minorities may find additional assistance here.

- U.S. Small Business Administration (www.sba.gov). The SBA is an informational powerhouse. Take advantage of what they have to offer.

- SCORE, the Service Corps of Retired Executives (www.score.org) is another resource where you can get free advice about business, management, taxes, record keeping, advertising, marketing, financial plans, and more.

- Many states have training resources to help your business succeed. Try your area's Department of Commerce and Community Affairs.

Full-Time or Part-Time?

You *can* run your music business as a sideline. Following my guidelines, it is very easy to make extra money every month for just a few days work. You can make as much (or as little) money as you want. If you're in a band or if you have a regular day job (music or otherwise), you can moonlight as a commercial music composer. Be aware that prospects and clients will expect you to be available during the day. For the typical nighttime band, this is easy, but not so for other day jobs. Voice mail, cell phone, email, and either many accrued sick days or an understanding boss can still make it possible. It's not easy, but it worked for me. I used my lunch hour for phone calls and took days or parts of days off for meetings. There came a point when it didn't work, so I started my business full-time.

However: *Never quit a gainful means of employment to pursue music full-time!* Start part-time and work your way up. Be realistic about your expectations and your goals. I want you to succeed. And I'll help you anyway I can. But please, don't make the jump until you are ready. Start out moonlighting and move steadily forward. You won't regret your caution. When I finally decided to go full-time, I already had an established track record and a list of satisfied clients to fall back on.

▶ Don't make a switch to running your own business if you have other conflicts in your life. Let your current stress subside before moving forward.

▶ Take time to prepare for your business. You may need to continue in your current job as you study your chosen business, sharpen your skills, and save enough money. Do your homework because it's better to make a $100 mistake than a $1,000 mistake.

▶ Start small, perhaps part-time, and see if running your own music business is right for you. Better to find out while your risk is lower than to commit and be dissatisfied and disappointed.

▶ Make sure you understand that running your own small business requires time and attention. It's not for the squeamish. Before undertaking this adventure, make sure the transition is right for you. While you may experience some fear, your gut should reassure you that you are on the correct path.

Get Help from Other Experts

Even if you run your commercial music business as a one-person shop, you'll still need the separate functions that all businesses share. While you'll probably handle most of these jobs yourself, in some areas you may need to seek professional advisers. Treat these people as an integral and crucial part of your business. Their advice and assistance could mean the difference between coasting along and bursting ahead. Spending a few dollars here may save you plenty over the long haul. And since all these fees are tax deductible business expenses, this is really a smart *investment* in your future success. So, take advantage of existing knowledge. You can and should learn from what others can teach you. Don't let your schooling stop. All that you need is out there for you to exploit. Take the vast information available and use it to your benefit.

What advisers will you need? Accountant and/or bookkeeper, tax adviser, lawyer, bank and investment adviser, insurance provider(s), and Webmaster. You may also want a publicist, graphic designer, photographer, travel agent, other musicians, recording studios, equipment rental houses, and an on-call electronics engineer. The people you decide to add to your team is a decision only you can make, based on your goals, situation, and the skills you possess. Contact these people and build a relationship *before* you desperately need their help. Explain how and when you will use their services and get their commitment.

Meet with your accountant/bookkeeper regularly. Mine set up my business structure and gave and continues to give tax advice. He approved an accounting system based around a few off-the-shelf resources. I handle my own year-end Uncle Sam stuff. My lawyer reviewed the various contracts I planned to use and has consulted with me occasionally on other contracts and legal matters. I don't call often, but he knows my business and is ready when and if I need him.

Don't forget your outside musicians, recording studios, equipment rental houses, and if your studio is complex, you might consider adding an on-call electronics engineer who can fix your broken gear quickly when you're on deadline. Also, promotional opportunities can often arise quite fast. That's why you might need people with expertise in these areas. Some quick print shops offer one-stop shopping. Other advisors round out your business network and fill gaps in your knowledge.

Another important part of your team is a dependable partner. You don't necessarily need a partner in the formal, legal sense. But what you do need is a cheerleader, someone to bounce ideas off of, someone who listens and understands your work and lifestyle. This partner can be a spouse or significant other, or it can be another business associate. When you're down, this friendship can help significantly. And when you're up, you can celebrate together.

I also suggest forming a "kitchen cabinet." Gather a few different people of varied backgrounds and form an informal, *ad hoc* executive board. The purpose of the group is to share valuable experience. These outsiders can show you a completely different perspective of your current picture. Try meeting quarterly (at your kitchen table, of course) to discuss the various aspects of your business. While it would be nice if this cabinet included your lawyer, accountant, and others, that might be cost prohibitive. I suggest you include a few family members, some friends, fellow business peers, and perhaps some good clients. Use this time to find solutions to problems and to bounce ideas around. You'd be surprised the kind of help you get from regular sessions such as these. This is information you can really use to run your business better.

Finding the right adviser requires some time and energy. Here are five steps that will help you make the right decision.

DETERMINE YOUR GOALS AND OBJECTIVES

Review your current situation and make sure you know where you've been, where you are right now, and where you want to go. Finding the right adviser is much easier when you have a clearly defined objective. This way you can evaluate how a specific adviser's strategy can help you get where you want to go.

CHOOSE THE SERVICES THAT ASSIST YOU IN ACHIEVING YOUR GOALS

When you know your objective and understand your position, selecting the appropriate adviser to match your needs is easier. Don't go to a general practitioner when a specialist may be more appropriate. You don't necessarily need an entertainment lawyer or accountant, because a good contract lawyer and small business accountant can do the job satisfactorily.

SELECT A FEW POSSIBLE FIRMS TO INTERVIEW

Once you know the kind of service that you need, find three or four candidates who provide these services. Try asking friends, family, and business associates for names of professionals who have success in your area. You may want to ask them to help with your evaluation, too. After you get your list of possible professionals, contact each one and request information about their services, qualifications, and past performance. This information should help you narrow down the field.

MAKE APPOINTMENTS TO MEET WITH THE MOST PROMISING FIRMS

This is the most important aspect of the whole process. Use this meeting to assess each adviser. You need to see if their services, performance, and philosophy match your needs and goals. There are certain key questions you need to ask each candidate. These include questions about services, philosophy, other clients, fees, licenses and registrations, and references. Even if your questions are answered satisfactorily, don't forget the intangibles. You should also use this personal contact to see whether you are comfortable with your possible adviser. Make sure you get the answers you want. Each firm should also have sufficient documentation to back up any claims they make. Ask for everything you think you'll need to make an informed decision and scrutinize everything carefully.

CHOOSE THE BEST PROFESSIONAL

If you've followed these guidelines, you should have what you need to make your decision. The key is doing your homework. Take the time to investigate possible firms, ask the right questions, and then choose the adviser with a philosophy that best matches your own. Your professional advisors are vitally important. You can't do everything. Take advantage of professional expertise in these and other areas where your knowledge may be lacking.

Protecting Yourself with Contracts

Louis B. Mayer said it best. "A verbal contract isn't worth the paper it's printed on." Contracts are a form of security for both you *and* your client. Contracts take on many forms, from a simple purchase order to multipage excursions into legalese and other obfuscation. Many contracts will come from your clients, and it will be up to you to make sure you fully understand it (hire a lawyer!) before signing. When you are asked to supply the contract, keep it simple and not intimidating. Call it a letter of agreement instead of a contract and use the guidelines set forth by a lawyer you retain. I prefer printing contracts on letterhead, which helps reduce the fear that more formal documents may instill in your clients.

On a base level, contracts state what you'll do, what they'll do, what it costs, and how they pay. They sign it and return it to you with some kind of initial payment. You invoice them for the remaining payments. Here are the essential parts to every contract:

► Print on your letterhead and date it. Include the client name, full contact information, project name. Next, list the services you will provide for this project. List any other special specifications. Indicate the due date and what materials will be delivered (i.e., master CD). Indicate the total fee for the project and the terms for how it is to be paid. Show how additional expenses are to be reimbursed. Indicate the amount of the advance (if it applies).

▶ Include any special notes about ownership, work-for-hire, or independent contractor language. This is the Grant of Rights section where you indicate if you are selling all rights or one-time rights, the territory (world, regional, local), and the duration (in perpetuity, one year, etc.).

▶ Leave room for both your signatures and date. Make two copies of the agreement and sign them both. Ask your client to sign both copies, keep one, and return the other copy to you with a check for the amount of the advance.

There are many boilerplate contracts on the Web that can serve as the basis for yours. Try a Google search for starter ideas. Have a lawyer review what you find and make sure that you understand what's there.

Try to get some money up front, typically one-third of the total fee. Writing music is a custom job, by nature, and once you begin, the music may not be appropriate somewhere else. By getting money first, you have more leverage should the client decide not to continue. Plus, this payment usually helps weed out the serious people from those who might try to take advantage of you.

Sample Letter of Agreement

Thanks for choosing me to compose the music for your production, ABOVE AND BEYOND, *for XYZ Productions.*
These are the services I will provide:

● Compose, arrange, and produce approximately 8–10 minutes of original music conforming to your specifications.

● Attend a spotting session with the director to determine the musical style, number and length of cues, etc.

● Create demonstration copies (on CD and/or MP3) of the music work-in-process subsequent to the spotting session, but just before the final recording session.

● Produce and deliver the final master recording as a 44.1kHz/16-bit stereo digital audio file on CD-ROM in Microsoft .wav format.

You will:

- Provide a digital file, preferably mini-DV tape or DV format saved in Windows .avi format, of the production in its final edited form.

- Review and approve the work-in-process before the final recording session. Revisions will only be accepted at that time.

- Provide attribution on the production's end credits to read: Original Music Composed and Performed by Jeffrey P. Fisher.

- Specify that Jeffrey P. Fisher (BMI) is 200% writer for all music composed on all performing rights cue sheets.

*PLEASE NOTE: This is **NOT** a work-for-hire agreement. I retain ALL copyrights, phonorights, and publishing rights to the music. With respect to any and all areas outside your market area, I have the unrestricted right to sell, use, or grant licenses to the music beginning one year from the date of this agreement and continuing forever.*

This agreement grants you single-use, non-exclusive rights to the music for use only for the ABOVE AND BEYOND project. You must seek an additional license and pay appropriate fees for any other or future uses of this music.

My base fee for the services I described above is estimated between $xxxx.xx and $xxxx.xx. That fee estimate is based on 8-10 minutes of original music at my standard rate for single-use, one-time rights of $xxx.xx per finished minute. This fee includes composing, arranging, producing, recording, mixing, and one master CD. Any out-of-pocket expenses incurred on your behalf for other material requests will be billed to you in an itemized fashion subsequent to your advance approval of such expenses.

Payment of the base fee will be made as follows: ONE-THIRD ($xxx.xx) of the above fee is due upon my starting the work; ONE-THIRD ($xxx.xx) is due upon approval of the demonstration work-in-process; ONE-THIRD ($xxx.xx - $xxx.xx) upon completion and delivery of your final master. If more (or less) music is composed than initially estimated, the increase (or decrease) in the fee will be reflected in your final payment.

Jeffrey P. Fisher shall be deemed an independent contractor and is not an employee of XYZ Productions. As such, XYZ shall not deduct withholding taxes, FICA, or any other required deductions. These taxes are the sole responsibility of Jeffrey P. Fisher. Also, Jeffrey P. Fisher further acknowledges that he is not entitled to any fringe benefits, pension, profit sharing, or any other benefits accruing to employees.

Please sign both copies of the agreement below, date it, and return one original to me with your check for the first payment ($xxx.xx). Keep the other copy of the agreement for your records. I will invoice you for the remaining payments when they become due.

Again, thank you for choosing me to work on your production. I'm very excited about it, and when you sign this agreement and return it to me with your check, I'll start composing.

Please sign here:
ACCEPTED AND AGREED BY:
Mr. Joe Sample, XYZ Productions, DATE

Talent Release

Besides contracts between you and your clients, you may want to use contracts between you and others you hire to provide a service, such as musicians who play on a recording. Have your contract talent sign a release that simply states that upon accepting payment, they release their work from further claims. In other words, their contribution is a work-for-hire, and the one-time payment for services rendered is all they shall receive or are entitled to. Here's a sample talent release to use:

For value received in the sum of $xxx.xx, I, the undersigned, give and grant Fisher Creative Group, its affiliates, successors, and assigns the unqualified right, privilege, and permission to reproduce in every manner or form, publish and circulate videotapes, audiocassettes, or films of recordings of my voice and/or my musical contribution arising from the production titled ABOVE AND BEYOND and I hereby grant, assign, and transfer all my rights and interest therein.

I specifically authorize and empower Fisher Creative Group to cause any such videotapes, films, digital media, and recordings of my voice and/or musical performance to be copyrighted or in any other manner to be legally registered in the name of Jeffrey P. Fisher and/or Fisher Creative Group.

My contribution to this work shall be considered a work made for hire, and as such, I, my heirs, executors, administrators, and assigns, hereby remise, release, and discharge Fisher Creative Group for and from any and all claims of any kind whatsoever on account of the use of such recordings, including, but not limited to any and all claims for damages for libel, slander, and invasion of the right of privacy. I am of lawful age and sound mind and have read and understand this Authorization of Release. Signed this first day of January 20xx.

Protect Your Ass(ets)

Do you own any tangible property, such as computers, musical instruments, other gear, or your own home? These are typical assets many of us possess and need to protect. Another resource you should safeguard is your health. Also, your talent, reputation, relationships, and any intellectual property you've created are just as valuable as any traditional property.

Talent is something that you must protect by constantly challenging yourself. Haven't new experiences—a new synth patch, relationship gone sour, or other life event—always sparked your muse? Doesn't it make sense that adding more experiences to your life should help you become a better music professional? Make improving your skills a top priority because the more you know, the bigger the well to draw upon for inspiration.

We all work very hard to build and sustain our reputations. Don't let mistakes tarnish yours because once ruined, it can take a long time to get back to where you were. Protect and grow your reputation by promoting your image and earning credentials, such as awards, media coverage, and so forth.

Who you know is often the most valuable asset you can have. Spend resources nurturing your network of clients, vendors, peers, media, mentors, and others who form your career bedrock. Healthy relationships require both give and take to really work, so never forget to support those who support your work. These priceless relationships are crucial to reaching your goals.

All creative works, including music and lyrics, are considered intellectual property. Since they are a revenue source, protect them by invoking the applicable rights and laws. While you can't prevent someone from stealing your original idea, the specific way you convey the idea is something you can protect. For songs, the copyright law provides rights to reproduce copies, make derivative works, distribute for sale, lease, or rental, and perform the copyrighted work publicly. For names, slogans, and logos, the trademark law helps you protect what you use to promote your music business career. If it applies, patent law protects your original inventions and formulas. Take advantage of these laws to protect what you create. There is an entire chapter devoted to this later in the book.

AN APPLE A DAY

There's more to protecting your health than leading a healthy lifestyle. First, staying healthy protects your capacity to make money. If you're sick, you'll be less able to work toward your goals. Second, staying healthy protects other savings you may have accumulated. With healthcare costs as they are, a single major illness could put you in the red fast, and you may be paying the tab for many years to come. Of course, there is health insurance to minimize your risks when unforeseen circumstances wind their way into your life.

Insurance is a game, sort of. You justify paying the bill knowing that help will be there when you need it. In the back of your mind, you hope you'll never use it, really. But peace of mind comes with a price that many of us are willing to pay. Of course, the insurance carrier knows that, statistically, you won't file a claim or your claims will be minimal.

Many countries, such as our Canadian neighbors, provide universal health care for their citizenry. In the U.S., however, we are on our own. Employers frequently provide coverage, but many of us are self-employed or work part-time where the health benefit is more the exception than the rule. Since buying a policy can be expensive, look for alternatives first. Can you get insurance through a working spouse? Can you join an organization, association, or union that has a group policy, such as the Musician's Union? For students, even those enrolled only part-time, there may be policies available or reduced rates on a parental policy. If none of these apply, you may be forced to secure a suitable policy on your own. Thankfully, the Web makes the research quite easy.

Here are two places you can look for health insurance on the Web: www.musicproinsurance.com and www. ehealthinsurance.com

---

HEALTHY, WEALTHY, AND WISE

Major medical policies cover the most health-related issues and let you choose the practitioners and facilities you want. They are therefore the most expensive policies you can buy. In contrast, HMO and PPO policies let you select from doctor and hospital networks, and you must use only those approved by your plan for the coverage to take affect. Any out-of-network expenses either cost you more or are not covered at all. Another benefit HMOs and PPOs offer is discounts on routine and preventative care and savings on certain medical conditions typically not covered under the medical policy, such as dental and eye care. Many HMO and PPO plans use local health care providers, so if you're on the road a lot, this choice may not be right for you.

Basic or catastrophic policies cover only emergencies and surgery; you have to pay for routine care yourself. For the young and healthy, this can be a good choice, as a major illness won't wipe out your savings. However, routine care or persistent illnesses can add up quickly.

The amount you pay, called the premium, for a policy depends on its type, medical coverage, deductible, and co-pay. Coverage for certain medical conditions, such as maternity, cost more. Typically, you are required to pay initial medical expenses out of your own pocket before your insurance coverage kicks in. This threshold is called a deductible. Costs accumulate until you meet the deductible. The higher the deductible, the lower your premiums, but you risk paying more yourself. Each person on a policy must meet his or her own deductible, with the family deductible typically three times the single total.

What is often misunderstood is that once you exceed the deductible, you still are required to share some of the medical expenses. For example, the insurance may pay 80% while you pay the other 20%. Also, HMOs and PPOs require co-payments in addition to the deductible for certain instances. For example, I must pay a $30 co-pay for each doctor office visit both before and after meeting my deductible.

Thankfully, there is an annual out-of-pocket limit of the maximum amount you must pay. Once you pay this amount, the insurance pays 100% of any additional covered medical costs. When the year is up, you start paying all over again. Be aware that policies have a lifetime limit on the amount they will ultimately pay, too.

Each policy explains what is covered and what is not in detail. Though it's not the most exciting reading, it's important that you understand the specifics of what you are buying and any limitations. If not, contact the insurance company and ask them to explain it to you. You don't want to think something is covered; you want to know!

Check for prescription drug coverage. Medicine can be ridiculously expensive, and a single infection could set you back a couple hundred dollars. If the additional premium costs fit your budget, drug coverage can save you money down the road. There is often a separate deductible for pharmaceuticals, though.

Self-employed business owners can currently deduct 100% of their health insurance premiums off their taxes. Healthcare expenses are tax deductible once you exceed a certain point, so keeping good records makes sense. Monitor your medical bills diligently. Always check the bills you get from doctors, hospitals, and labs and carefully compare them to insurance company statements. If you find errors, take time to get them corrected, as they frequently work to your favor.

ME, MY, MINE

Property insurance is the primary way to minimize risk related to what you own. Chances are you already have a homeowners or rental insurance policy protecting your physical property (and if not, why not?). Your music gear or anything you use for your business may or may not be covered under that policy. Talk to your insurance agent and describe your situation specifically. You may be forced to buy a separate policy to insure your business property or all that may be required is a rider to your personal policy and a slightly higher premium.

The insurance realm has changed dramatically post 9/11, so check the policy carefully to see what perils are covered by the insurance and which are excluded. Generally, fire, water, theft, and natural disasters are covered, except floods and earthquakes. Those last two require buying incredibly expensive policies. Make sure you know both when and where you are protected. If your policy only covers your home, and something gets stolen from your car after a gig, you need to know if your insurance will pay for it.

How much you pay for the premium depends on the coverage amount. Property insurance policies also have a deductible that is your responsibility. The insurance carrier pays the amount over this, if any. However, unlike medical policies, these deductibles do not accumulate. The deductible applies to each individual claim. If you need to file many loss claims, your total out-of-pocket costs could be considerably more than you expected.

Take time to determine the real value of what you are insuring. Read the policy carefully so you understand the policy limits. This is usually a total dollar amount; make sure it's enough to cover you should you lose everything. Also, check to see if your policy pays replacement cost or actual cash value. The replacement value pays the full amount needed to replace the item. The cash value pays the market value of the item, sometimes only 10–20% of the original price. You also need to know how to file a claim. Stolen items require a police report, for example.

When it comes to keeping records, follow the guidelines established by your insurance carrier. Most require documented inventory of your property. The greater the detail, the easier the claims process will be. I suggest recording the model name and number, serial number, and original purchase price and date for all your gear. If you have vintage equipment, have it appraised regularly. File this paperwork with your agent and keep another copy in a remote location, such as a bank safety deposit box. Photos and videotapes are more evidence that many people consider, too.

NEVER 'NUFF PROTECTION

Auto insurance is another special form of property insurance. It is the law in many states, and you should insure any vehicle you use for your music activities. If your vehicle is for both business and personal use, check with your insurance carrier to be sure that your coverage suffices.

Disability insurance pays a portion of your lost income should you be unable to work either short- or long-term. These policies can be rather expensive and only pay 60–70% of your income prior to the disability. Unfortunately, it can take several months for the insurance to start, even after approving your claim. If permanently disabled, Social Security would be available to you.

Did you know that in a lawsuit your assets can be liquidated to settle the claim? We live in a litigious society, and an umbrella liability insurance policy can protect you. These make sense for people with a lot to lose. If that's you, then check into one.

If you work with a partner, what's to prevent that person from walking away and competing with you? Did you draw up a suitable agreement to protect assets that you control together, including each other? If not, take steps today to save problems down the line.

Finally, there is life insurance that pays beneficiaries when you die. Insurance companies determine the premium based on the death benefit amount, your age, and lifestyle. Do other people, such as children, depend on your income? You owe it to them to have such a policy in place.

Protecting your health and property needs to be a top priority. However, you may now have more questions than answers. Take these pages with you as you contact your insurance provider so you can discuss the options and make informed decisions.

Office Equipment

A computer is a necessity for running your business. As mentioned earlier, I have a dedicated computer for music and an additional one just for business. I use the business one for bookkeeping, order processing, email, Web site maintenance, quotes, contracts, and invoices, writing and promotions, and so forth. You will want a quality printer, too. I prefer laser printers to inkjets. Get an ample-sized desk for holding your computer and other work. Invest in a quality chair as your posterior will be parked in it for many hours every day. Most of all, choose software that works together well and that matches *your* personal working style.

▶ **Word processor.** For many people, a solid word processing program is all you'll ever need. Use it to draft and store all your promotional material, keep track of clients, meetings, long-range goals, and more. I have no other business forms as I create everything I need on computer and print as needed. Some programs even have a rudimentary database that you can use for both contact and mailing list management. Other than a separate financial program, my word processor and PDA give me everything I need to run my commercial music business activities.

▶ **Contact or personal information manager**. You will be reaching hundreds, maybe even thousands, of people throughout your career. Keeping track of all those details in your head is impossible. This software helps you track inquiries, clients, meetings, to-do lists, and more. My PDA and its parent program, Palm Desktop, help manage business contacts, all my appointments and deadlines, to-do lists, and memo drafts. Synchronizing data between my office and the Palm is a snap. I'm not sure how I ever got along without it (a refrain I've heard from many *digerati* cohorts). For meetings, I take along a portable keyboard for the Palm, which makes taking notes and jotting down ideas a snap.

▶ **Small business accounting software**. A simple money management program can make your business life so much easier. Lest you think that the software will be the equivalent of balancing your checkbook on a computer, you are in for a huge surprise. You will always know your true financial position when you meticulously track both income and expenses. And this software makes it all a snap.

You need a dedicated business telephone with voice mail. The choice for making this a land line or a cellular phone is up to you. The cell gives you added portability and the ability to keep the same number should you move. If a land line is your choice, have the telephone ring only in your office. You'll avoid lots of embarrassment when your two-year-old hangs up on an important client.

Having a fax machine is less important today than it was a few years ago. Email has all but supplanted this technology. I have a cheap fax machine that I use for the 2–3 times each year that I must fax something. For receiving, I use the E-fax service (www.efax.com), which put the faxes in my email inbox. I rarely photocopy because my computer can print an extra copy for my files. For copies of check stubs and other things, make a trek to your local copy shop.

For shipping, establish an account with one of the main shipping carriers, Fed-Ex or UPS. When it doesn't have to be there overnight, try the U.S. Postal Service's Priority Mail. I buy stamps and use the flat-rate envelope for everything under a pound. You can even print labels, pay online, and schedule a pick-up with the postal service now.

Of course, you'll need some general business supplies like paper, labels, oversized envelopes, staples, clips, etc. Shop at the local office supply superstore.

Home Work Help

Earlier I suggested using your home during the initial phases of your burgeoning commercial music business. Unfortunately, the versatility of a home studio brings many other temptations and distractions. Friends call, relatives stop by, and many people may not think you are *really* working.

▶ Get into a routine. You can't run your business occasionally. You must set a schedule of some kind. Though it need not be precise, it should be functional. Since most clients call between nine and five, you need to plan your day accordingly. Recognize your limitations and personal preferences and know what to do to complete each project. If you're not self motivated, you might need some nudging to get going. Do what you must to make sure you start working toward your goals.

▶ Explain your situation. Make sure you include your family in your plans. They are an integral part of your success machine. Spouses, significant others, and especially children need to understand what you are doing. Show them what you do and what you plan to do and share your goals with them. Work out a schedule so they recognize when you are working and when you are available to them.

▶ Set up a specific work space. A spare bedroom or basement home office will help you avoid household distractions. Plus, you can close the door when the day is over and leave your work behind. Walking past your work can be too much of a temptation when you're supposed to be relaxing.

▶ Child care may be a viable solution. If you're choosing to work from home so that you can spend more time with your family, you may encounter difficulty. One solution may be to combine some child care with your home routine. Even a sitter for a few hours each day can free you for important, uninterrupted business tasks.

Time Management Tips

We all get the same time allotment each day: 24 hours. Spending those hours productively is what separates those who accomplish more from those who only wish they could. When you complain about not having enough time, you probably mean there's not enough creative time available. That's the paradox. You need time to create your best music, but you don't have enough time to do it.

Creativity and time management don't mix. Therefore, the real secret is managing everything else that you do. Then you'll free up time to focus on your music where cutting time corners simply doesn't work.

Lack of time can really stress you out. You're forever moving and getting nowhere. And that can seriously interfere with your music. Stop. Take a step back and evaluate your life. Keep a journal of how you spend your time for a week or two. Include as much detail as you can, including your feelings about what you did. After the fortnight, take a long, hard look at how you fill your days. Identify the time wasters and stuff you hate doing. Reduce the time you spend on them or jettison them completely. Weed out those commitments that interfere with your music goals. Also, look for unproductive time and decide how to fill these scrap moments with more productive musical undertakings.

Grab a piece of paper and write your most important need-to along the top: make more music. Below this, make a list of your have-tos—all those things you must do to maintain your current lifestyle. Include the obvious, such as sleep, eat, and earn a living, along with the mundane, such as laundry, pay bills, and so forth. Notice how your have-tos and need-tos conflict? Emotions pull you to your dream; logic drags you back to reality. If only you could remove the have-tos, you'd have more time. So circle the least important have-to on your list. Is there some way you could eliminate it? Pay somebody else to do it? With this have-to crossed off, you instantly create a time gap that can be filled with your music. Not only that, but you've forced yourself to carefully choose what is really important in your life right now. You give yourself permission to pursue that which holds the most meaning and satisfaction for you.

It's possible to accomplish more with your music using whatever time you have available. Jerry Cleaver, in his *Immediate Fiction* book, offered this simple, yet effective method for making time for your creative pursuits. Set aside five minutes each and every day to work on your music for a month. Take no time off. Ever. For any reason. And don't bank the minutes. Five minutes every day for 30 full days. Now five minutes isn't much time, but the two and a half hours you accrue can add up to some significant progress. And you make music part of your daily, must-do routine. This is important: If you have a day job, work your five music minutes *before* your regular job. Your mind is fresher, and your subconscious learns that music is more important to you. After the first month, bump up the time to 10 minutes, then 15 the next month, on to 20, 30, then more. By slowly making time in your schedule for music, you establish a genuine groove that both satisfies your musical needs and increases your output substantially.

A major time vortex is your job. If music isn't your main gig, your day job can zap a considerable chunk out of your time allotment. If music is your main gig, you still must spend time managing your affairs. It all comes down to money (doesn't it always?). If you have any number of adult responsibilities, paying your bills is your albatross. Can you work less and free up more time for your musical pursuits? Examine your lifestyle and see if you can cut back on expenses. Living on less money precludes your need for working as much. Focus on gigs that pay well and eschew nickel-and-dime clients. Volume sales mean more work and less time for other pursuits. Well-paying gigs mean you can work fewer hours on client projects and gain more time for other pursuits.

Create a logical filing system both in your computer and for physical files. Have both short-term storage (for current and pending projects) and long-term storage for completed items, recordkeeping, etc. On my computer, I set up folders for each of my projects and carefully file everything pertaining to the project in subfolders off the main one.

Set aside specific work time each day and don't let anything or anyone interfere with it. Even if your music is a part-time venture, keep regular hours. Music people often dread the tyranny of a daily grind because routine and creativity just don't mix. Instead, schedule flexible time blocks for music creation and other sessions to take care of everything else that needs your attention. You can group related duties together, too. For example, make one errand run that hits all the spots you need in one trip. Better still, shop via the Internet and have stuff delivered (or download it right away) instead of wasting time driving to the store.

Know and understand your particular strengths. For example, I'm sluggish and less creative in the morning. Therefore, I use my mornings to catch up on all those little things that steal time away from creative endeavors but have to be done anyway. I then hit the ground running with main projects after lunch. This really works for me because I rid my desk and mind of daily details before pursuing more creative possibilities.

Distractions from telephones, email, and people can really soak up your time fast. Let the voice mail grab your calls while you work on your music. Leave the email for later. It really is OK to say "no" to people. Tell them that you're busy and then give a time when you will be available to them. Don't let paperwork, phone calls, email, and such pile up, though. Putting them off only exasperates your time crunch. Set aside time each day to deal with them promptly. Handle your email once or twice a day. Use email filtering that automatically deletes spam, sends personal messages to a separate folder, and leaves important business information in your inbox. Make all your phone calls in one marathon session. When postal mail arrives, shred the junk, separate personal mail from business, and take care of it right away. Play too much phone tag? Send an email or fax instead. Schedule telephone meetings just as you would an in-person meeting. Also, make people come to you instead of wasting time traveling to them.

Set up your work area for efficiency. If your room is nothing but a big hassle, rethink it. Put the stuff you need within easy reach. Find the right basic settings for your gear, keep it set up, and dial up what you need quickly. Use templates and other shortcuts to automate your work in whatever ways make sense for you. Organize separate workspaces for specific tasks, such as a shipping area stocked with labels, tape, envelopes, and products. Most importantly, get to know your music tools really well. You'll waste less time learning new software/hardware or troubleshooting. With a few well-chosen tools, your productivity will increase exponentially.

Big projects are scary. Cut them into smaller chunks and digest them until the whole meal is finished. Planning a new CD? Set a future date for the finished product and then set interim deadlines for major milestones (composition, tracking, mixing, mastering, and duplication) by working backwards through your calendar. When scheduling large projects, add a 20–40% margin of error because it will take longer than you think. Finally, establish deadlines and do whatever it takes to meet them! Also, work on the project every day—even if you only do a little work—to keep you on track.

GET HELP

You'll gain precious time when you concentrate on the work that you do best and find other means to get the rest done. First, start with your family and friends. Can they remove some of your workload from you? Second, hire subcontractors to fill in the gaps for you. Third, hire an employee. If you feel that's a big step, consider this. Let's say you charge $100 an hour for client work, and you waste an hour running errands. You not only lose an hour, you lose $100. Hire a helper for $10 an hour and have this person run your errands for you. You gain an hour for work and lose only $10. However, you can make $100 during the same hour and net $90 instead. That's wise time and fiscal management.

Technology will definitely help you get more done in less time, especially computers. You already know I depend on my three computers to get more done. While music (and video) production requires a more robust system, use any low-end machine for basic tasks. You'll accomplish more and easily justify the extra cost. Get a PDA, too. The typical handheld packs an address book, calendar, to-do list, and more into a few inches. Add-in programs bring you additional power. For keeping track of the people, appointments, and projects that comprise a busy music life, these wonder boxes can't be beat. Plug in all your contact information, use the to-do list, track and manage your short- and long-term goals, schedule your days with the calendar, program reminder alarms, and keep all this with you as your portable office. When you waste less time keeping track of information, you'll gain more time for your music.

I travel on business quite frequently, and it can really wreak havoc on your ability to get things done. Travel itself is tiring, and when it's accompanied by long, busy working days, it takes its toll. I find myself thinking I'll get a lot done on the plane and in my hotel room at night/in the morning. Instead, I'm often exhausted and find it hard to keep up. But you must. Obviously, the ubiquitous cell phone helps you stay in touch. Pay attention to time zones when connecting with people. Many hotels and venues offer free Internet access so you can keep up with email (a laptop with a wireless connection is a must-have on the road). If not, try an Internet cafe or coffee shop. An assistant back at the office can help, too, even if that's a significant other who can attend only to certain matters.

Set yourself a quota of tasks to accomplish when away and work hard to finish them. When you return, spend part of a day catching up and then move forward.

Finally, give yourself permission to mess up now and again and don't feel guilty about it. So what if you took half a day off and neglected other business and personal chores? To use time wisely, you do not need to fill every waking moment with productive activities. When you're particularly inspired, let your creativity breathe and music flow. When the muse wanes, grab the to-do list and check off a few items. And now and again, give yourself permission to slack off.

Dealing with Stress

Too much stress can adversely affect your mental and physical health. When you take charge of your musical career, you become responsible for so many details that the stress of handling it all can be overwhelming. What makes running your own commercial music business so exciting and challenging is the same thing that can really damage your life. Try these tips to either prevent or minimize the effects of stress on your daily life.

▶ **Try physical activity.** Release all that pressure through exercise. Just a brisk walk may help tremendously. Or you can try a more strenuous workout to alleviate the bad vibes. Personally, I'm fond of Tai Chi because it strikes a wonderful balance between a hard workout and enriching relaxation.

▶ **Share your stress.** It may help to talk through matters with a friend, family member, or fellow business colleague. Don't just unload your troubles. Make the session productive by working through your stress and arriving at possible solutions.

▶ **Know your limits.** If a problem is beyond your control, don't fight the situation. Learn to accept some things as they are. Don't sweat the small stuff (it's all small stuff anyway).

▶ **Take care of yourself.** Get enough rest and eat well. Starting your day stressed out will only make matters worse down the line.

▶ **Make time for fun.** You should schedule time both for your work and your recreation. Play is as important to your health as work is to your wallet. You need an occasional break from your routine to just relax and have some fun.

▶ **Find a quiet place and go to it.** This doesn't need to be some idyllic scene in the country. Create your own quiet place in your mind and take some time to bathe in the mental picture. I grab some headphones, a Mahler CD, close the door, crank the volume, and float away.

▶ **Consider scheduling a regular vacation time**. Let your clients know you will be "closed" and don't budge on it. This is your time to refresh. It will take preparation, though. First, make sure all your clients know about your downtime. Second, make sure you complete any projects and deliver anything else you've promised. Third, tie up all the loose ends, including a "vacation" message for both voice- and email. Fourth, have fun on the trip knowing everything is fine. Fifth, when you return, pick up where you left off and move ahead. You need time off and truly deserve it.

An Ounce of RSI Prevention

Watch out for Repetitive Stress Injuries (RSI). Musicians are at greater risk because many of us play an instrument and log quite a few hours at our computers. This double-whammy can irreversibly damage your body in ways that interfere with your ability to play your musical instrument, work at the computer, and accomplish other tasks. A balanced mix of playing, computer use, alternative activities, and frequent rest can all help you avoid the debilitating RSI specter.

Obviously, make sure that your computer workstation is set up properly. Position the monitor directly in front of you with the top of the screen at eye level. Position the work surface at the proper height so that your wrists and arms are parallel to the floor. Leave ample room for your knees and legs. Get a good, comfortable chair that easily adjusts to your body. It should have lumbar support and arm rests. Sit up straight in your chair, feet flat on the ground. You should feel comfortable at your workstation, not awkward, and you shouldn't strain to reach the keys or mouse. Every half-hour, take a break, get up, move around, and work those neck, shoulder, and back muscles.

While arm and wrist rests are fine for relaxing, you shouldn't use them while keyboarding or mousing. Wrist supports in particular often create a condition where your wrists are bent back when they should be in line with your arms. Lift your hands up above the keyboard/mouse when working. Lightly touch the keys while typing and hold the mouse gently. If you're not typing or mousing, move your arms and hands to different positions instead of leaving them in place.

Try to reduce overall mouse use by learning keyboard shortcuts. Also, cut back on your computer time altogether by finding alternatives, such as using the phone instead of typing emails. I also use the Contour ShuttlePro V2 to control some software, which gives my left hand more to do than simply typing. As with a mouse, position the ShuttlePro comfortably and use it gently without bending your wrist or reaching awkwardly.

Because RSI is caused by many repeated small movements, give your affected body parts something different to do. Put them through larger ranges of motion. Do stretches and other exercises that move them counter to the routine of playing, keyboarding, and mousing. Consider regular, vigorous exercise as part of your plan, too, such as taking a power walk at lunch.

Treat the affected area to some deep massage. Don't just rub gently; really get in there and palpitate the area aggressively. Keep the room warm. A chilled body is more susceptible to injuries than a warm one. Especially make sure that your fingers, hands, wrist, arms, and shoulders are warm. The human body is primarily water, so be sure to keep yourself hydrated. Caffeinated drinks and alcohol actually dehydrate you. A glass of water is the ticket, and several glasses a day is first class.

Take a break. For maximum benefit, take shorter, more frequent breaks. Be sure to stop what you're doing for at least five minutes out of every hour. Really relax during your time off and give your fingers, wrists, arms, shoulder, back, and more a much-deserved respite. Additionally, perform some mild stretching exercises that work RSI-susceptible muscles and tendons contrary to your playing/working positions. Refresh yourself with some gentle self-massage. Most importantly, get plenty of extended rest so your body can properly rejuvenate and recover from overuse.

Success for You

How do you gauge your own success? Is it money? Recognition? Satisfaction? What? Don't equate your own success with someone else's measure of it. Work on your own level. Do what *you* want to do and in the way *you* want to do it. Don't be concerned with other's perceptions. You must be happy first!

There will always be someone who writes better lyrics, composes sweeter melodies, and uses fancier recording tricks. Forget about all that. Each of us has a unique gift to share. Stop worrying about the other guys and get on with it. Because the rewards of finding and following your life's work can be great. This is a creative business. Be innovative, stand above the crowd, project a successful image, and you will succeed.

Special caution: Be conservative. Don't go over the edge. Be realistic and practical. Write down your goals and the steps you must take to reach them. Then take each small step and learn as you proceed. Don't stifle your exuberance, but don't bleed yourself dry either. And don't spend untold money on this venture, or you'll lose your shirt. Don't expect to make a fortune, but do expect success. Monitor your progress, cover your costs, and put some cash in your pocket. Do it on your own level, make some money, and grow. You'll find the work more satisfying, rewarding, and fun!

Industry Insight

Keith Kehrer

Kamakaze Music, NYC/Arlington, VA
kkehrer@msn.com, www.kamakazemusic.com

Recent credits/past projects:
Film Score–*Standalone* (independent full-length feature)

Why did you choose this career (and how did you get started)?
I have wanted to be a composer since I first heard Carl Stalling's music for the Looney Tunes cartoons. I studied composition with various private teachers and honed my craft in NYC, NJ, and the West Coast, playing in bands, arranging, doing studio work, and producing and engineering mine and other projects. Starting in 2000, I had built up my studio and felt confident enough to pursue film, TV, and other multimedia projects. Using Jeffrey P. Fisher's books and other business resources, I created demos, marketing materials, and a weekly follow-up routine to land film, TV, and game work. Some of the contacts I made, I am still negotiating to work with.

What was and how did you land your first project?
I found the production company doing *Standalone* through a tip sheet and connected well with the director. From the fall of 2004 through March of 2005 I composed, edited, and built the score, evolving a good work routine with the director. We have other films and TV pilots in the works based on the premise of the original film.

What are you working on now and how did you get this current project?
I am waiting to work on the next film and TV pilot with my current director and marketing myself to other production companies in my local area and NYC.

What do you feel makes a good music score (or jingle)?
A good score or jingle supports the dialogue and drama of the production in a subtle but powerful way. You don't notice the music, but if it were not there, it would lessen the impact of what is on the screen.

What gear do you use?
My studio is based around my Macintosh using Cubase and a plethora of plug-ins, soft samplers, orchestral libraries, and soft synths. I also have a PC with Gigastudio and Sony Acid and lots of soft synths. I have a rack of pre-amps, compressors, guitar processors for vocals, and guitars for getting performances into my computer.

Explain your promotional strategies (what works and why).
I am marketing to local VA production companies to build my reel and a base of income and to NYC for larger projects, using my old and new contacts to build my reputation and repeat clients. I use a combination of phone calls, direct mail, my Web page, and email to find and qualify prospects; then I follow up leads and stay in touch with past and future clients. I am still figuring out what works.

What skills do you feel someone needs to succeed in the area?
Obviously, the ability to create quality music fast and on-target for any project you take on. You need to be relentless, organized, personable, a good listener, flexible, eclectic, and willing to learn and not be afraid to fail.

How do you approach projects, technically or creatively?
I will sit down with a client and talk about what their vision is for their project. I will find out what music they like for their project, going so far as to watch movies and listen to CDs with them to get a feel for what they have in mind. Once I know what direction I will be going, I create a Cubase template and a palette of instruments and sounds that I will use throughout the project.

How do you get paid (typical pay for projects, royalties, etc.)?
I generally will ask for a deposit to start work and use a three-tier payment plan (start, deliver, final master), though it depends on the project. I am starting to use PayPal to allow people to pay by credit cards.

What do you wish you'd known then that you know now?
How to invest and keep the boatload of money I was making in the past so that I had a nice nest egg to use instead of a day job to support my business.

What are your plans for the future?
To work on more films, build my relationships, grow with my directors, take on more game projects and quit my day job to go independent.

Can you comment on financial strategies you use/used to start/run this career/business?
I really did not have any strategy besides investing in top quality gear and samples. I wish I were better at planning my finances.

Can you comment on using employees, partners, and outsourcing?
Up until now, I have done everything myself. I am in the process of hiring interns to help with my promotion.

Is there anything else you'd like to comment on that you feel is important?
Don't get into this business unless you are willing to be relentless, have a thick skin, and are willing to work hard and put a lot of time in it. I love creating, so I will never stop doing this. Now it's time to make money and do what I want in life.

CHAPTER 11

Money Matters

"An investment in knowledge always pays the best interest."—Benjamin Franklin

Obviously, every dollar you make with your music is important. Guess what? Every dollar you spend to earn that cash is equally significant. Why? It's that five-letter word we all love to hate: *taxes*! Business expenses offset your income, thereby reducing what you pay in taxes. Missing a legitimate, deductible expense is the same as not getting paid—you're throwing money away. Also, without real information about your business finance, how will you know if what you're doing is actually making money?

Keep the Books

There's an old joke that goes something like this: "There are three kinds of bookkeepers in the world. Those who can count and those who can't." If your idea of bookkeeping is to get a check, cash it, and spend, you'd better listen up. It's time to revise your approach into something more meaningful and useful. You need a method for tracking all your income and expenses as they relate to your musical pursuits. We'll take the journey down the tax road a little later in this chapter. Here's how to set up and use a basic bookkeeping system to get control of your finances and make tax preparation easier.

Bookkeeping is a detailed method of accounting for where your money comes from and where it goes. To be effective, you will need to keep some records, learn to file receipts, and manage your cash flow. The reward for your diligence will be knowing how much you earned, how much you spent and on what, and if there's anything left over. Having an accurate picture of your financial situation helps you make better decisions about what you're doing. Plus, you have all the supporting documentation Uncle Sam requires every April 15th.

This is known as a cash system. You enter every transaction as each one is incurred. You get a check, you deposit it, and you record the credit. You get a bill, you write a check, and record the debit. Your balance is always up-to-date. Another form of accounting, called accrual, is beyond the scope of this book. It does have certain advantages, best explained to you by a qualified accountant. For now, the cash system is simple, efficient, and effective.

When it comes to taxes, the entire burden of proof falls on you. The IRS has to prove nothing. You must provide tangible evidence of every claim you make. A shoebox full of receipts does not a bookkeeping system make. Setting up your books and proper bookkeeping is something you can't take lightly. It's vital that you record all your music business income and expenses diligently.

The simplest way to manage your music business finances is to open a business checking account. Shop around as the fees for these accounts can vary widely. Even paying 10 or 15 bucks a month adds up quickly. Deposit all your business income into this account. Also, use this checking account to pay all your business expenses. Record the reason for the expense in the memo section of each check. Since it's hard to be without one, get a credit card and use it just for your business (more on that later). Pay the bill with a check from the business account. Keep all the canceled checks, bank, and credit card statements in a file with enough sections in it for each month's activities.

This no-entry bookkeeping system is fine for the humble, part-time venture. Unfortunately, it lacks the real detail you need to both monitor your income and control your expenses. This technique also doesn't provide all of what you need for filing your taxes. The exception is that you can file the Schedule C-EZ form if you have less than $2,500 in expenses, no employees, don't claim the home office deduction, and a few other restrictions. Chances are that you'll need or want to use the regular Schedule C form, so this bookkeeping method won't cut it for long.

CATEGORICALLY SPEAKING

The real benefit to bookkeeping comes from the details. You need a specific way to record all of your business financial transactions either on paper, in a spreadsheet, or with money management software. But what transactions do you record and how? There are five steps to keeping your books. First, categorize your income and expenses. Second, create and use a ledger to record each transaction. Third, start a filing system to manage the paperwork. Fourth, monitor your bills and income. And fifth, use the information you learn to run your business better.

Even as a kid, I kept track of my money. (There's probably some pathology to this behavior that a qualified therapist could root out.) Anyway, I recorded my money sources (allowance, gifts, etc.) and where I spent it (comic books, candy, and such). This monetary diary matured as my finances became more complicated into the system I continue to use today. I now use a computer instead of a notebook, though.

How you decide to divvy up everything depends on your situation and how much detail you want. If you have several sources of income, you may want to track them separately. Since I compose, produce, record, teach, and write about music, sound, and video, I set up multiple, independent income categories. By spreading revenue across numerous accounts, you'll see which of your activities are the most profitable and which gigs either need a jump-start or should be reconsidered.

Divide up your expenses by following the tax deductible categories from IRS form Schedule C—Profit or Loss from Business that apply to you. Chances are you won't use every category every year. There is only one income category on the form, though: gross receipts or sales. The remainder of the form deals with offsets to your revenue. That alone should indicate why bookkeeping is so critical.

EXPENSE CATEGORIES FROM IRS TAX FORM SCHEDULE C–PROFIT OR LOSS FROM BUSINESS

Advertising

Bad debts

Car/truck expenses

Commissions, fees

Depreciation and 179 deduction

Employee benefits

Insurance

Interest

Mortgage

Other

Legal/Professional

Office expenses

Pension, profit sharing

Rent or lease

Vehicle, machine, equipment

Other business property

Repair/maintenance

Supplies

Taxes, license

Travel

Meals and entertainment

Utilities

Wages

Other

After many years in business, I've settled on several primary expense and income accounts. Some are subsets of the Schedule C categories that help me monitor certain expenditures more closely. At tax time these individual accounts sum to just one Schedule C line, though. For example, I lump the total income from the separate categories into the gross receipts or sales category on the form.

INCOME CATEGORIES

LS   Live and session performances

SJ   Composing scores and jingles

PA   Project studio audio-only production

PV   Project studio video production and post-production

MS   Music CD sales

BK   Book sales

OW   Other writing

ES   Equipment sales or rental

TL   Lessons and teaching

EXPENSE CATEGORIES

A   Auto expenses

B   Business meals and entertainment

E   Cost of equipment over $400 (for section 179 deduction)

F   Fees and commissions paid to vendors

G   Travel expenses

J   Purchases on behalf of clients for resale

K   Goods purchased for resale

L   Legal and accounting fees

M   Musical equipment and supplies

O   Office supplies

P   Printing (paper and CD/DVDs)

R   Equipment or studio rental

S   Postage and shipping

T   Telephone

V   Advertising

X   Taxes and licenses

The two-letter income code and the one-letter expense code are for quickly recording the proper category on receipts, invoices, and in the money diary, ledger, or with software. The coding idea came from a long-forgotten off-the-shelf resource. My sincerest appreciation goes out to those persons who created it originally because it has served me so well for 25+ years!

With your categories taken care of, toddle on down to your local office supply warehouse. Pick up enough 6" x 9" envelopes so that you have one for every expense. You'll use these envelopes to file your receipts. I prefer envelopes over file folders because all those slips of paper don't fall out so easily. Also, buy a one-inch, three-ring binder, some blank paper, and a three-hole punch.

When you get back to your office, label each envelope with the tax year, an expense category, and its letter code. You'll use the binder both for your money diary and for other financial paperwork, such as business checking account statements, credit card statements, and invoices.

If you decide to do your books on paper, draw lines on a few sheets to create a six-column ledger. Here is where you'll record your transaction details, including date, activity, income/expense category, amount, and miles driven. You could set up a spreadsheet in a similar manner. Either way it should look something like this table:

Example Paper Money Diary

DATE/TIME	ACTIVITY	CAT.	AMOUNT	MILES
11/27–1:00	AAA video spotting session			48
11/27–3:00	Post Office: Web CD orders	S	(12.85)	8
11/28	AJF invoice #102006	SJ	1942.23	
12/3	Cell phone bill, check #444	T	(79.11)	
12/4–3:00	Office store: envelopes, paper, binder, and paper punch	O	(19.63)	21

When you receive a payment, record the transaction, being careful to attribute the income to the correct revenue category. Also, make a copy of the check (or other income record), staple it to a copy of the invoice, and file it in your binder.

For expenses, record the transaction to the correct category. Write the expense code on the receipt and file it in the appropriate envelope. Keep all this paperwork for tax purposes as it backs up your claims should you be audited. When buying multiple items, try to keep similar items (e.g., office supplies) together. If one receipt carries many expense categories, it can be a pain to file (make copies and copious notes).

Ultimately, you'll probably want to use dedicated software for this task. The look may differ, but the fundamentals remain the same. Whether you use Microsoft Money, Quicken, or Peachtree, you'll enter the date, the payee, and the amount and assign specific categories to each transaction. Include details in each transaction's memo section, too. File and keep those pesky receipts.

Software easily handles more sophisticated transactions where you split one receipt among several expense accounts. You can generate many informative reports, too. I use the monthly reports and often compare prior years to current year-to-date totals. Software tools usually include accounts receivable for recording money due and accounts payable for listing upcoming bills. The business editions of the popular programs even funnel expenses into the proper tax form categories, making filling out your taxes a snap.

Also, software makes recording reoccurring transactions easier. Though I spend more days doing bookkeeping, I spend less overall time (probably 30 minutes a month and a couple of hours at tax time). When a bill comes in, enter the amount and due date and file the statement. Once or twice a month, print checks (don't write them!), stuff them in the envelopes, and mail them. I do check runs once a month, postdating checks and sealing envelopes. I write the date the envelope should be mailed in the lower left corner and drop it in the box when it's time. Better still, sign up for direct debit from your business checking account for all the bills that you can.

The handwritten diary is still useful for recording business mileage, though, because the IRS demands evidence of mileage driven for business purposes. There are a few programs for handheld computers that also record mileage. See the "Tax Tips" section below for more details on vehicle-related deductions.

GETTING PAID

You also need to establish procedures for billing your clients. You can either bill your clients on delivery or you can invoice them with payment terms. Sometimes, you get cash before delivery, such as when someone buys from your Web site and then you ship the product. You may also ask for an initial deposit before a project begins.

Billing upon delivery is ideal when you perform a single service. You want to be paid at the end of the session or you won't release the files/CD. For new clients, this is the best tactic to ensure you get paid. If they won't agree to those terms, ask for 50% up front and the remainder 10–15 days after the project finishes.

Often, especially when dealing with larger companies, you'll need to offer credit terms. The most common is net 30—the total bill is due in one month. I prefer to bill net 10 or 15 because shaving a few days off really helps the cash flow. Some may even ask for net 60 or more. Again, try to get some money up front with the rest paid on credit terms. If a gig is substantially complex and will take a significant amount of time, consider creating a series of progress payments, such as 1/3 up front, 1/3 at a major milestone, and the final 1/3 on delivery.

Specify your payment terms up front either in your contract or in the purchase order provided by your client. Prominently feature the payment terms on your invoice. Print invoices on letterhead with the word INVOICE big and bold on top. Assign each invoice a unique number. I base mine on the date e.g. , 062406. Itemize everything because the more details you include, the less clients will call you with questions. Carefully show exactly what each item or service was and what it cost. Make the total amount due big and bold and indicate your payment terms prominently. Mail invoices promptly and keep a copy of each one in the binder. For immediate sales, hand the invoice to your client so they can pay you. Separate your open invoices from the already paid ones. This way you can see who owes you money and can then call and remind them. Alternately, use software to monitor unpaid invoices.

To avoid collection problems, a few days before the bill is due, call your client and remind them. Do they have everything they need to pay you? Send past due notices after the deadline has passed. If you're having trouble collecting, start documenting your contact. If it goes on for a long time, either A) have a lawyer send them a letter on his letterhead demanding payment or B) consider taking them to small claims court. In court, your documentation (contract terms, original invoice, follow-up information, etc.) can help your case. It can be hard to be the "creative" person and the bill collector, so consider having another person be the "bad cop" for you. Have a friend, significant other, or relative make the calls and do your collections.

Fight for payment and help your cash flow by getting at least one-half before you release the final master. For new clients, never give up the master until you've been paid in full. You can be a little lenient with long-standing clients, but for new ones, be firm!

EBB AND CASH FLOW

One unfortunate downside to your running your own commercial music business is the erratic income coupled to regular (and sometimes unexpected) expenses. Managing your cash flow becomes crucial. Stay on top of money owed to you. Watch for out-of-control expenses. Keep a little extra money in your business account to help ride those ebbs and flows. Still, no matter how hard you try, you may become strapped for cash occasionally.

To be successful in this business means having credit when you need it. For example, many rental companies will charge you the full amount of the equipment rental and then credit your account when you return their equipment. I'm not a huge advocate of debt, and I prefer to buy items only when there's cash to pay for them. However, a credit card can be a useful and convenient short-term financial tool. There are many ways to use the power of credit to your advantage without getting mired in high-interest debt.

For example, often you will need to buy things on behalf of your clients and bill them later for these expenses. This might include material, talent fees, and even travel expenses. You will pay these expenses initially yourself and then add the charges to your invoice. The client will then pay you so that you effectively recoup your out-of-pocket costs later. You need to be able to support this cash flow, so a credit card is handy for these situations.

Use one credit card specifically for business purposes. Credit helps the cash flow since you are not paying for expenses until after the client pays you. Use your credit wisely and make sure you pay the balance in full every month. Use it for convenience and to float costs that are due you from clients. Do not use your credit card to finance your business or your life. It's best used as a short-term, stop-gap measure only.

Know your card's billing cycle. Buy what you need after the rollover date and get a whole billing cycle plus the grace period before you have to send a check. For me, that can mean 55 days or more before the bill is due. This strategy works best when you have to buy items for clients and must wait for reimbursement from them.

Look for "same-as-cash" deals offered by many companies, such as the three payments of $29.95 variety. They charge you equal installments over time. Time the first payment with a rollover, and you spread the installment payments even further. Other incentives, including no payment and no interest deals for a few months, can make more expensive purchases easier to acquire. Be sure to pay off balances before the due date to avoid interest and other finance charges. Recently, I bought a new computer on one retailer's no interest for 18 months plan. I've been sending in enough each month to pay it off before the due date and will save nearly $500 in interest.

ROI WHO?

When you see your monthly and year-to-date income and expense totals, you'll always know how good business is or isn't. You'll see where you're overspending, so you can cut back. You'll see where you're wasting time on activities that bring little return. In short, having a handle on your finances gives you real insight into what you should and shouldn't be doing. You'll plan better and make more informed career decisions.

Monitor and evaluate your music career financial progress using the return on investment calculation (ROI). First, subtract your expenses from your income to get your profit. Second, divide your profit by those same expenses. Third, multiply the result by 100 to get your ROI percentage.

▶ $10 - 9 = 1 / 9 = .11 x 100 = 11.11% ROI. Not bad. To put that in perspective, every dollar you spend brings in $1.11.

▶ $10 - 1 = 9/1 = 9 x 100 = 900% ROI! For this example, every dollar you spend brings in $9. Great!

Do this calculation monthly and compare to the previous months (compare year-to-year, too). Are you making progress? Since there are two parts to the equation, increasing income *and* decreasing expenses are the only ways to improve your numbers.

All this bookkeeping may sound like a lot of work, and at first it can take some time to get everything running well. Don't neglect its importance, though. I've been managing my finances with these methods for decades now and have never regretted the effort I've put in. Spend a little time each day or once a week to keep everything updated, and you'll be rewarded. Hire a book-keeper, if you prefer. Take steps to reduce your business bookkeeping considerably. That frees up more time for music activities.

Tax Tips

Everybody complains about taxes. But few do anything about it. Well, there are several actions you can take to improve your tax situation and save a bundle, legitimately, with your business compos-ing scores and jingles.

If you're making even the tiniest amount of music-related scratch, there's no reason to pay more taxes than you have to. To reap the most tax benefits, start running your music career as a legal small business (see the previous chapter). The IRS loves small businesses. According to the Small Business Administration, there are 25 million small businesses in the U.S. today. And a large per-centage of them are sole proprietorships—one person shops. As a sole proprietor, you report your music business income as part of your personal income, using Schedule C (and a few other forms). Partnerships report income and expenses similarly. Corporations file their own taxes, but that doesn't diminish the advice the follows.

Taxes are all about income and expenses—the money you make and the money you spend. The more you make, the more you pay in taxes. Simple, right? Even the most convoluted of IRS instruc-tions make that point painfully clear. That means the inverse is also true. Since the IRS taxes only your business profits, cut back on the profit and pay fewer taxes.

"But, dude, I gotta eat." Whoa there, buckaroo. I'm not saying that you should earn less. Quite the contrary, really. Get busy selling your music scores and earn some substantial scratch. At the same time, look for all the possible ways to convert expenses into legitimate business deductions. Even some personal expenses may be deductible against the business. The more expenses you have, the more you reduce your taxable income. And since you were going to spend the money anyway, you might as well realize some tax benefits, too.

Basically, all the expenses you incur to run your music business are deductible. To be fully deductible, however, these expenses must be "ordinary and necessary," according to the IRS. That's just fuzzy enough to be dangerous. Ordinary means the expenses must be typical for the kind of business that you operate. Buying a new guitar could apply; buying a dishwasher wouldn't. Necessary just means the expense is vital to the success of your business. Office equipment, postage, phone charges, Web site hosting fees, recording studio costs, duplication, dues, magazine subscrip-tions, and other such related items are definitely necessary for the success of the typical soundtrack and jingle composer. See the Schedule C expense categories in the previous section for examples of what's deductible.

For every $100 you earn, you pay approximately $43.30 in taxes (if you're in the 25% tax bracket, pay the 15.3% self-employment tax, and send an additional 3% to your state). Of course, that also implies that for every legitimate $100 business expense you incur, you also *save* $43.30 you would otherwise pay in taxes. That's like getting everything you buy at a substantial discount.

Why does the IRS let you deduct all these expenses? They want you to succeed. So they let you invest money in your business as incentive for you to earn more. And the more money you make, the more you'll pay in taxes. You see they have an ulterior motive; they ain't jus' bein' neighborly. But there's a caveat (isn't there always?). You need to be gainfully engaged in making a buck. You must turn a profit in your business three out of every five years or your business will be classified as a hobby, and you forfeit the expense deductions. Bottom line: very bad news and very high tax bill. (And one dollar in profit those three years won't make you popular down at the Treasury Department, either.)

Another important gotcha: If you're just launching your commercial music business, startup expenses can't be deducted all at once. You must amortize them—spread them out—over five years by taking 20% portions of the total startup expenses and deducting them over five consecutive years.

GEAR LUST = TAX SAVINGS

Did you know that the gear you buy for making your music magic could be a sweet tax deduction? Under section 179 of the tax code, you can deduct or "expense" up to a whopping $102,000 of tangible property (2005) and write it all off when you prepare your taxes. This amount used to hover around $25k, but in 2003 Congress passed the higher amount to "kick start" the economy. Be aware that this limit may go up or down in the future. Define tangible property as expensive, long-lasting items, such as a new computer. This amount is above and beyond many other normal business expenses you might incur.

If you've had a particularly strong earnings year, you might want to offset some of that gain by deducting all the cost of large purchases in one year (up to the $102,000 limit). Alternately, you can choose to depreciate what you buy and deduct a portion of those costs over the next several years. The choice really depends on your specific tax situation.

HOME SWEET HOME

If you set up and perform the majority of your music activities in your home office, you can deduct a portion of the same expenses that now do little or nothing to lessen your tax burden. You can write off rent paid or mortgage interest, property taxes, utilities (gas, electricity, water/sewer), homeowner's insurance, repairs, and depreciation. First, dedicate a portion of your home entirely for your music business. Keep it free of personal items and make it your primary business location.

Beware that if do most of your work elsewhere and only use this home office occasionally, your deduction may be limited or entirely *verboten*.

Here's how to figure your allowable deduction. Total up the square footage of this exclusive and principal place and compare it to the total square footage of your crib. Say your math works out to 10% (100 square feet of a 1,000 square foot home—you need a bigger place!). You can then deduct 10% of the aforementioned expenses using Form 8829 *Expenses for Business Use of Your Home.* The total deduction then flows through to your Schedule C, reducing your income and therefore your taxes.

There is a recapture clause, which doesn't apply to renters. If you sell your home and make a profit, those profit dollars become taxable business income at the same percentage rate as your deduction. Score a $50,000 gain, and following the above example, $5,000 of it belongs to the business (subject to self-employment tax and regular income tax, of course). Note that the personal income you make from a house sale is generally not taxed, though. If you stop taking the home-office deduction for two tax years prior to the home sale, this recapture clause doesn't apply.

SELF-EMPLOYMENT TAX
Self-employed have a special tax just for us. Actually, every worker pays the same tax—funding for Social Security and Medicare—it's just a little different when you're on your own. You must contribute both the employee *and* employer contributions, which total up to a whopping 15.3%. Yep, just over 15 pennies on every buck you earn goes right into the Social Security kitty. This is, of course, before you start paying any regular income taxes. Although it's a small consolation, you get to deduct half of any self-employment tax you pay on the first page of your 1040 tax return. It's not a dollar-for-dollar deduction, however.

You must pay these self-employment taxes, along with regular income taxes, quarterly. You need to predict what you are going to earn this year and the taxes that would be due on that dollar amount. Then you send in 25% of that money on April 15, June 15, September 15 of the current year, and January 15 of the next year. These estimated tax payments are important because if you don't pay enough, there's a penalty due the next April 15. If you pay 100% of the previous year's taxes and 90% of the current year's bill, you won't owe the penalty. It takes some experience in this area so that you don't over- or under-pay.

HEALTH INSURANCE
You can deduct the premiums paid for health insurance. This doesn't come off the Schedule C but is actually a front-page deduction on your personal 1040. So, once again, it is not dollar-for-dollar. It took until 2003 for self-employed individuals to earn the right to finally deduct 100% of the premiums they paid. Congress may change its collective mind, though. Corporations have always had the 100% deduction. Other typical medical costs are deductible as personal expenses on the Schedule A (if you qualify).

EAT, DRINK, AND BE MERRY

When you entertain your clients, the money you spend is another write-off. However, these meals and entertainment are subject to a 50% limitation. Spend $100 on a pizza party and take $50 off on Schedule C. Give clients gifts, up to $25 per client, and you can take that as a full deduction.

When you travel as part of your music business, those expenses are deductible, including airfare, lodging, and meals. You must support your travel and lodging deductions with receipts. However, instead of keeping track of your meals, you can take the government's standard per diem allowance of around $30 for Meals and Incidentals. Other cities may have higher amounts, so check the official Web site (www.policyworks.gov/perdiem). Meals on the road are still subject to the 50% limit. The IRS figures you gotta eat anyway, so they limit the expense.

VEHICULAR REDUCTIONS

Yes, that old beater is worth money! Keep track of actual vehicle expenses (gas, repairs, etc.) or take the standard mileage rate (which changes every year; check with the IRS). In either case, you must document the miles you drive for business, the dates, and purpose of trips, along with expenses incurred. A dedicated notebook/diary earns a gold star from the IRS.

Even if you use your ride for business *and* personal use, the business portion of your expenses is still deductible. Determine your business percentage by dividing your business miles by the total miles driven (2,500 business/10,000 total = 25%). If you just use the standard mileage rate, multiply your business miles driven by that rate (2500 x $/mile = deduction) to arrive at your deductible expense amount. You can also deduct the full cost of tolls and parking fees incurred while on business. This is in addition to the standard mileage rate. Also, the loan interest on your car is deductible (subject to the business use percentage, if it applies).

FEED THE NEST EGG AND SAVE, TOO

You also save money by contributing to a qualified retirement plan. The IRS makes it easy to sock away some cash for a rainy day and rewards you with a nice, fat deduction each year. This is another 1040 deduction, not Schedule C. The more you put away, the more you save. And since you're really helping yourself down the road, it's a smart way to manage your taxes and your future. More on this important subject below.

EOY TAX TIPS

At the end of each year, you have another opportunity to reduce your tax burden: accelerate expenses and decelerate income. Look for ways to either reduce the money you have coming in or uncover major purchases you can make *before* the end of the year. First, spend some cash on business expenses. Don't just blow the wad. Make sensible purchases this year that will reduce your taxable income. Ideal last-minute purchases include postage, gear, general office supplies, and promotions. You can also pay your mortgage and health insurance premium before the year-end to realize some other tax savings. Second, put off collecting money this December to January of the next year by billing your clients a little later or by offering more liberal credit terms. Though you'll have to pay taxes on the money eventually, you defer that payment for a whole year.

While we all have to pay taxes, we are only required to pay our fair share. Make sure you are not throwing money out the window. Talk to your accountant or tax planner for all the details about these issues. Take advantage of these and all the other tax breaks available to you. And put more music money in your pocket where it belongs!

GET HELP FROM THE IRS

Surf on over to the always exciting IRS Web site (www.irs.gov) and download the free guides that explain the specific tax benefits for small business owners.

▶ #334, Tax guide for small business

▶ #463, Travel, entertainment, gift, and car expenses

▶ #533, Self-employment tax

▶ #535, Business expenses

▶ #583, Starting a business and keeping records

▶ #587, Business use of your home

Retirement Savings

As Congress dukes it out over Social Security's future, don't sit idly by and wait to control your retirement destiny. There are proactive alternatives to just collecting government checks in your golden years.

A personal Individual Retirement Account (IRA) lets you contribute up to $4,000 for the years 2005–2007 and $5,000 a year starting in 2008. If you are 50 or above, 2005's deduction is $4,500, $5,000 for 2006 and 2007, and $6,000 in 2008. You personally direct how and where to invest your money.

The traditional IRA lets you deduct your contribution amount from your income each year, therefore reducing the taxes you may owe. Money deposited into the account also grows tax-deferred, and compound growth can be substantial. Instead, you pay taxes when you withdraw the funds at retirement, including taxes due on the account's investment growth. This tax-advantaged account is based on the principle that your tax bracket may be lower in the future.

Conversely, the Roth IRA doesn't let you take the contribution amount off your taxes today. Rather, the Roth gives you tax-free withdrawals. Roth IRAs are very attractive for younger investors. Your investment account could grow considerably, and your withdrawals, including the account's investment growth, would be tax free. People who already have funds in a traditional IRA need to investigate what conversion costs would be—having to pay taxes today on previously tax-sheltered contributions.

A personal IRA should be part of everyone's retirement planning. In addition, the self-employed and those with incorporated companies should investigate three additional retirement options: SEP, SIMPLE, and Keogh plans.

SIMPLE SEP STEPS

Simplified Employee Pension (SEP) and Savings Incentive Match Plan for Employees (SIMPLE) are the most common retirement plans for businesses. A SEP is a good choice for sole proprietors; SIMPLE plans are more suited to incorporated companies.

Both plans are easy to set up and administer and allow contributions of up to 25% of income, with a 2005 total cap of $42,000 based on a $210,000 income maximum. I know, that math doesn't add up (see below). Like traditional personal IRAs, contributions are tax deductible with tax-deferred growth. The assets in either plan must be managed by a financial institution (bank, investment firm, etc.), but plan members have control over their account's *specific* investments.

A company must offer its SEP/SIMPLE plan to all employees and let them deduct the same percentage as the owner. The SIMPLE plan also lets the company match employee contributions. Since both plans are based on income, the deductible amount can vary from year to year. When you have an especially strong earnings year, contribute more. If times are tough, scale back.

Have you ever wanted to learn math the exciting IRS way? Here's your chance. For SEP, SIMPLE, and Keogh plans, the maximum allowable contribution is 25% of income; however, the math is somewhat convoluted. Essentially, you can contribute the percentage of your income only *after* you reduce your income by that same percentage amount. Huh? First, determine your business profits (net after paying self-employment taxes). Second, divide that number by 1 plus the percentage you want to contribute (e.g., 1.25 for a 25% contribution amount). Finally, multiple the answer to the second step by the actual percentage you want to take. The final figure is your contribution amount.

100,000 / 1.25 = 80,000 x .25 = $20,000 is your maximum contribution.

KEOGH DOUGH

Another retirement option for sole proprietors and partnerships (but not incorporated businesses) is the Keogh plan. Again, this plan is tax advantaged (deduct now, defer growth, and pay taxes later) but may be set up in several ways. A defined-benefit plan pays a fixed benefit amount to retirees. The profit-sharing model is similar to the SIMPLE plan with employer-matched contributions. The money purchase Keogh plan requires establishing a contribution percentage and sticking to it every year, with strong penalties for noncompliance. Keogh plans require more work to set up and run and therefore require the help of a professional pension manager.

When you're young (and foolish), you just want the cash *now*! It can be hard to imagine retirement and even harder to start planning for it. But the reality of it is if you don't plan for your golden years, nobody will. Whether you choose a SEP, SIMPLE, or Keogh retirement plan, you can save a substantial amount of your earnings (at far higher levels than personal IRAs and light-years beyond Social Security), direct the growth options to maximize your investment, and then retire on your own tidy little nest egg. Don't ignore this advice because saving for the future is an important part of running both your music business and your life.

Grab IRS Publication 560, Retirement Plans for Small Business, from www.irs.gov.

If you'd invested $10,000 when you turned 21, by age 65, assuming an 8% compounding growth, you'd have a whopping $295,559 *without* having contributed another penny to the account. If new parents placed a *single investment* of $10,000 that equally compounded at 8%, their son or daughter would be a millionaire at their retirement without ever contributing to the account again. You kind of wish the U.S. government would encourage such a practice, wouldn't you?

Invest for Today and Tomorrow

I'm always amazed at how many creative people ignore their need to invest for the future. Now my particular idea of investing goes way beyond merely saving money and depositing for growth in a bank, stock, bond, mutual fund, etc. While I know those forms of investing are crucial to real success, there are a few other forms of investment to consider, too.

Since I advocate running your music career as a business, the first place to invest is in your business itself. That doesn't mean running out and grabbing more gear. Invest in your business to make it grow. Add new music products and services and spend resources to promote them. Next, invest in your business relationships. Nobody achieves success in a vacuum. You depend on people to help you achieve. Today is the perfect day to start building those crucial relationships. Always invest in yourself. Become a better person by mastering new skills and savoring new experiences. Of course, you should also invest traditionally, such as in tangible goods like real estate, and invest in the economy through a variety of conventional investment choices, for example, stocks and bonds. Making all these forms of investment a part of your daily life is the true path to success in your life.

Always think of the money you didn't make as the investment in your career. If you work for free or get paid little, quite griping. Instead think of the experience this way. The money you didn't make is nothing more than an investment in your future. For example, you could spend a few hundred (or thousand) dollars to take a course. Or you could write a score for a student film and not make any money. You'd get a credit, a viable recommendation, and some samples for your demo, though. I'd say you "invested" that money well!

If you diligently follow the methods described in this book, you will make money. Just like a salary, these business profits bring you purchasing power to support your lifestyle. Additionally, money earned today can pay a portion—if not eventually *all*—of your future lifestyle. Your money, when saved and invested, has the ability to earn more money. Your savings pay you income, which is the income you use to support your chosen lifestyle. You become financially independent, not having to work for money. It doesn't happen overnight. You need to get (and stay) out of debt, make more money, save more money, invest your savings, and work your way toward that goal.

Let's see how this can really work. For example, you sell a single music project one year and earn $600. You would need $10,000 in the bank earning 6% interest to make the same $600 bucks in one year. It can be hard to save $10,000. Even socking away $100 a month takes almost seven years! However, the fact remains, a $10,000 accumulated capital base has the ability to pay you a dividend of $600 a year or $50 a month without further intervention on your part. Add that to the original $50 from your business and in less than seven years your business and investments together generate $100 each and every month.

That's not a lot of cash for most lifestyles. However, you must make sure you understand the *principle* of this example. Earning, saving, and investing is the path to building a self-sustaining business. Make money from your music, save some of those funds, invest them, and you'll watch your nest egg grow. Can you use your music career to make and save $1,000 a month? If so, in seven years you will have $100,000 in the bank paying you a whopping $6,000 a year in interest (assuming a 6% return). That's a $500 a month income without touching the original 100 grand.

"Yeah, right," I hear you saying. There's no way you could *earn,* let alone *save* $100,000. I used to agree until one day I clicked a report in my financial software that showed my earnings for a certain range of dates. I'd brought in $99,559.83 during that time period. Of course, this wasn't *net* income, but the exercise instantly proved that I did have the ability to bring a hundred grand into my hands. Grab your tax returns for the past several years, total up the gross income, and see how much money you've brought into your life. You just might be amazed at your fortitude.

Next, you need to control your expenses and *keep* more of that money. Track your expenses for a few months, business and personal, and then look for ways to trim the fat. You need to keep track of every little expense and avoid the tendency to lump expenses into larger piles. What you are looking for is waste—money you've spent without considering its consequences. As your music helps you maximize your income and your diligence helps you control expenses, you'll be left with savings. Invest those savings so you don't have to work for money. You earn income from investments instead. What choices do you have to make right now to allow yourself to earn money from your music, save a sizable chunk of it, invest it, and ultimately reap the benefits of all your hard work? This is the path to financial freedom.

A FEW MORE FINANCIAL IDEAS

Have the amount of cash equal to six months of your basic living expenses in a safe, interest-bearing account. This can help you in emergencies. Also, have another source of quick cash for an immediate, dire emergency, such as house equity. Consider medical emergencies and other catastrophes to be a real emergency, not needing a new keyboard. Also, pay down your mortgage faster. For example, on a $100,000 30-year mortgage at 8.5%, paying just $70 more each month will pay off the loan in 22 years and save $55,728 in interest.

Have a fallback. What if your primary source of income dries up? Do you have another way to generate income in your life? Can you do something else? Teach music lessons or work at a music or pro audio store? This way you can capitalize on some other skill until you get things back on track.

If you choose to invest in mutual funds or stocks, the most important thing to remember is to invest the same amount regularly. For example, contribute $100 a week to your investment account. What this does is let you take advantage of dollar cost averaging. This minimizes your risk during wild swings in the stock market. In essence, you buy more shares when the price is low and fewer when the price is higher. When you average out the costs, you usually come out ahead. Having too much credit hurts your ability to get credit when you *need* it. Experts suggest you pare down to one credit card and cancel all those others. Make sure you never carry balances on your credit card. The interest rates are too high and the temptation to spend beyond your means is too much. If you're heavily in debt now, use your initial savings to eliminate your debt before you move down the road to financial independence. Also, studies show that people spend 20% more when they use credit (even more when you count the interest charges). I've been guilty myself. When I know I'm going to charge a purchase, I'm apt to add a few extra items because of the convenience. Fight this temptation!

If you've never invested before, *start right now.* The sooner you take advantage of all the options available to you, the better off you will be. Make sure that sound financial planning and investing are a major part of your business and personal life. By familiarizing yourself with possibilities and by taking advantage of professional experience and services, you will reach your objectives sooner.

Get the Money You Need

Every small business faces the problem of needing either seed money to start or to fund a major capital expenditure, such as equipment. Here's how to tap into the money stream when you're tapped out.

BRING IN MORE BUSINESS

Double your efforts and land some additional business and increase your cash flow accordingly. What promotions can you run to get clients fast? Though it may take a little money before you can make money, it's a prudent investment. Offering a discount—a sale of some sort—is a sure-fire way to generate new business and reactivate old accounts.

INCREASE YOUR FEES

When was the last time your raised your rates? It may be time for an across the board 10–15% fee increase. Also, are you charging the right amount that reflects your experience? Do some research to see what others who do similar work are charging. If you are more experienced and successful, charge more than the average. If you're starting out, try 80–90% of the average.

DECREASE YOUR EXPENSES

The primary step toward reducing expenses is organizing your business financial records and then carefully monitoring them. If you don't keep track of what's coming in or going out, you'll never know where you stand. It is just simple arithmetic: If you spend less, you'll make more money. Look for excessive fat and other bad spending habits and give yourself an instant raise. Take a long, hard, methodical look at your business expenditures and find ways to reduce your overall expenses such as rent, telephone, supplies, etc. and eliminate frivolous spending altogether. Most of all, keep your gear lust in check. Do you really need all the latest toys?

BARTER PRODUCTS AND SERVICES

Let's say you need a guitar part for a project but have no money to pay the player. Offer the guitarist free studio time in exchange for her playing on one of your tracks. The guitarist can use her time to record a demo, for instance. You need to be aware that the IRS has specific rules covering bartering in business situations. You must record these exchanges as regular business income and expenses. However, when this trade is like/kind, the effect on your taxes is zero. Following the above example, let the guitarist bill you for her time on your track and then you bill her the same amount for your studio time. The two invoices effectively cancel each other out. She owes you no money, and you owe her none, either. More importantly, you both have the legitimate paperwork you need for your tax preparation.

FRIENDS AND RELATIVES

Your first source of cash is often to ask those closest to you to help you out. Be careful with this strategy, as it can often ruin even the hardiest relationship. You should be very clear with your intentions. Spell out precisely the amount you need, how you intend to use the money, and specifically how you plan to pay it back. Create a simple, amicable, and equitable loan agreement to protect all parties involved. This does not need to be a long-term loan either. I know someone who borrowed $1,000 for one week and paid back $1,050. Where else you could get that return on your money for doing absolutely nothing? A better strategy is to trade in-kind services with friends and relatives. Have an uncle with a print shop? Instead of borrowing money, ask him to donate print services to you until you get your project off the ground. Or trade your time by working part-time at the print shop for future services.

YOUR CURRENT CLIENTS

This is the easiest method to raise cash and often the most overlooked. Instead of extending credit to your clients, ask to be paid in advance for some products and services. On big projects. always insist on getting some money up front—from 33–50%.

YOUR VENDORS

After asking your clients for money in advance of services, turn your attention to vendors next. Ask for credit terms of 60–90 days on the products and services *you* buy. You might not get this at first because you may need to build up their confidence in you. Build a good relationship by paying on time. When the day comes that you need to ask for extended credit, they may grant it to you.

Not too long ago I faced a $5,000 production bill and wouldn't have the cash to pay until after my client paid me. At first I considered the home equity course mentioned below, but later decided to ask the supplier. After explaining the situation to her, she agreed to offer me 45-day credit terms. I then convinced my client to expedite payment to me. This let me pay the production tab in 35 days, and now I never have any trouble getting liberal credit terms from this vendor.

YOUR HOME EQUITY

If you own your home, you can secure a line of credit from your bank. This credit line is based on a percentage of the equity you've built in your home. Equity is defined as the difference between what you house is worth and what you currently owe. The bank may extend credit usually no greater than 80% of that amount. This financing option is often cheaper and easier to get than most conventional loans. The interest rate is well below credit cards, and qualifying is frequently simple. The interest may even be deductible. There is a downside, though. You are guaranteeing the loan strictly from your personal assets—you put your house on the line!

BANK, SBA, AND OTHER LOANS

These are by far the hardest ways to get cash. Basically, you go to a bank and apply just as you would for a mortgage or auto loan. The only difference is that you'll need a detailed business plan. Suffice it to say that building rapport with your local banker means you'll have an ally when the money crunch comes your way. What are the elements of a formal business plan? Follow this outline: introduction or executive summary, financial plan, promotion plan, growth plan, detailed cash flow projections, and personal information, including copies of tax returns. It can be wise to include additional items such as pictures, example promotional material, audiovisual presentation, and testimonials or other letters of recommendation.

Include these fundamental details:

▶ Business name

▶ Vision or mission statement

▶ Product and service definitions

▶ Marketplace description and market research findings

▶ Production and distribution methods

▶ Business organization

▶ Capital and start-up costs

▶ Sales projections for the first five years

▶ Expense projections for the first five years

▶ Business assets

▶ Personal assets and liabilities

▶ A list of strategic goals and the action plan to achieve each one

LEASING

This is always a good alternative when your cash is tight. New equipment, cars, and more can all be leased. The considerably less up-front costs make leasing very attractive. On the plus side, you get the latest and greatest equipment for your business or choose better, more expensive options that you otherwise couldn't afford. Make sure you carefully consider the leasing restrictions. Don't get into long-term leases on equipment or materiel that outdates quickly.

While I have no formal leasing agreements, I do *rent* regularly. This strategy gives me access to state-of-the-art music gear without paying the sometimes exorbitant price tags. Instead of buying that new digital gizmo, I rent, borrow, or visit a commercial studio. You pay far less than you would by buying the deck and pay it one tiny morsel at a time instead of all at once. I often bill clients for these charges, so the money doesn't really come from my pocket anyway.

Industry Insight

Lori Rae Martin

AudioGirl Productions
Los Angeles, CA
Lori@AudioGirlProductions.com
www.AudioGirlProductions.com

Recent credits/past projects:
California Lottery, Intel, State Farm, Jiffy Lube, Infiniti, The Golden Nugget, L'Oreal, RCA, Mission Tortillas, Estée Lauder, Safeway, Gillette, Southwestern Bell Yellow Pages, Basic Four Cereal, Elizabeth Arden, The Mojave Resorts, VA Hospitals, Oscar Mayer, Aero Mexico, Smokey Mts. Visitor Center, Creative Ceed Beauty Company, Children's Hospital San Diego, Al Dente Pasta, Direct Web, and KBIG, KABC, and KNAC radio.

Why did you choose this career (and how did you get started)?
I was singing at Disneyland, working towards my music degree, and also working as a music minister. One day my electric piano (a cool Wurlitzer) was stolen from church. With the pastor's generous reimbursement, I bought my first synthesizer, a Roland Juno 106. That led me into recording and MIDI programming. This girl singer could have her own band at her fingertips—and it was always on time and sober! I was hooked and from that point on, I've had my head buried in equipment manuals.

What was and how did you land your first project?
My business partner in AudioGirl Productions, Sylvia Aimerito, is a professional broadcaster and voice-over actress. She was a DJ and Music Director at a radio station that hired me to produce their station jingles and IDs. And in 1997, we combined our related skills in voice-overs, production, and music to form AudioGirl Productions.

What are you working on now and how did you get this current project?
Currently, AudioGirl Productions is producing employee-training modules for a car company. These will be used both online and on DVD to acclimate the employees to the new car line-up, specs, and features. This includes voice-over, original music, and some on-camera. This client was directed to our Web site by an outside recording studio.

What do you feel makes a good music score (or jingle)?
I aim for a score that is musically interesting and enhancing to the voice-over or visual message. It must never overpower the all-important copy. A jingle should be memorable, concise, and capture the "attitude" of the ad. And it's a given that the production be pristine and the performance skilled.

What gear do you use?

For just VO, we often go directly to PC using Adobe Audition. We use Audio Technica AT 4047 and 4033 condenser mics run through a Tascam USB/FireWire interface and PreSonus TubePre. For music and VO, we love our Roland 2400CD and plug-ins. For programming, I mostly use the Roland Fantom X7. And since we work frequently from the home studio, we also have a 4x4 SoundSucker sound booth that we couldn't live without.

Explain your promotional strategies (what works and why).

We advertise on a few trade Web sites and one print publication: *Encore Directory*, print and online, (www.encoredirectory.com) and the OCMedialist online (www.OCMedialist.com). Most of our clients are found by word of mouth. And that includes our mouths! We tell everyone what we do and always carry business cards.

Another great promotional tool is our Web site. Since it's often the first impression for a client, we strive for a polished, professional, and welcoming presentation that will convey trust in our abilities to deliver a superb product and ultimately motivate that person to contact us.

What skills do you feel someone needs to succeed in the area?

Being courteous is imperative; return calls and emails promptly. Make sure the client feels well taken care of. Also, doing something productive every day for your business is critical. Keep learning. Be fair and professional and make an effort to be organized and balanced in your work and life. And stay positive and fun to be around. Trust me, these are the skills that positively affect your client list!

How do you approach projects, technically or creatively?

After getting a feel for the mood of the project, I play various music beds in my library of already composed grooves to see if I have anything that may remotely work. This is where "ideas" for incomplete songs come in handy. Usually, I can find something I can work with as a foundation. Or I pick up the guitar or sit at the keyboard the "old school" way and try to think outside the box. And I'm always studying the work of other composers, too.

Can you comment on financial strategies you use/used to start/run this career/business?

The only debt I have is my home. I have always been a financially sensible person (thanks to Mom and Grandma) and have never borrowed money to grow the business. For example, I always pay cash for a new piece of equipment or I don't buy it. When I use the company credit card, I pay it off immediately. And if I'm still getting a great sound with a 10-year-old piece of gear, I'm going to keep using it (maybe I should have kept the Juno 106!). I don't want to have to take a job just to pay off a plug-in. What I value most is peace of mind, and being frugal contributes enormously to that for me.

Can you comment on using employees, partners, and outsourcing?

I am blessed with having a great business partner in Sylvia Aimerito. She is at the top of her game in the field of broadcasting and voice-overs and has been an immeasurable source of contacts and job leads for me. I, in turn, have provided her with a practical knowledge of audio engineering, music, and marketing ideas. We're a fabulous team, each with our own unique strengths and talents but like-minded in our vision of AudioGirl Productions. Regarding outsourcing, I've learned that I don't have to know how to do every little thing. We maintain an up-to-date list of contacts that are invaluable to our business. For AudioGirl Productions, it's definitely a team effort.

How do you get paid?

I've learned from experience and knowledgeable sources that like any business, it's what the market will bear. I've also learned that it's very important to have a healthy respect for one's hard work and talents and not give it away. For one minute of finished original music, we currently charge a flat fee of $1,500. Our average rate for voice-over work is $395.00 for the first hour, $200.00 each hour after that.

What do you wish you'd known then that you know now?

I'm glad I have my music degree and know how to write a good fugue and arrange horn parts, but I wish I had taken more business classes in college.

What are your plans for the future?

My immediate plan is to expand AudioGirl Productions' happy clients list and ultimately our charitable contributions. I'm also working towards the completion of a CD of original songs.

Is there anything else you'd like to comment on that you feel is important?

Yes, I'd like to take the opportunity to personally thank Mr. Fisher for generously sharing his invaluable "insiders'" knowledge about the industry. His enormously practical advice was instrumental in helping me crystallize what direction I wanted to take my company and musical talents. His materials are filled with a wealth of ideas and information for not only the neophyte, but also the working pro.

CHAPTER 12

Rights Right

"We make a living by what we get; we make a life by what we give."—Winston Churchill

Few topics have as much misinformation surrounding them as the copyright issue. Composers the world over seem to live in fear that somebody, somewhere will steal their creative work. The fact remains that copyright infringement is a remote possibility for most of us. It does happen (and has happened to a friend of mine), so you must understand your rights, whether you keep them, retain some, or give them all up.

Copyright protection is automatic. As the creator, or author, of an original music composition, you earn certain rights as soon as you create and record your music in some way—on paper, CD, digital file, etc. You do not have to mail a registered letter to yourself, file with the U.S. Copyright office, or put the copyright symbol (©) on your music to get copyright protection. These are all surreptitious myths perpetuated by the ignorant. And while there are certain merits to *all* of those steps, they are not required for full copyright protection. Why? Because copyright protection is automatic.

Copyrights cover literary, artistic, and musical works (including words and sound recordings). However, ideas, procedures, processes, methods of operation, concepts, or discoveries never get copyright protection. Only the exact way an idea is conveyed, like the words on this page, is protected. Trademarks are brand names or designs applied to products. Service marks are words and symbols used to identify services, such as a slogan. Patents protect inventions and improvements to existing inventions. You can't copyright your business name, but you can trademark it.

The owner of the copyright is the author of the original work who has the exclusive rights to do and to authorize any of the following:

▶ To reproduce the copyrighted work in copies.

▶ To prepare derivative works based upon the copyrighted work.

▶ To distribute copies to the public by sale or other transfer of ownership, or by rental, lease, or lending.

▶ In the case of literary, musical, dramatic, and motion pictures and other audiovisual works, to perform the copyrighted work publicly.

▶ In the case of literary, pictorial, graphic, or sculptural works, including the individual images of a motion picture or other audiovisual work, to display the copyrighted work publicly.

These five rights are exclusive and can be enforced at the owner's discretion and at any time. The differences between the last two need further clarification. To perform a work, showing a video for example, is to show the work in its entirety. To display a video would be to show individual frames nonsequentially. Also, a sculpture cannot be performed; it can only be displayed.

The copyright for an original work created after Jan. 1, 1978, lasts for the life of the author plus an additional 70 years.

Work-for-hire is a special case. Ordinarily, if you create it, you own it. However, a work that is prepared by an employee within the scope of his or her employment is considered a work made for hire. The copyright ownership belongs to the employer. Work that is "commissioned for use as a contribution to a collective work" is a work made for hire *only* if the parties expressly agree in a written instrument signed by them. Put simply, an employee automatically forfeits copyright ownership. A freelance, independent contractor automatically retains copyright ownership. Both situations can be reversed through a signed, written agreement.

The owner of a copyrighted work may transfer the ownership, and therefore his rights, to another party by using a written instrument of conveyance signed by the owner. If the music you produced was a work made for hire, this is unnecessary.

For the value received, Jeffrey P. Fisher hereby sells, transfers, and assigns to XYZ Production, its successors, assigns, and personal representatives, all right, title, and interest in and to the following music copyright:
(Describe the nature of the copyrighted work.)
The certificate of copyright is attached. Jeffrey P. Fisher warrants good title to said copyright, that it is free of all liens, encumbrances, or any known claims against the said copyright. Signed under seal this first day of December 20xx.

It is a common misconception that your work is not copyrighted until it is registered. Your music gets copyright protection *the moment it is fixed in a tangible medium*. Remember that copyright protection is automatic. Registering the work doesn't prove authorship, either. Registration allows you to stake a claim to the work in question. The Copyright Office does not determine the validity of the submitted work. The burden of proof falls to you.

However, registration *is* required in two instances: first, to correct publication without notice of copyright on works published before March 1, 1989; second, to be able to sue for infringement, the copyrighted work must be registered. Please note that statutory damages awarded for copyright infringement are awarded from the date of registration forward.

Until March 1, 1989, it was mandatory for a copyrighted work to display the copyright notice such as: Copyright, Jeffrey P. Fisher, 2005. Failure to affix the notice to the work effectively eliminated the copyright, and the work automatically entered the public domain. Following the International Berne Copyright Convention, the United States copyright law was amended. It is no longer necessary to display the copyright notice on works, and failure to do so no longer results in loss of rights to the owner-author. The "circle c" and the word "Copyright" are interchangeable: ©2005 Jeffrey P. Fisher.

If you decide to file, use form PA to register the music only or SR to register the sound recording, which registers the music, too. You must also send two nonreturnable copies of the song. The filing fee is $30 per song (2005).

▶ The Copyright Office, Library of Congress, Washington, D. C. 20559 (www.copyright.gov) has all the forms and details about this important issue.

▶ A quick note about trademarks/service marks. You may apply the "TM" or "SM" designation to any trademark or service mark that you plan to use. However, you must register the mark with the U.S. Patent and Trademark Office (www.uspto.gov/main/trademarks.htm) to use the "circle R" (®) designation. Part of the registration process requires making sure that nobody else owns the mark already.

▶ Need to know if a music work is in the public domain? The fee-based Public Domain Music Works (www.pubdomain.com) claims to have searched the U.S. Copyright Office and built the largest public domain music database on the Web.

Know Your Rights

The music you write, whether a score or jingle, with or without lyrics, is called a *song* for copyright purposes. Songs get afforded certain rights that the copyright owner can license. These rights include mechanical, performance, synchronization, master use, and print. Your income comes from how you license the use of your songs. Some of your income may come from fees charged for composing, while other earnings come as royalties from the licensing of these rights. Essentially, the copyright laws allow you to earn income from your music beyond any initial fees you may get to compose and record it. Royalties are, in effect, an ongoing payment for your creative work.

There are two parties with an interest in every song: writer and publisher. Your share of the music you compose is called the writer's share. The other share is the publisher's. Royalties earned are split 50-50 between the writer(s) and publisher(s). If a song is unpublished, the writer earns both shares, or 100% of the royalties. If there is more than one writer or publisher, the corresponding share is split accordingly. In other words, all writers, no matter how many there are, divvy up only the writer's share.

It may shock you, but jingles rarely, if ever, earn any of these rights. Jingles have always been the exception to these rules and show no signs of changing. Your sole payment for a jingle is the fee you charge your client. However, other music that you compose and sell has the potential to earn some or all of the money from these licenses.

MECHANICAL

This is the compulsory royalty payment for songs reproduced on media (e.g., CD). The statutory fee that must be paid by the company selling the CD is 8.5 cents per song, per unit (2005). If somebody covers your song for their CD, or if your song appears on a soundtrack album, you would earn this royalty.

The National Music Publishers' Association/Harry Fox Agency, Inc. (www.nmpa.org/hfa/licensing.html) is the primary collection point for mechanical royalties.

PERFORMANCE

A song performed in public, including radio, TV, restaurant/club, and concert venues, earns a royalty. Those companies that play music publicly pay the fees. The three primary performing rights organizations (PROs)—ASCAP, BMI, and SESAC—collect, administer, and distribute these royalties. The fees paid depend on the specific use. For example, a featured performance would pay more than an underscore, a song on network TV would pay substantially more than one on PBS. Each PRO has a fee schedule on its Web site.

To collect these royalties, the writer and the publisher must belong to one of the PROs. You can only belong to one for your lifetime, so choose wisely. The publisher's and writer's PRO can be different for a song, though.

▶ ASCAP, American Society of Composers, Authors, and Publishers (www.ascap.com)

▶ BMI, Broadcast Music, Inc. (www.bmi.com)

▶ SESAC (www.sesac)

You should join a PRO once your work begins to appear in public performances. You will need to register your works, a quick and painless procedure via the Web, so that you collect performance royalties. Essentially, you will register the name of the song, its use (underscore, theme, music library), and the writer(s) and publishers(s) and the percentage of each. Make sure you keep this information up to date, including your contact information, and check it regularly for any mistakes.

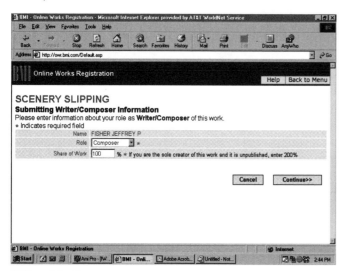

BMI registration.

Stay on top of cue sheets for music that hits the broadcast market. You want to ensure that those who use your music report the selections played, file the necessary cue sheets required by the PROs, and pay the appropriate fees. Major TV outlets are 100% cue sheet compliant, so your worries are few. Still, it's a good idea to remind your clients when your work is destined for broadcast, and even put a clause in your contracts.

Verance (www.verance.com) provides a service to composers that places watermarking technology into your music files. When your music plays on TV, Verance generates reports for the PROs to use to pay performance royalties.

SYNCHRONIZATION

When songs are used along with moving images, such as in a motion picture or TV show, another fee must be paid. Fees for these synchronization rights must be negotiated on a case-by-case basis between the prospective licensee and the writer/publisher. Some fees can be low and others quite substantial. Note that when a TV show grabs sync rights, they still also pay performance rights to the song.

EMG, Inc. (www.clearance.com) has valuable information about the synchronization rights issue.

MASTER USE

This is another negotiated license to use the actual recording of a song synchronized to moving pictures. If a song is covered by a no-name artist, then only a sync license must be sought. If the actual song by a recording artist is used, then both the sync and master use rights must be purchased.

PRINT

Sheet music also earns royalties for a song, typically 10–15% of the retail price, less for compilations and publication in magazines.

CLEARING RIGHTS YOURSELF

This job usually falls to the music supervisor, but that may turn out to be you. Should you need to use an existing song for a project, you will need to clear its rights. For mechanical royalties, use the National Music Publishers' Association mentioned above. Performance royalties would be part of the cue sheets filed by broadcasters. You would talk to the song's publisher to clear sync and master use licenses. Search for publishing information through the PROs. They may turn you down flat, charge an exorbitant fee, or be very accommodating.

Rights in Action

As you make sales with your music (song), you will typically be faced with one of four scenarios.

1. You keep all rights to the song and continue to earn royalties from its use. You also have the unrestricted right to sell and license the song repeatedly. In short, you are simply renting your music. You still own it! Feel free to sell the same music to as many people who are willing to license it.

2. You give up all rights to the song and never see any royalties or additional money beyond the initial fee you charge for composing it. This is better known as a work-for-hire or copyright buyout. The person or company buying the song then becomes the copyright holder and will earn royalties accordingly. National jingle spots are typically purchased this way.

3. You give up some rights while keeping certain other rights. For example, you give up the publishing to your client, but keep 100% of your writer's share. Any revenue received from the aforementioned rights would be split 50-50 between you and the publisher (your client). This is typically how music library licensing works and some film/TV scores.

4. Any one of the preceding situations may apply, but in addition you may earn a royalty, or points, based on some other factors, such as units sold. This would apply to soundtrack albums and when scoring for the gaming market.

Obviously, you want to hold on to as many rights as possible. Your clients may want some of the action, too. At the very least, try to keep your writer's share so your music continues to earn for you.

ALL-IN OR PACKAGE DEAL

In the soundtrack and jingle world, there is something known as the package or all-in deal. In days past, composers charged a single creative fee, and the client buying the music paid all the other costs to realize that music, including recording, material, and talent fees. Today, the general approach is to pay a single, larger fee and require all costs related to delivering the completed music be paid by the composer. That means you are responsible for paying musicians, studio charges, material costs, and so forth yourself. Whatever is then left over after all these bills are paid remains as your creative fee. The package deal is the norm for jingles, TV shows, nonbroadcast music, games, and most low- to mid-budget motion pictures. You will need to become rather adept at figuring costs to make sure you don't lose money. This is the subject of the next chapter.

However, just because the project is a package deal doesn't mean there still won't be rights issues. If the package deal is also a work-for-hire copyright buyout, then there will be no rights involved on your end. If it is not, try to hold on to both the writer's and publisher's share. You may only get the writer's, however. That means you can still earn performance royalties and possibly mechanical royalties (if there's a soundtrack album). One small caveat: Music in films does *not* earn performance royalties when played in movie theaters, only when played on TV.

Also, it's important to recognize that when you score a film or a TV soundtrack, the package deal includes the sync and master use licenses. You are getting paid to compose, record, and deliver, and these two licenses are implied in that commission. Yet, there may still be a separate contract that grants those two rights to the client. The money paid will be something akin to a token dollar.

Union Thoughts

Another source of income for you comes from being part of the Musician's Union. If you play on your recordings, as many of you will, there may be advantages to being a union member. Personally, this hasn't been an issue for me, and when I contract out, I'm primarily nonunion because I hire my friends and fellow musicians.

The decision to join is all yours. They do offer several benefits such as referrals, networking opportunities, pension and insurance plans, a pension plan, and wage scales. Contact your local chapter and see what advantages there are for your situation.

▶ American Federation of Musicians (www.afm.org)

Industry Insight

David Jaedyn Conley
Mydnyte Productions (USA), Seattle, WA and Mydnyte Productions (Australia), Melbourne
jaedynconley@yahoo.com, www.mydnyteproductions.com

Current projects:
Clean, a feature film by Neil Bilas
Recent Projects:
"*Frankenchicken*" Television pilot for Film Victoria and BigKidz Entertainment, "*Small Ant Syndrome*" for BigKidz Entertainment, "*Benny's Hook*" for BigKidz Entertainment, "*Object of My Affection*" for Peta Manning and Natalie Vella, "*Wet Dreams*" for Peta Manning, and "*Rabbit in the Moon,*" an Emmy award-winning film by Emiko Omori.

Why did you choose this career (and how did you get started)?
Initially, the nature of my career vision was much different. I was a guitar player/vocalist in a band during the Seattle music explosion in the late 80s and early 90s. We did very well and managed to garner a reasonable following, eventually attracting an indie-label deal. This band toured extensively for about three years. The band was a progressive rock band, and ultimately during the heyday of grunge and flannel, we found it increasingly difficult to stay visible. Numerous factors led me to believe that this vehicle had gone about as far as it could, so I departed for something different.

Anyone in progressive rock will tell you that they are concerned with pushing the music to the next level. Truth is, after I departed, I really didn't know where to turn. I began recording a solo album that featured my compositions exclusively, and I performed every instrument in the recording. I really wanted to take both my compositional skills and my performance abilities to a new level, and I had become fiercely independent and self-reliant.

Eventually, I decided to return to school and undertake music composition studies. During the course of this study, I learned digital audio production, orchestration, harmony, counterpoint, and many other concepts. I was immersed in classical studies and found myself writing music for orchestra and other various ensembles that I would never have dreamed I was capable of.

To me, composing music for the moving image requires a higher understanding of music as a whole. To manipulate music and make it belong to the visual action requires a vast array of knowledge and abilities in different fields. It is not enough to just be the composer—sometimes, you must also be the performer, or the conductor, the engineer, or the producer, business manager, arranger, programmer, audio tech, secretary, psychologist, or even the janitor! It truly requires you to be a "jack-of-all-trades." The job requires an amazing amount of self-actualization and carries a heavy responsibility.

While in school, it became clear to me what I wanted to do, and I began to adjust my studies to facilitate this endeavor, Somewhere around the third year of my bachelor's degree, I got the idea to take old black-and-white silent films and compose musical scores for them. This earned me a scholarship to go to Hollywood and study briefly with an Emmy award-winning composer. I attended large-scale recording sessions of orchestral film music, and believe me when I say I learned heaps very, very quickly.

I didn't just learn from this composer, but the engineers running the sessions as well. During lunch breaks I took the opportunity to pick their brains regarding production techniques, and I learned a great deal about digital audio production—knowledge that I still rely on to this day.

What was and how did you land your first project?
Following graduation, I began searching for film projects to be involved in. I posted my details on an Internet callboard and was contacted shortly thereafter by an independent producer who was finishing his first film. He wanted to know if I could send him a demo and asked me if I was interested in having a look at his film.

He sent me a copy of the film on VHS, and I quickly digitized the video into QuickTime, scored the movie from beginning to end, re-reduced it to VHS, and sent him back the film, as well as the black-and-white silent film that earned me the scholarship.

He was so stunned by these actions and the quality and speed of my work that he gave me the job. Incidentally, we kept none of the original score that I composed for him in that demo, but that doesn't matter. I managed to show him I was capable of producing the service he needed, and my flexibility impressed him.

What are you working on now and how did you get this current project?

I am currently in Australia working on a feature length film called *Clean* by director Neil Bilas. The film is a dark tale of a family fragmenting apart and descending into madness. I was contacted by this director by email after he found my details on the University of Melbourne Web site. The Internet is, and always has been, one of the most effective tools in my business arsenal. I landed the gig because of the quality of my previous work and demos. And while I am very eclectic and diverse, I have a special affinity for composing music with a darker, more sinister, and dramatic edge.

What do you feel makes a good music score (or jingle)?

Film composers must put themselves second to the picture they are scoring and put the needs of the film first. A good score or jingle is created when the composer can determine what the film needs and what will serve the film. Sometimes, it may be that single unwavering note in the background that nobody notices, or it can be a fully realized orchestral score. There are so many steps in the process of film scoring, and so many people may have their hands in your score—rewrites are common, and you have to be careful not to become too attached to what you are writing because it is all subject to the approval of the director and producer, and possibly the production team. After all, we aren't creating a music video, but rather a film that has music in it.

Whatever your preferences may be, I feel that a good score or jingle is achieved when it augments the emotional subtext of the film. Sometimes, the messages of a film or jingle aren't so overt, and it is possible to arrive at what these messages are and play on people's feelings somewhat subliminally by scoring to these elements. It means a broader depth, not only to your score but the movie itself.

I believe that the best scores are achieved when there is an element of selflessness by the composer. It lies in the motivation of the work and what forces are driving you to compose the score. Concerns about turning out a hit score that will win awards or how much money you want to make given a certain project can cheapen your motivation, and it can show in your work. It's a careful balance of knowing when to push the envelope musically and when to back off.

What gear do you use?

The technology I use in my studio is composed primarily of nonlinear digital audio recording systems. I have begun incorporating software-based synthesis and sampling into my projects and am leaning away from purchasing costly synthesizer and sampling keyboards and hardware. I have found that software-based synthesis and programs like Reason and Logic Pro have now reached points where the sounds now rival the quality of outboard gear or hardware. I have also abandoned any use of SMPTE VCRs and composite my temp scores in QuickTime Pro. The ease and facility of use made that step a natural evolutionary step in my production process.

This was forced on me, though; it wasn't easy to make this step, and I made it reluctantly. One day I came home and found water pouring from the ceiling of my studio. Apparently, a pipe burst in the building, and the result was an inundating rush of water that flooded my beloved Roland keyboard. I had a film on the table and was expected to produce a score within the week.

Reluctantly, I turned to Reason and began scoring the film utilizing its sampling and synthesis capabilities. I was actually amazed at how well the score turned out, and as such I have found myself returning to this more and more—now coupled with the "Rewire" capabilities of Logic Pro. The amount of time I saved was amazing, and now even if I am creating a score that will utilize a live orchestra, I may still map things out in Reason ahead of time to illustrate to the director what the end result may sound like. Ultimately, I never use my Emulator sampler anymore and only occasionally use the subsequently repaired Roland keyboard for recording.

Explain your promotional strategies (what works and why).
These days my promotional strategies are centered mainly on the Internet and direct marketing. I spend a fair amount of time networking my existing relationships to meet new people who are making films and commercials. I have found that direct mail works best for me after I make personal contact either by phone or meeting in person. Initially, the client usually asks me questions like, "What type of gear do you have in your studio?" and the direct mail brochure that I send outlines these kinds of details, as well as past credits and projects. Usually, however, I find that my demo does most of the speaking for me, and after they get copies of my DVDs and CDs, such details seem less important to the client. I think what it comes down to is the client is trying to figure out whether or not you simply have the capability to deliver what it is they need, and this should be self evident in your demo. It should reflect the level of quality and craftsmanship that make it hard for them to say *no* to using your services. Directors and producers take huge risks in going with a composer they have never worked with before. Production companies spend huge amounts of money realizing these projects, and any breakdown on the production process reflects on them. If they hire you to compose a score, and in the end you are unable to deliver what they hired you to do, you may not be the only one who loses his job.

The Internet, oddly enough, seems to draw in a great deal of work for me. The thing that I really like about the Net as a marketing tool is that it is capable of disseminating a great deal of varied materials for a minor cost, and the access is global. It is also nearly instantaneous—if I get a call from a director that is headquartered far away from me, I can send them to my Web page and, depending on their Internet access connection, they can have near instant access to my demo materials. This is great and saves me the time of preparing DVDs and waiting for them to be shipped and arrive.

This works best if you maintain some sort of regular Web presence and have listed yourself with a few major search engines and industry-related directories. When I get an email from a prospective client, I am always amazed at how they found me, because there are always some new links popping up for me on the search engines. Occasionally, these links are set into motion by other people cross-referencing my sites, posting reviews of my recordings, or even auto-generated. The Net as a marketing tool can be difficult to get started initially, but eventually you can build some momentum, and it begins to move with minimal thrust.

What skills do you feel someone needs to succeed in the area?

I think the most important skill for a composer to have is the ability to speak the lexicon and languages of both the trade and art, which can sometimes be divergent. The ability to convey information effectively is of paramount importance, but so is comprehending what the director is telling you, as sometimes directors and producer lack the musical language to really state what they want. This requires a great deal of patience and mental translation because sometimes what they tell you and what they mean are two different things entirely. You sometimes need to take that extra step in the communication process because this is an industry where there are no second chances.

I also think that it is important for a composer to understand the entire production process of film scoring. o A great deal of flexibility is required as well. You need to maintain an open-minded detachment with your work—what happens when you spend hundreds of hours perfecting the opening sequence of your film and it is what you believe is the best piece of music you ever written, only to have the director say, "I like it, but it isn't going in this film!" There is a time to fight for that score you believe in, but more times than not, the director being the customer, he should win the argument.

How do you approach projects, technically or creatively?

My creative approach to each project is different, as no two methods of my production seem to be the same. Sometimes, I spend a great deal of time playing the piano before I compose; other times I simply sit down and begin notating in Finale. I think that each film has its own character and style, and depending on the nature of the style of music I must create, the creative process is largely dictated by these factors. If the music style is electronica, my process will be much different than it would be if I were composing for string orchestra. If the score will be comprised of recordings by live players, soloists, or orchestra, again my process will be much different than that of a score where I am playing it all in using samples and my keyboards. Again, flexibility is the recurrent theme in my process, as is a great deal of eclecticism.

How do you get paid (typical pay for projects, royalties, etc.)?

I have specific policies regarding payment and billing. When I am asked to quote, I first determine the nature of the score—is it live players or do they want me to use electronics or samples? If they require a fully orchestrated score with live players, I am quite frank regarding the costs and make sure they understand that these costs will be factored into the quote. I then consider the length of the film, how many hours the project will likely take to complete, factor in any gear rental I may need, special supplies, or specific requests from the director like the costs of a certain player, instrument rental, or voice talent. I then usually add 5–10% for unknown expenditures, which almost always emerge.

Typically, I ask for half of the money paid when I start the project and the other half when I complete the project and hand over the masters. I almost always try to retain my performance royalties and rarely give buyouts on film scores unless I am compensated adequately and appropriately. Jingle work, however, can be different as many production agencies are seeking buyouts. My quotes all depend on the circumstances and nature of the production. I always make certain in written agreements that I have permission to circulate the film in my demo kit and place excerpts from the score online in my online demo kit. I also stipulate that as long as my score accompanies the film, my screen credit cannot be removed, nor can the film be exhibited without the said screen credit. In one of my last films I also clearly spelled out how much score could be used to advertise the film, that such advertising was free of performance royalties (these were friends so it was a bonus), and that they had permission to include excerpts of this score in the video game that accompanied the movie production. I no longer do anything on verbal agreements, not even with my friends. I have predesigned music agreements, which can be modified to suit the production at hand. My feeling is "I trust you, you trust me, and now it is in writing so there is no reason to ever mistrust each other." I lost a very close friend over a verbal deal, which got worse and worse for me as time went by, as she breached each and every point we ever agreed to verbally. If I had gotten all that in writing from the beginning, we might still be close friends. I also lost heaps and heaps of royalties, as this was a high-level, network production.

What do you wish you'd known then that you know now?
Anything is possible if you truly believe in yourself, what you do, and your capabilities.

What are your plans for the future?
My plans for the future are to continue composing music for film and to score films that are bigger in magnitude in terms of visibility and production. I plan on continuing to operate in Australia and capitalizing on this burgeoning market, as well as open a Los Angeles office in pursuit of larger films with wider distribution. I also plan on creating a team of composers for the specific purposes of capitalizing on creating music for advertising and multimedia. I am also currently in talks with a corporate entity that wishes to create a next-generation source library business operation.

Is there anything else you'd like to comment on that you feel is important?
Only that it is extremely important to secure even the smallest deal in writing. Verbal deals have a way of crumbling the instant that money of any sort becomes involved. I do not keep employees, and I am extremely careful about collaborators and would-be partners. If I need outside assistance, I hire people as independent contractors. That way they do their own taxes, and I do not have to provide benefits, health insurance, and other expenditures I couldn't afford because my business is so small.

I am even careful with performers in the score. All of my musicians and performers sign "work-for-hire" agreements. Occasionally, a performer will come back and say they want a cut of the profits because they claim, "Without me, my special touch and talent, your score wouldn't be what it is today, and therefore I am entitled to a part of the reward." I have a very good composer friend who composed and recorded a score utilizing the string orchestra of a local high school. He failed to get these agreements signed before the recording session and after the fact one very greedy set of parents decided that because of their daughter's participation as a violinist in the orchestra, the score was an amazing piece of music that it wouldn't have been otherwise had she not performed in it. They refused to sign the document, wanted a cut of the royalties, and ultimately this score was never used because of one simple document. Had he passed these documents out before the session and required them to be signed before each respective musician entered the studio, he wouldn't have sustained this loss. This musician would simply have been excluded from the session.

CHAPTER 13

Set and Get Your Fee

"Big shots are only little shots who keep shooting."—Christopher Morley

You create music and now somebody wants to use it. What do you charge them for that use? The answer depends on many different factors. This chapter provides some insight into how to approach this subject with confidence. Please note, though, that the following information comes from my personal experience and research. As the saying goes, "your mileage may vary." Use this information to guide your own research and adapt what you learn to your own particular situation.

First, understand that there are two sides to the pricing equation. One, how much money you want to make, and two, how much the client is willing to pay. Rarely are these two sides equal. More often than not, the client has a specific budget, and you'll need to decide if the pay is right for the work you'll do. From their perspective, clients want to get the most for the minimum. On your side, you need to earn enough income to support your lifestyle *and* make a wage that reflects the creativity and technical excellence that you put into the project.

The reality of these two positions means that pricing and negotiations are closely related. You may have a dollar figure in mind; the client a completely different number. Together, you will need to compromise on a final music charge that pleases both parties. It is a combination of all the information discussed in this chapter that works together to form your pricing formula. No single method works for every project. It is up to you to take what's presented here and determine what's right for a given situation as you quote fees or decide to take what's offered.

Tough Talk About Money

Many artists are reluctant to mix art and commerce. It's a necessary evil in this little corner of the music world, though. Traversing the money tightrope requires a delicate blend of humility and candor. You don't want to be seen as a money-grubber, but you can't risk being taken advantage of, either. However, money talk doesn't need to be contentious. Keep negotiations friendly but professional. You won't talk about fees during your initial contact with a prospect; that's too early. You can't wait until after you've turned over the master; that's far too late. You will discover the right time through experience.

Meanwhile, clients may open up the discussion, in which case, you'd better be prepared to answer. If the subject doesn't seem to come up, initiate it yourself. The best time to broach the subject is when it's obvious they've hired you or when they begin to talk specifics. As you capture the project details, you are in the prime position to quote your fees for what they require. Alternately, the money issue makes an ideal gig for a partner. This approach lets you remain the music *artiste* while your partner functions as the hard negotiator.

What about working for free or very little money? While volunteering can be an opportunity to gain some experience, you risk being unable to climb out of the bottom tier of music fees. Those who get your music for nothing or next to nothing will usually not start paying you big bucks down the line. They will always expect a deal. An exception to this would be as you build a relationship with a media content producer and become the go-to composer as they move up in the ranks, taking you along with them to bigger and better-paying projects. Otherwise, offer free music services only to a project or two where *pro bono* work is seen differently, such as scoring music for a charitable organization. This can let you build your demo, credibility, and reputation without the "cheap composer" syndrome plaguing you.

Occasionally, you will hear the "we don't have any money for music" argument, "but we really like your stuff and want to use it for our film/video/game/etc." If you are just starting out, perhaps consider the offer (under a few conditions outlined below). If you've been around a bit, you must weigh the ups and downs before deciding. Do some research on the people and see if they have a track record. Talk extensively about the project and get a true handle on how it will benefit you. Think about all the options and listen to what your head says. Then ask your stomach. If your gut has a funny feeling in it, pass. If it feels rights, go for it.

If you do decide to offer the music score *gratis*, do so only under the following requirements:

▶ Ask for a small stipend anyway to cover some material costs. Tell your would-be client that few people like or can afford to work completely for free. You may be surprised when they manage to come up with a few bucks after all.

► Draft and have them sign a simple contract that gives you *all rights* to the music. Don't give them any rights to the music at all, ever!

► In that same contract, have a clause that says if/when the project makes money, you expect to be paid a certain amount. You will need to define what "makes money" means and the dollars you expect as your usual fee. Include any initial stipend as a sort of "down payment" toward the score, with the remainder payable in the future contingent upon the project making money.

► Insist on a screen credit in both opening and closing titles (if that applies) and that your music credit be used on all advertising materials used to promote the project.

► Request several copies of the final work (on DVD, etc.).

► Ask for a glowing testimonial from the project producers that you can use with your promotions. Also, request that you can use them as a reference for your latest prospects to call to check on your work.

► Leverage this project in publicity and other promotions.

► Do all this as amicably as possible. I'm a firm believer in building relationships with people. They do pay richer dividends than any other career investment.

Don't let this talk about low-cost/no-cost music dissuade you from making a quick buck now and then. Not every gig will pay as well as you hope. I see nothing wrong with handling lower paying gigs if you can do them with a minimum of fuss. There's also nothing wrong with working on projects for which you have great affection and passion (even if the pay is low). For example, most video producers can't afford original music for their productions and opt for library music instead. Selling your own library music is one way to capture that market. However, those same video producers might want a short, original theme to use with the mostly library-based score. You could offer to do the work for a minimal charge. The secret here is to do the work fast. Hunt through some old tracks and ideas and transform them to meet the client's need. Or put together something quick using software such as Sony Acid Pro. Don't forget to keep all rights to the music; no reason you should give away the store for a small stipend.

Two Sides to Every Coin

As you compose, produce, and sell your original soundtrack music and jingles for movies, games, radio, TV, and the Web, there will be two primary sources of income.

▶ **Front end**. The money you make as you complete a project. Whether you keep some rights or the client buys out your copyright, you will collect your fees when finished. The elements that comprise the front end include your creative fee, any production charges, material costs, and talent charges.

▶ **Back end**. The money you could *potentially* earn in the form of royalties after you complete the project. Notice I used the word "potentially" because there is no guarantee that you will ever earn any ongoing income from your creative work. The back end includes all the rights—mechanical, performance, sync, and master use—profiled in the previous chapter, along with any other royalty participation, such as profit points or percentage of sales (on games, soundtrack albums, and so forth).

If the project is a buyout, you must make *all* your money on the front end; there is no back end to speak of. When you retain some or all your rights, you make money on both the front and back ends. Some swindlers may try to tell you a tale of incredible back end monies that you will make. They'll use this same con to avoid paying you any front end, too. Don't fall prey to their fantasy. The back end is mostly speculative income. Get sufficient front end dollars.

However, when you know—for an absolute fact!—that your music will play on major television outlets where performance royalties are guaranteed, *then* you may eschew a smaller front end for the back end you will indeed earn (provided you keep your writer's share, of course). For example, it's not uncommon for episodic television to pay a small all-in package fee to a composer who then earns the real money from performance royalties when the shows air. Composing 15 minutes of music for 20 TV episodes can earn in excess of $60,000 in performance royalties (on network TV)!

We've already discussed the back end royalties in the previous chapter. Here let's concentrate on the front end dollars.

CREATIVE FEE

The creative fee is the composer's fee charged for the music that you provide. The amount varies due to several considerations, such as the nature of the project, where it will play, the rights involved (back end), and so forth. A great deal of the fees you will receive will be based on client budget and prevailing rates. More on these two subjects later. For now, here's how to come up with a basic rate.

Let's say you want to earn $50,000 this year from your music. There are about 2,000 hours available each year to work (eight hours per day; five days per week; two weeks vacation). Unfortunately, you will use many of these hours promoting your business, managing it, and so forth. If you are fortunate, you may make music half of the time available or about 1,000 hours. To reach your goal of $50,000 you would need to charge $50 an hour (50,000/1,000 = 50). A daily rate would be $400 (8 x 50 = 400).

But what about taxes, health insurance, and other business costs, called *overhead*, related to your salary? Overhead is the umbrella term for all those pesky costs related to being in and doing business whether you have paying clients or not. These include such costs as rent, health insurance, gear payments, telephone, Web site/Internet access, utilities, etc. Some of these costs may be fixed (the same every month), while others may be variable (different each month). Don't estimate these costs. Figure them out to the penny. Also, know your tax rate as that enters in to the equation, too.

Overhead and taxes can easily double your gross income needs to $100,000 a year or more. You will need to gross $100k just so that you net your $50k income goal. Therefore, a more realistic rate, in this example, is $800/day, provided you invoice 125 days each year. That's how you can reach your income levels and pay all the costs of being in business.

If it takes you two days to write a minute of music (jingle or longer score), you would charge at minimum $1,600 for your creative fee. Any other charges (detailed below) would be added to the creative fee, too. *But there's a genuine problem with this pricing approach.* What if it takes you 10 minutes to write the music? What do you charge? $16.66? What if it takes you 10 days? Few clients will pay $8,000 for a minute of music (unless it's a rare national jingle buyout). Therefore, there's a little more to this pricing issue than at first seems apparent.

While this exercise is an ideal method for figuring what you *should* charge, it doesn't always take into account the reality of the situation. For example, you land a national commercial jingle and get $15,000 for the buyout. Let's say it takes you three days to pull it together. You did pretty darn well financially. Now you manage to land $15,000 for an indie film score that takes you two months to complete. You didn't fare as well in the wage department there. However, you wouldn't turn either project down, would you? In this example, you've made almost a third of your salary goal with two projects and did it in a little over two months. You'd have to do almost 19 $1,600 gigs to earn the same scratch, but that will take some serious promotional scrambling to win as many clients.

The point is that you must have an income goal. And that same goal must be based, partially, on what it costs for you to be in business. With that goal established, you will know what you *should* charge your clients to reach the goal you've set for yourself. Now, with a real figure in mind, and an idea of the "going rate" for the music you will deliver, you can quote rates with some confidence that clients will accept them. You will also know what kind of pay rates you need to earn. You will know immediately whether a project is worth doing for the budget that's proposed. And, you'll really know when you should get out of Dodge…fast.

If you are expecting $1,500, and the client is offering $150, you are a long way from common ground. Run (unless you desperately need the scratch). If the client offers $1,250, though, you are a lot closer. I'd say go for it. And if the client offers $2,000, you know that "Let's get started" or "Can I have a PO number?" will be the next words out of your mouth! These examples, of course, presume you will keep all or some of your rights and therefore have the potential to earn back end money or resell the music again to another client (earning more front end money again).

So take the time to establish a realistic income projection based on the time and resources you have now. If you've never done anything in the arena before and have no reputation whatsoever, a huge income goal is probably unrealistic in the early years. If you already have had some success and now are willing to move to the next level, then establish income goals that require you to push yourself harder.

BUYOUT FEE

Typically, your buyout fee should be about 10 times more than what you would charge for music where you keep all rights. For example, if you charge $1,500, keeping all rights, the buyout fee would be $15,000. Also, be sure it is a *true* buyout where you sign over the copyright to the client and never, ever receive another dime from the music. Some projects may confuse exclusivity with buyout, for example, when licensing music to a client for a specific use. You may keep rights in other areas. This would *not* be a copyright buyout.

MINIMUM FEE

Fast projects don't pay. I once spent a whopping 10 minutes altering a track—tempo change, sound palette revision, muted a lead instrument, and presto: new music track. How do you bill for 10 minutes of work? Well, it took my entire life to get to the point where in 10 minutes I could create an acceptable music track. Since I didn't bill clients for all that time spent honing my craft, I need to make up for it now. Therefore, set a minimum fee for all projects you will do. My suggestion is to look for the average rate for the kind of music and licensing you offer and make that the minimum creative fee you always charge.

PRODUCTION CHARGES

These are the costs realized to produce the final music master. These would include recording studio charges, engineer salaries, equipment rentals, and similar costs. Since you have your own project studio, bundle your in-house charges into your creative fee. Charge back any and all outside production costs to your clients (with a markup added in).

Personally, I own my equipment outright and find it a better tactic to charge a higher creative fee and include the free use of my studio in that charge. Therefore, I don't sell my studio time on composing projects; I sell only my creative services—my music. That's my niche. However, when I use a commercial facility for projects or rent equipment, those charges are added to the invoice along with my basic rate.

MATERIAL COSTS

These are the costs incurred for actual, physical material used to create or deliver the music, such as CDs, hard drive, etc. This material typically would belong to the client when the project is over. You may buy this material yourself on behalf of your client and then charge them back for it. Don't nickel and dime your clients. A couple of blank CD-Rs will not kill you to throw in for free once in a while.

TALENT

These would be all the costs associated with the hiring and recording of musicians, singers, and so forth. Get the various union rate cards (AFM for musicians, AFTRA for voice talent) to use when estimating what's needed for a project. Should you use non-union talent, get a handle on the fees from these people, too; it's usually 50–60% of comparable union rates.

PACKAGE OR ALL-IN DEAL

As was mentioned earlier, it is typical of today's commercial music industry to bundle all these fees—creative, production, material, and talent—into a single fee. The client pays this fee, and you, as composer, pay *all* out-of-pocket costs from this single fee, keeping what's leftover as your creative fee. The package deal may or may not have back end participation (jingle, no; TV documentary score, probably yes).

You are responsible for all costs related to delivering the completed music. Obviously, you must know those costs when either quoting or accepting a package price. It is in your best interest to spend as little money as possible or do as much work as you can by yourself with your own equipment. When you lower those expenses, you make more money. Juggling all these costs can be a nightmare. Pay yourself first. Allocate between 35–50% of the money to cover your time and experience. Use the remainder of the budget to pay for everything else. If you have cost overruns, there will be a contingency in reserve to cover those charges. It means cutting into your pay, though. If you're smart, you'll estimate carefully and come away with a better check at the end of the project.

Therefore, I can't emphasize enough how you *must have a clear idea of what your costs will be* in order to effectively quote or accept proposed package deals. Can you meet a project's goals based on the budget available? Don't guess; figure this out. For example, if you compose a piece using your own in-house project studio, hire no additional people, and deliver a file via FTP, the package price can be significantly lower than what would be required if you hired an orchestra, recorded in a world-class studio for a week, and delivered multitrack stems on hard drives. For the former, $2,000 wouldn't be a bad payday for an up-and-comer; for the latter, $200,000 wouldn't be nearly enough to cover the bills.

MARGIN OF ERROR

Especially when you are in the position of quoting the package fee, add in some wiggle room for unforeseen circumstances. For projects that seem relatively straightforward, add 20% to the figure you estimate before telling the client the final charge. If the project appears difficult or the client indecisive (or the equally grueling nitpicking client), add a 40% margin to cover what you know will be problems.

MARK-UPS

When you will incur either production or material costs and will charge them back to your client, always add in a markup so that you make a little more money on these items. My general rule is higher markups on cheaper items and smaller markups on more expensive items. For example,

I may double the charge for a spindle of CDs but add only 20% to a recording studio charge. Hide these markups from your clients; they should be already included in the fee your client sees.

Still More Pricing Intelligence

There are four additional key areas that contribute to the pricing equation: competition, price positioning, typical (or market) rates, and client budgets.

COMPETITION

You need to discover the typical fees paid for music in your area. This information comes from the same people you are trying to convert into clients. Asking about music budgets is the only way to get this information reliably. It can really help if you have a solid rapport with a client or two on whom you can spring this money question. Honesty is the best policy here. You want them to know that you want your pricing to be in line with their budgets so that you can continue to work together.

Also, you will need to shop the competition to find out their prices. Contrary to asking client, this research may require some harmless subterfuge. You will need to contact the competition and ask what they charge for certain situations. Rarely will this information be readily available (on the Web, for instance). Once you find out these rates, you might try slightly undercutting their prices. Try the 80–90% range. If XYZ down the street charges $2,000, try $1,895 for your bid. Don't undercut by too much because you'll start a price war that only drives everybody's prices down and soon clients will demand music for pennies. We all lose in the end. When Budweiser emerged on the beer front, they could have undercut their competition and started a price war. In fact, that is what the top beer brands did. They started lowering their prices in an attempt to grab market share. Instead of lowering their prices, Budweiser spent that money on promotion. They were an expensive brand, but ultimately became better known because of their advertising and promotion campaigns. That's a lesson you can take to the bank.

POSITIONING

You have three choices for positioning your prices.

▶ **Skim:** You charge higher prices but have lower volume. You don't do a lot of work, but you charge significantly larger sums for that work. Designer clothing is an example of this pricing strategy. Here you dip your toe into the premium waters and charge higher prices, usually with more amenities. This is an ideal tactic for a well-known or established composer.

▶ **Penetration:** You charge low fees and make up the difference with high volume. You have to do a lot more projects because the money on each project is so low. One example of this pricing approach is a fast food restaurant. With the low end, you promise no frills, just basic service. Personally, I feel it doesn't pay to be the cheapest composer in town. Perhaps, when first starting out to build a demo and a list of referral clients, it may be acceptable to work for lesser pay. The problem is that you'll have a harder time raising those rates once your expertise and reputation grow.

▶ **MOR (middle of the road)**: You price your services somewhere near the middle of these two extremes. Essentially, you charge what the market will bear—what clients are willing to pay. This is, by far, the pricing formula most of you should take. To live here, though, you must know the typical rates.

TYPICAL RATES

Through research, interviews, experience, and so forth you will discover the going rates for the music you compose. Make staying up-to-date on prevailing music fees a critical component of your business planning. Here are some general guidelines circa 2005.

▶ Nonbroadcast soundtrack underscores range from $500–1,500 per finished minute (keeping rights; far more when a buyout).

▶ Local jingle packages range between $1,500–15,000 while national jingle packages fall between $5,000 and $50,000 or more.

▶ Episodic TV scoring is almost always a package deal falling between $3,500–25,000 or more per episode. Animated shows fill the low end, cable programming takes the middle ground, and network TV pays near the top tier. TV movie packages may start in the $25,000 area but be as high as $100,000. Note that music played on TV earns performance royalties, which can be quite substantial for multiple reruns on a major network.

▶ Game music fees range from $500 to $1,500 per finished minute. There are typically sales bonus points available, too.

▶ Major motion picture package deals start at $25,000 and go up to over a million dollars. Independent features stay in the $5,000 to $100,000 range. Points participation is rare except for soundtrack albums. Composers may keep their writer's share, thereby earning back end dollars.

▶ Library music pay ranges from $2500–$5000 per CD (12–15 total tracks). Composers keep their writer's share, though. Sample libraries usually pay a 15–20% royalty based on net sales only.

I regularly conduct a rate survey of subscribers to my *Moneymaking Music Tip of the Week* email newsletter. Here are the results of some recent polling:

▶ **Indie film**. $1,250 (10-minute film)

▶ **Games**. Main title, $800–1,200; underscore (per finished minute or one-minute loop), $500–1000; sound effects, $100 each

▶ **Jingles**. :30, $4,620; demo, $1,848; company theme: $500 (8 seconds); Nonexclusive music track, $750

▶ **Music library**. $300 per track

There is the annual Film & TV Music Salary and Rate Survey *published by the Film Music Media Group (www.filmmusicworld.com). There is a charge for the PDF download (www.theindustrystore.com/fitvmuboandr.html), but it's well worth the cost when planning the pricing strategies for your music business.*

CLIENT BUDGETS

As has been mentioned, more often these days than not, the client has a specific music budget. Most will gladly tell you what that figure is. Then it's wholly up to you to decide if the fee proposed is reasonable for their specifications and your objectives. Hopefully, you've done your homework and will know the answer quickly. Sometimes, there are other benefits, besides cold hard cash, that may influence your decision (such as when a project offers inroads to other gigs).

Clients may not offer the music budget but may quote a range. Alternately, they may quote the budget for the entire project. That can be just as good. On average, between 1.5% and 3% of the total production budget would be available for music, including creative, production, material, and talent fees. For an example, with a $100,000 production budget, you can expect between $1,500 and $3,000 available for music. Quote your package price accordingly, and you stand a good chance of getting the gig.

Clients are far more knowledgeable about the art of commercial music than ever before. They used to be at the mercy of the music house, but now they are quite savvy about productions costs (they know your costs are virtually nil because you have your own project studio) and rights (they try to keep some or all of *your* rights and pocket the money themselves). That puts us poor composers at a disadvantage. When the clients name a fee, knowing your own costs and income goals will make you far more savvy as you decide whether to accept or reject a music project. Also, recognize that clients today are very price sensitive and want to pay less and get more. They are not as loyal to one composer as they may have been previously, especially when tighter music budgets dictate price shopping.

Quoting Fees

When asked how much you charge, make sure you get as much detail about a project as you can *before* proffering your price. I usually try to turn the tables and get a feel for the budget from the client. At that point, you might say that the budget is sufficient or counter with another offer. Additionally, you might quote typical rates, as a range. It really varies by project and client (and as your experience and confidence grow). Don't be shy. You are a professional and deserve to be paid accordingly.

Even if you offer a verbal quote, provide a more formal estimate. Once the estimate is approved, follow it up with a contract.

Thank you for choosing Mr. Composer to bid on the music score for your film, Indie. For the fee of $xx,xxx, Mr. Composer will compose, produce, and deliver approximately 30-40 minutes of music. This fee includes all costs related to the final master recording, except for any licensing of additional music not composed by Mr. Composer. Mr. Composer shall retain both the publisher's and writer's rights and royalties on all music composed. Mr. Composer is affiliated with (name of PRO). Payment of the above fee will be one-half ($xx,xxx) when starting the project and one-half ($xx,xxx) after delivering the final music master.

During a negotiating session, you may have to tip your hand and quote a price. The client may then counter with a lower fee. *Don't cut your price* at that point. Instead, change the project guidelines. Listen to what the clients says and then counter with something like this, "My usual fee for what you describe would be $1,500, as I said. However, I can meet your $1,250 budget if we cut the music under the second segment." This way you didn't lower your price, but, in effect, you *changed the project specifications*.

Stand firm, quote your fee, and wait for a reaction. He who opens his mouth next usually loses the negotiation. Don't let that be you. Remember not to apologize or give up. You provide a unique and valuable service and should be paid accordingly. Not everyone can afford your original music, so work hard to gets those who can.

OVERCOME PRICE OBJECTIONS

Consider these when faced with a price objection. Make sure you focus on the benefits your client receives from original music when you state your price and answer their objections. Here are a few other strategies you should use to overcome objections to your quoted fee:

▶ Divide your fee into smaller units. For example: $5,000 is a lot of money, but $500 a minute for 10 minutes of music sounds far less.

▶ Demonstrate how your fee is but a small fee percentage of the overall production budget yet brings greater impact to the audience. Without your music, the project will be something less. That fact alone must be worth it to the client.

▶ Make sure the specifications are the same. If your client is comparing your fee to library tracks, you need to differentiate your service. Don't let them compare apples and oranges.

▶ Remind them that a cheaper price often means inferior goods.

▶ Create payment terms that lessen the impact of your price. Perhaps one-third now, one-third upon delivery, and the final one-third 30–60 days later. Only extend this credit to those clients you know or trust will pay.

Industry Insight

John Seguin
Seguin Sound, Missouri
jseguin@seguinsound.com, www.seguinsound.com

Recent credits/past projects
KTA Tennis (computer game), Lugaru (computer game), Madtak, Juggle Master (computer simulation demo/interactive), *For You I Scream at Me* (animated short).

Why did you choose this career (and how did you get started)?
I've always wanted to be a professional musician. Back in grade school, where I first played Orff mallet instruments, I always loved the way that music sounded and the different moods it could create. I followed this dream up through college, completing a Bachelor of Music Education from the University of Illinois, Champaign-Urbana.

What was and how did you land your first project?
Commercial work was not really what I was planning on doing at the time, but a friend of mine had started going to school at the Art Institute of Seattle. He wanted to get some music for this short

animation piece he had created. I literally did *"For You I Scream at Me"* almost overnight and was very energized by the experience.

What are you working on now and how did you get this current project?
I'm currently working on scoring a small handful of computer games. I obtain most of the work by putting up ads in very key locations (such as bulletin boards on game development Web sites with high visibility) or by joining IRC chat rooms where other developers are hanging out. I found I was probably the only composer there. It's better than a big convention where everyone goes, and it's a huge frenzy. Find a development community that matches your skill level, abilities, and equipment. Volunteer to work for free. These folks are on their way up, and hopefully they'll bring you with them if they like what you do. I've done a few games (and am still working on a few) for free and am working on my first paid (albeit extraordinarily cheap) gig now. Right now, I'm targeting strictly independent developers and working to gain credits and experience.

What do you feel makes a good music score (or jingle)?
The most important thing is how well it fits the piece you are working on. I've found that fewer people are concerned with how high quality your sample library is when compared to how appropriate the music is to their project.

What gear do you use?
I run my studio around a dual processor power Mac G4 and Logic Pro 7. I also use KRK6 monitors, a Technics 88 key weights digital piano, and an M-Audio Oxygen-8. For live recording, I use a Rode NT2 condenser with hardware compressor/limiter/expander. I have a handful of real percussion (mostly ethnic stuff) instruments and guitars as well.

Explain your promotional strategies (what works and why).
Currently, my promotional strategy is to pitch that I am brand new to this business and looking to gain experience. I explain my experience, education, and drive, and because of the community I'm pitching it to (independent game developers), most of them can really connect with that.

What skills do you feel someone needs to succeed in the area?
You need a ton of determination and drive to get things done. It can be very disheartening to put lots of effort into something that your client outright rejects. However, as in all business, "the customer is always right," so you have to go back and start again.

How do you approach projects, technically or creatively?
I try to get a clear idea of what the client wants to have. This is often far more difficult than it would seem. To aid in this, I often require a demo of the software/film in rough form or at least screen-shots/stills and thorough description before I agree to score. Also, when working for free, you want the game to be released, and some of the independents, without investors on their backs, can just decide to call it quits and your music will never see the light of day. I then try to get some of the confining parameters worked out, such as delivery formats, length desired, etc. I've been setting up

various templates in Logic Pro in order to jumpstart the technical stuff and get right to the music making.

How do you get paid (typical pay for projects, royalties, etc.)?

I charge by the finished minute, with a one-minute minimum charge per cue. I hope to continuously increase this rate as my experience and sound improves. I've also occasionally sold sound effects that I've created or adapted, which are done on an individual sound rate.

Can you comment on financial strategies you use/used to start/run this career/business?

Initially, there is no getting around it—it costs a good deal of money to start making music that people are willing to put into their projects. However, if you already have a computer, a good set of speakers, and MIDI gear, the extra expense is fairly minimal. I set up a Web site for myself, which I pay for, but that is now my only overhead. Besides snail mailing my paper contracts and master CDs when projects are completed, I do everything else over the Internet via email, instant messaging, or IRC chat.

What do you wish you'd known then that you know now?

It is extremely difficult to do work for someone who has already bought library tracks or is using free tracks from elsewhere. Even if they want you to do the music and would love original work, it's hard to compete with something they've already latched onto and have been listening to for weeks or months. Repetition is a very strong persuasive force that is hard to ignore. I've now started to sort of "screen" for this sort of thing. Otherwise, you wind up with requests like, "make it just like this, but different and better," which is an extremely difficult thing to do!

What are your plans for the future?

I have a good day job, so I can take my time in doing projects as I find them and build a name for myself in the independent game community. My hope is to do some work for some very talented young developers who will then go on to the big leagues and take me along with them. Developing relationships is probably the single most important thing in this business. Everybody wants to work with people they know will deliver and who they can communicate with.

Is there anything else you'd like to comment on that you feel is important?

Stick with it! This is a hard business to get started in, but there is a lot of opportunity to obtain repeat customers. Most of the people I have worked with have expressed interest in working with me again on future projects. It is a fun and exciting career that I hope in several years to be doing full time.

CHAPTER 14

Diversify and Thrive

"Put all your eggs in one basket and—watch that basket.*"*—Mark Twain

One of the primary means to grow your commercial music business is to diversify into related areas. Start thinking about the different ways you can package and sell your musical talent and use your equipment to its fullest capacity. Evaluate your talents and then determine what ancillary music products and services that you could offer. Diversity really is the path to profiting from *all* your musical and technical skills. Your motivations for pursuing these ventures could include:

▶ Wanting to make extra money.

▶ Building your reputation through cross-promotional efforts.

▶ Needing to do it for the sheer joy of it.

There is no mandate that says you must start and maintain these sidelines. On the contrary, if your commercial music business is both rewarding and paying the bills—*don't stop*. If not, these add-on businesses can complement your work and artistic vision. In my case, I need a few different challenges for my creative sanity. That's why I offer original music, recording and audio-post, writing and training, and albeit rather infrequently, playing solo gigs. Learn from these examples and apply them to your own particular situation.

What follows are a few ideas for you to consider. This concept works best when the activities you offer are related and interactive, and obviously, music based.

BAND (OR TWO) THANG

Many musicians, myself included, need to perform. Although your soundtracks and jingles are one way to deliver your performances, they are not the same as being in front of an audience. Make playing in a group part of your commercial music business. Inviting clients and prospects to your gigs is a terrific promotional strategy. Don't limit yourself to one band. Having a band dedicated to a specific genre or that only plays original music is one thing. That doesn't mean you can't have a party/wedding/cover band, too—even if it's the same people. Taking both approaches can really multiply your chances for success.

SOLO MONEY

If you have decent keyboard or guitar chops, consider playing at weddings, small clubs, lounges, coffeehouses, and such. There are plenty of places out there starving for live entertainment. These gigs can be low risk while offering you the opportunity to stretch your performance skills. You may not get paid a bunch (tips and a small stipend), but how many people get paid to hone their craft?

SESSIONS/SIDE PERFORMER

Traveling acts and even established local acts often need the services of great players hired for a gig or two. That's a great way to earn some extra dough. Also, go after the lucrative jingle, soundtrack, album, and other project gigs that may be available. The competition can be fierce, but outstanding skills (both technique and sight reading), coupled to a willingness to promote yourself ruthlessly, can pay off handsomely. You may even expand your network and make some other contacts that lead to more commercial music gigs. Not to be redundant, but hanging out in your local commercial music scene is an important way to promote your own success. Get on the inside and join the clique, and you'll be far more successful.

SONGWRITER

The natural adjunct to commercial music ventures is to write and pitch original songs for others to record and release. Search for producers and small labels that are looking for material for their artists. This takes some research; there's no sense in pitching to a group that always writes their own music. However, there are other acts that always cover tunes. Go there!

SOUNDWARE (PATCHES, SAMPLES, AND LOOPS)

Can you make sounds, make samples, or produce loops? This can be a lucrative sideline business. This subject make so much sense for media composers that there are additional details below.

MIDI AND KARAOKE

An adjunct to the soundware segment of the music industry is preparing and selling MIDI sequences or finished recordings for weddings, churches, schools, karaoke, and more. Of course, you'll have to clear the songs that you sell by paying mechanical royalties.

AUDIO ENGINEER

Are you a more behind-the-scenes person? Look for work that lets you push the right buttons. Live mixing and studio engineering can help you gain some valuable skills, make contacts, and earn some money as well.

PROJECT STUDIO PROFITS

There's no reason your well-equipped home project studio can't become a moneymaking machine. There are musical acts and voice-over talent to record, on-hold messages to produce, radio commercials to make, Podcasts to create, audio-post projects to complete, and so much more. Even selling just a few hours or days a month can put some extra cash in your pocket. I believe in this idea so much that I've written another book dedicated to this subject.

> Profiting from Your Music and Sound Project Studio *(Allworth Press, 2001) offers the definitive approach to establish, promote, manage, and succeed with a professional music and sound project studio.*

LESSONS

Why not make some money showing others how to play? Don't ignore the older folks out there; kids aren't the only ones wanting to learn how to play an instrument or two.

WRITE/TEACH

Writing articles not only functions as a promotional tool, but they can also make you money. Have knowledge up in your head? Write it down and share it with the rest of us. You may write for Internet sites, magazines, or even books. I co-host a few technology forums that have me answering questions and helping people from around the world. Also, teaching and lecturing are other opportunities. I teach audio and video production at a college and lead training sessions for professionals at industry events and privately. Writing and teaching both build tremendous credibility for me *and* bring in additional funds.

INDIE CD MP3 RELEASE

Today's music world is a crowded place, but that shouldn't prevent you from creating and selling your own music creations. You can offer downloads or a physical CD through i-Tunes, Amazon. com, CDBaby, and so forth or just sell them from your own Web site. This release could be related to the original commercial music you sell or a completely different departure. Your own CD can make a nice premium or gift for clients, too. The beauty of your self-published release is that you can start small and do it for personal satisfaction or slowly and steadily build your audience. You can even go full tilt. These choices are up to you.

CD FUNDRAISER

Try this fundraiser for schools, churches, etc. Record a school band holiday album and duplicate it in-house. They agree to sell the CDs at their concerts, keep a royalty, and pay you the remainder. Let's look at the numbers. Give them a good royalty of 25% on what they sell. On a $10.00 CD, they'd get $2.50 for each unit sold. Let's say it costs you $2.50 to record, duplicate, and package the Holiday Concert release, so $10 - 5 = $5 profit per unit. Even after giving the school a big royalty of 25%, you still *net* twice your production costs. If they sell 100 CDs, you clear $500. And the school clears $250 (a lot more than they'd make selling candy bars).

This situation is perfect for school bands, choirs, and theater groups. You could record cast albums for the school's musical and sell them before, during, and after the shows. It's hard to beat this as a fundraiser. However, don't forget that if you record copyrighted material, you must pay mechanical royalties to the music publisher. Stick with a medley of public domain holiday classics, and you avoid that issue entirely.

AND NOW...
Brainstorm all the possibilities that you, with your talents, experience, and gear, can turn into separate music-related business ventures. While you can't do everything, you can experiment and find the work that you like best, as well as putting cash in the bank.

Also, consult my other book, **Moneymaking Music** *(Artistpro, 2003) for more details about making, keeping, protecting, and growing your music success fortune.*

Selling to Music and Sample Libraries
There is another way to get your music on radio and TV (and even films). While neither will be a primary source of income, sample and music libraries are viable alternatives that can put some real money in your pocket doing what you love best, which is making music.

Do you have some unused tracks, songs, sketches, mini-scores, and more sitting around somewhere? Do you feel you have a unique sound design or playing style that you are willing to package and share? Don't let all that music and sound gather dust when it could put money in your pocket. I chatted with Rudy Sarzo, Douglas Spotted Eagle, and Brian Tarquin about this subject to get their insight into this lucrative sideline. Also, this chapter concludes with a rather extensive interview with Fresh Music's Wes Talbot.

Rudy Sarzo is a well-respected bass player with Ozzy Osbourne, Quiet Riot, and Whitesnake on his long list of credits. He's an avid digital media buff who spends his road time putting together music and promotional videos, instructional bass DVDs, and his own music projects. His signature playing can be found on the popular *Workingman's Bass* (Sony) loop library.

Douglas Spotted Eagle is an award-winning musician and producer who has worked on over 300 records and, thanks to libraries, over 1,000 projects. He works from his Native Restoration studio in Utah on a bevy of audio and video projects. He's produced two sample libraries of his unique Native American music and worked on many *Loops for Acid* CDs for Sony.

Brian Tarquin works from his Jungle Room Studios in New York, splitting his time between scoring *All My Children* (for which he's won two Emmys) and writing for both sample and music libraries, including full-length CDs for Megatrax, Sonoton, FirstCom, Zomba, and ABC TV's Fifth Floor Music. He also managed to find time to release his own recordings, *Electro Ave.* and *Enjoy This Trip*, with collaborator Chris Ingram under their Asphalt Jungle moniker.

START WITH AN IDEA

Music libraries look for instrumentals only in a wide variety of music genres. While there is always a demand for knock-offs of today's hottest trends, there continues to be a need for good solid tracks in common styles: upbeat sports themes, big, bold corporate themes, New Age ditties and other low key tracks for use under narration, and ethnic/world pieces. The typical track lasts between two and four minutes. "Producers like it better when there is one CD with a lot of variations on a theme—long versions, 59- and 29-second versions, short 10- or 5-second stingers, and alternative mixes without the lead instruments," says Tarquin.

All three musicians agree that a good sample library should have a wide variety of elements, but avoid overdoing it or getting too complex. "The loops or samples must offer tempos and grooves that are usable," says Sarzo. "Approach it like a studio musician—playing for the song rather than your own ego. If you're just soloing and showing off, it may sound great, but will it work in the context of somebody else's song?"

"Think simply and provide material that works with other things," Spotted Eagle echoes. "If you're going to do weird stuff, you'd better offer riffs that go with it and grooves for underneath. If you play an unusual chordal structure, provide other things that relate. Odd meter? Include drum loops and/or percussion to support it."

Before you approach this market, be fully aware of the soundware and library music that's currently available. You will find that typical sample and library CDs stick to a single theme or musical genre. The companies marketing these products want either something new or a unique spin on a tested theme. If you're just offering the same old thing, you won't make the sale. Before you pitch your idea, see if there's a need or a gap first. A quick surf to a few Web sites will easily let you survey the landscape. Try the following ideas for samples.

Sample Libraries

▶ Big Fish Audio (www.bigfishaudio.com)

▶ East-West (www.soundsonline.com)

▶ Ilio (www.ilio.com)

▶ Sony Pictures Digital, *Loops for Acid* (www.sony.com/mediasoftware)

▶ M-Audio (www.m-audio.com)

▶ QUp Arts (www.quparts.com)

Music Libraries

▶ Digital Juice (www.digitaljuice.com)

▶ Firstcom Music (www.firstcom.com)

▶ Fresh Music (www.freshmusic.com)

▶ Killer Tracks (www.killertracks.com)

▶ The Music Bakery (www.musicbakery.com)

▶ Omnimusic (www.omnimusic.com)

▶ VideoHelper (www.videohelper.com)

Pay careful attention to what's already on the market; then gauge how your idea stacks up against the competition. Don't lose hope if you find a disc similar to your idea already out there. Check its release date. It may have been out for a while. Rethink your approach to bring a fresh take on the idea, too.

DEMO TIME

While Tarquin, Spotted Eagle, and Sarzo possess extensive industry credentials, the rest of us need to put together a demo of the idea before taking it to possible buyers. "Music libraries are very approachable," admits Tarquin. "Research what they have already; then put together a demo of your best stuff that fills a gap in their catalog. When I worked at a jingle house in Manhattan, we had tons of demos and shelved projects that we earmarked for music libraries."

For a recent pitch to Fresh Music, I assembled 18 music tracks on CD, some full-length, some shorter pieces, all in a similar style and approach. They accepted a few tracks as is, made suggestions for a couple of tracks, and trashed the rest. I then went back and finished up the CD per their requests. The final track count was 13 on the finished CD, *Dark New Age*, available from Fresh Music (www.freshmusic.com).

"When writing for a sample library, have a clear-cut project and an idea of who the audience really is. Show the company how you can fill their gap and put together a demo CD that proves you can do it," suggests Tarquin. He also feels that adding a biography and a list of credentials can help reduce any skepticism a company might have. "You don't need outstanding credentials as long as you have a good idea, can do the work, and appeal to the people you're selling to."

For Douglas Spotted Eagle, two events convinced him to do a sample library. "I was getting a ton of calls from directors and producers to do flute cues. Then I heard a sample from one of my recordings used without permission on a major film. I thought that putting together a sample CD with Native American vocals, drums, and flutes would solve both issues."

Spotted Eagle approached QUp Arts at a NAMM show and explained his vision of mapping drum hits and velocity for samplers. "They loved the idea, and the result was my original *Voices of Native America, Volume 1* for Akai/Roland samplers. Later it was optimized as an Acid loop library.

"To do an ethnic vocal library like *Voices* was a big risk. The response was amazing. QUp has since put together other groundbreaking ethnic libraries, including my follow-up: *Voices of Native America, Volume 2.*"

Tarquin also pitched his sample library idea at a NAMM show. "I was a fan of the Big Fish sample libraries, having used a few of their drum loop CDs for some projects. I researched a few other libraries and saw a gap in the Big Fish roster. So, at NAMM I met with them and pitched the idea for *Big Fish Audio Guitar Studio.* They asked me to prepare a short demo, and once they heard it, they loved it.

"*Guitar Studio* was unique at the time because it was live guitar performances as two-bar loops. I tried to cover as many styles, keys, phrases, chords, picking, arpeggios, and so forth using a variety of guitars," recalls Tarquin. "They asked me to do a sequel because the first sold so well. For *Guitar Studio 2*, I used many different amps, guitars, and mics to get a variety of sounds and tones."

Rudy Sarzo first approached Sony at a NAMM show and expressed how he was such a big fan of their Acid software. "Soon after that, they approached me directly and asked if I'd put together a bass-only library for their growing *Loops for Acid* product line. I agreed to do the first bass-only library: *Workingman's Bass.*"

DOING THE WORK

If you're fortunate enough to have your work accepted, you then have to get busy producing the CD. All production costs to create a finished CD—recording, talent, editing, mixing, and mastering—come out of your pocket. Having a well-equipped home project studio helps keep your costs lower because you can do virtually everything yourself.

Turnaround times range from two to four months after acceptance, with audio CDs or digital files (.wav or .aiff) on CD-ROM the preferred format. Some companies prefer a complete finished project, while others will handle the final editing and mastering in-house.

Tarquin spent four months recording *Guitar Studio*. "It was hard, meticulous work. I had to keep the recordings quiet and avoid breath and fret noise. I recorded it all on analog 16-track 2" tape and mixed it to stereo DAT. Big Fish loaded the tracks into ProTools for all the editing."

It took Sarzo about six weeks to put together *Workingman's Bass*. "I tried every riff, groove, and one-shot I could think of in a variety of tempos and keys. Bass notes don't stretch as readily in Acid, so I had to cover more ground.

"I recorded it all in my home studio using 4, 5, and 6 string Peavey Cirrus basses with Dean Markley strings through a Rupert Neve preamp into a Delta 1010 interface and directly into Acid. I used Sound Forge for editing. I kept the playing raw with very little effects so the end users could tweak it to fit their music."

CASH CONSIDERATIONS

One great reason to get involved with both sample and music libraries is that they handle all the promotion and sales. That means you can concentrate on your music. If you've ever just wanted to compose, record, tweak, and mix without most of the hassles of the music business, this little side-line may work for you. Tarquin says, "Big Fish and the other companies who buy my music handle all the marketing and advertising. I just compose and play."

According to Spotted Eagle, "Sample libraries are usually a standard publishing deal ranging from 5 to 20% of net sales, paid quarterly. There may be an advance against those royalties, but usually not." Since samples and loops are sold royalty-free, there are no back-end royalties, just the sales royalty.

Music libraries have many different methods of payment. Some composers may get a royalty based on sales, but that's rare. The usual deal is a one-time, up-front fee ranging from $250 to $1000 per song. However, when writing for music libraries, you keep the writer's share of the publishing. Therefore, any publishing money collected by the library gets split 50-50 between the publisher (the library) and you, the writer. Since you won't sell sheet music and people won't "cover" your songs, your money comes from performance rights.

"Libraries are a great way to get performance income," summarizes Brian Tarquin. "You may even do better than commercial radio."

DIY

If you want to take on a heavier workload, consider putting together your own music or sample library and promoting and selling it yourself. These are the steps I used to create, promote, and sell my own *Melomania* music library. For a sample or loop library, record your ideas from scratch or edit them from existing performances. Make sure you provide enough material to fill a CD/CD-ROM to keep buyers happy.

Think 10 full-blown tracks for a single music library CD. Use music you've already recorded or sit down and write something new. You can either provide a mix of popular music styles or stay in one genre. Typical tracks last between two and four minutes. For the radio and TV commercial crowd, you can also create 59- and 29-second versions from that master track along with a short 5–10 second stinger. You can also provide alternative mixes of some music tracks, rhythm section only, for instance. Title each cut and write a description about the music including instrumentation, tempo, musical genre, and accurate track timings. Include this information (see a sample of what I mean below) in the CD booklet, tray card, and on your Web site.

▶ "Happy Jazz" (3:17) Nimble guitar lines punctuate this pleasant tune.

▶ "Shades of Blue" (3:03) You can feel the heartache in every phrase.

▶ "Backroads" (1:45) Take a shortcut down memory lane.

Sell the library as a buyout and make money by licensing the same CD repeatedly to different buyers. They get to use the music nonexclusively. Draft a royalty-free license to accompany the finished music. This simple agreement should clearly grant buyers nonexclusive rights to the music.

By purchasing this music library, [Your name/company name here] grants you a nonexclusive, single-site, lifetime license to use any of the music on the CD within your own audio-visual productions. This music is protected by the copyright laws of the United States and other countries. You are in no way permitted to reproduce, resell, share, or otherwise transfer the music itself to another individual or company. Any attempt to do so will be subject to criminal prosecution including fines, imprisonment, and injunctive relief.

Join one of the PROs and tell buyers who use your library to indicate your authorship and affiliation on cue sheets. That way you'll get paid your performance royalties when you earn them.

This music is cleared through BMI. Please indicate: "Music composed by Jeffrey P. Fisher (BMI)" on your productions and make sure you list all titles used and timings so that BMI-affiliate broadcasters can file accurate cue sheets with BMI when your productions are aired.

Here's an important point: Buyout music is not copyright free. The copyright holder has chosen to make the music available on a nonexclusive basis for people to use. Buyers pay one fee and can use the music within the boundaries of the license agreement. The music copyright still belongs to the music supplier.

To promote the library, assemble a demo of the tracks comprising short snippets from each track. Alternately, give away a few free samples to encourage people to try before they buy. Promote your work via your Web site. You may even be able to sell your music via online retailers, such as Amazon, CDBaby, and so forth. Put together the promotional material you need and start getting the word out to music buyers. Essentially, you can contact the same people to whom you pitch your original music services (video production houses, radio stations, advertising agencies, and so forth).

Finally, make and sell the library. Selling online? You need to accept credit cards. Choose either PayPal (www.paypal.com) or CCNow (www.ccnow.com) to process your orders securely. It really doesn't make sense to mass produce your library, either. With a color printer and CD burner, you can manufacture your library or sample CDs on demand or a few copies at a time. You could even offer your library as downloads only. You might also consider offering your library as .wav and .aiff files on CD-ROM/DVD. This way end-users can import the music tracks directly into their DAW/NLE and remix them.

WHY I DID MELOMANIA

I never conceived my *Melomania* music library to be in competition with the bigger music libraries out there. To me, it was just an expanded demo of my work. It showed that I could cover a lot of styles. It lent some credibility, too. Now, I use it as a premium when people buy music from me, as something I throw in to sweeten the deal. I do sell it to clients with tiny budgets, and I've given it away to nonprofits. Of course, I'm looking for cue sheet compliance and therefore earning my back end performance royalties.

Industry Insight

Wes Talbot
Fresh Music, Hanover, NH
www.freshmusic.com

What is production or library music?
Library music is the musical equivalent of stock photography or stock video footage. People get music that is cleared for almost any use—radio, broadcast TV, corporate videos, and so forth. They pay a license fee and can then use the music nonexclusively. Library music is a collection of songs usually organized by genre, style, and other thematic elements, such as high-energy, corporate, sports, etc. Typically, they are purchased as whole CDs, but increasingly more people are just downloading single songs from the Web.

Why do content producers use library music?
There are three main reasons: budget, time, and the high "cost" of an original score. Library music is the most cost-effective way to get music for projects. Using library music also saves time. For example, at Fresh Music we've organized our Web site to make it quick and easy to find the right

track for a specific need. When I say the "cost" of original music is high, I really mean that more resources must be committed to realizing a finished original score—for example, time, money, approval, recording costs, and, yes, the creative fee. That's what takes using original music out of reach for many production companies. Today, music users want it good, fast, *and* cheap!

That said, some producers use library music as temp tracks while they wait for the original score or supplement original musical segments with some library tracks, too.

How and why did you get into this area?
It was a case of "if you can't beat 'em, join 'em'!" As a music composer in the late 80s, I kept butting heads with music libraries. I'd left NYC for western Massachusetts and had to find a way to market my music beyond this small region. I started investigating the music library phenomenon and discovered there was an explosion of library sources, driven no doubt by MIDI and cheaper recording technology. Before that, music library choices were few, and the music quality itself was inconsistent. I found some composers who were writing for libraries and making money doing it and thought that this could be an adjunct source of income for me.

Who uses library music?
Really just about anyone who needs music might look to libraries. TV and radio stations go through libraries like water. Bigger clients, such as corporations, use music in their sales presentations, training videos, conferences, and more. Of course, independent production companies, whether they are doing corporate, broadcast, or special interest work, all need music. And library resources fill their need readily.

How is library music licensed?
First, understand the nonexclusive nature of library music. Individual tracks are rarely licensed for exclusive use. Instead, music libraries license the same tracks repeatedly to different users who recognize that the same music track might be used somewhere else.

In the past, music libraries licensed their tracks per "needle-drop." That meant that when you used a cut, you paid for the music. The fee paid depended on the specific use. There were large fees for use on national TV and lower fees for nonbroadcast corporate use. Later, libraries started offering a blanket license that let buyers use a certain number of cuts per month. The problem with both of those methods was that the music user had to report every use to the music house and pay their fees.

Contrarily, the buyout, royalty-free business model was born. Instead of paying a fee per use, you pay a one-time fee and can then use the music nonexclusively forever. Outside of the initial purchase, the music user has no records to keep or additional payments to make (except for cue sheets, which we'll get to later).

At first, there was a perception that buyout music was junk. Partially, the initial offerings were not of the same quality as the needle-drop choices. That changed when Fresh Music came on the scene. We worked hard to change that perception by running our company like the big guys, having great service, terrific music, and generating buzz at tradeshows and such. Add to that, there was competition in the buyout arena, which I feel brought both credibility and legitimacy.

Let me add that the term royalty-free is a bit of a misnomer, though. While it is true that the library music buyer pays no fees beyond the initial one-time buyout license, there are performance royalties involved with specific uses. For example, when the composition is played at a venue, the venue pays a fee. And, of course, when the composition is broadcast on TV and radio, the person broadcasting must pay the performance royalties. (More on that subject below.)

Are there other licensing issues?

The music library business is really music publishing. Therefore, you can negotiate anything. There is always the opportunity to negotiate different fees and exclusive use. For example, one corporate group wanted to license John Fogarty's *Centerfield*. Fogarty asks for at least $10,000 to license the song, with the money sent directly to the baseball players' retirement home. Another artist licensed a song for free because it was being played at an awards presentation for outstanding students.

We had an inquiry about using music in information kiosks located at professional offices. All the other music libraries turned the producer down. We countered with $25 per office, per year license. He started with five offices but now has over 1,000 installations. He stays with Fresh because we were the only ones who even talked to him about his needs.

What do you feel makes a library successful?

Obviously, the music is what people buy. Beyond that, what's important about operating a music library is the music you license must be well organized. The search engine on the Web site must make sense. Customers want to find, audition, buy, download, and use the music fast. If people can't do that, the music won't matter. Fresh Music was the first to have a search track where customers could search for styles, genre, emotion, and other keywords. If the customer can't find melancholy corporate strings in 10 minutes, they move on to another supplier.

Though some people buy CD collections to have around, most are far more selective and just buy what they need. Most of all this is a fast business. Most of our CDs go FedEx with the rest as downloads. Every morning when I check the orders, I see how much will go out that day in FedEx envelopes. Customers want their music *now*!

How does the music end up on TV/radio/cable?

The bigger music libraries have staff who constantly pitch the networks to get their specific music on the air. They also hit music supervisors at TV series rather aggressively. Record labels have also jumped in, realizing that breaking new artists on popular shows is worthwhile. Even infomercials are pitched by the big guys out there. So there is a lot of competition.

That said, we don't have the staff to work this way, but our music regularly ends up on broadcast TV. We are the kings of the Outdoor Channel, Lifetime, and Discovery channels. All those documentaries and reality shows that get on the air need music, and they often turn to our library.

Are there opportunities for composers to write library music?

At the start, I had to convince people to write for the library. Now I have to turn many down. I average between 5–15 submissions a week. Half are these are Web links; the other half CDs. I'm always looking for something I don't already have or a new twist on a solid idea. And as the library grows, that becomes more and more difficult.

There is a definite style and feel to production music. Sadly, some composers look down on what we do and just send us the junk they have on their computers. It's condescending, really. Others send good music, but it doesn't work for the music library. And then we find the compositions that we know will work; music that is, dare I say, fresh!

The best works are well recorded and well thought out. They convey a specific emotion and stay in a definable genre. Real library composers know there's more to what we do than just noodling over a drum loop and synth pad.

How should a composer pitch to a library?

Visit the Web site (www.freshmusic.com) and search the catalog to see what we already have. If you can't bring anything new to the existing material, or if you're just going to copy something I already have, don't bother to go forward. The music library business is no different than the traditional music business. Even if your music is fabulous, but I already have too much similar stuff, I can't, and won't, go for it. Don't copy what I already have. I'm loyal to my composers and prefer to give them a shot at doing more rather than buy something similar from somebody new.

However, if you feel you have something we can use, make a short introduction via email. Try to give me a hook that I can market. I read these emails and get back to those that sound promising fast with a form letter containing submission guidelines.

What you send doesn't need to be elaborate. Send me a cover letter with a summary of the music, a line or two about each song (use keywords people would search on), a brief bio, and then the CD clearly labeled with your contact information.

People do send me links, but I feel a CD carries more weight. I can pop it in the car or whatever and listen at my leisure. With a link, I must be at the office, and I'm at the mercy of the Web site and the composer who puts together a 12-second crummy encode that doesn't tell me anything. For me, the CD is the better presentation.

Keep it simple and let your music tell the story. There is no need to go overboard on presentation as some people do. I'm going to hear what you do in the tracks. If I don't hear it in the music, the rest won't matter. If the music really grabs me, again the presentation doesn't matter either.

Out of 100 people who contact me this way, maybe only 20 actually follow up and send a demo. Of those 20, typically four are worth contacting again. And out of those four, maybe one gets it, and we end up working together.

What I find is that many composers are unrealistic; they don't operate in the business world. What I'm trying to do is start a dialogue and see if the composer is willing to make changes and revisions. I might find three songs that I like and ask them to expand upon those. Or I might make arrangement and mixing suggestions, more of this, less of that, that kind of thing. Too many composers feel the tracks are "as is" when they submit them. I don't work that way. It's about commerce. Can I sell it? Will my customers buy it? With our track record and longevity, I feel I have a good sense about what will work for us. Few composers are willing to work with us that way, which is really a shame. Real composers take this seriously. And Fresh Music is very serious about this industry, too.

Also, make sure you return phone calls and emails, deliver material when promised, be willing to work with us to get it done right, and don't drop the ball. The composer who understands all this and recognizes the money to be made will be more successful. You don't just mail in a CD, sit at home playing video games, and wait for checks!

It's not all commerce, though. There is an opportunity for art, too. Take your CD you did for us, *Dark New Age*. It's great. I loved it when I put the CD on. Your music was very specific, dark and brooding, and well conceived and recorded. There was thought, composition, and chops put into it. It wasn't a throwaway. It's obvious you took it seriously.

How do composers get paid?
In the old days, composers received a percentage of CD sales, which was determined by how many songs they had in relation to the library as a whole. The problem with that was that as our library grew, they made less money.

Today, we negotiate a single buyout fee that gives us the music to use on an exclusive basis. The amount we pay really depends on the tracks. If somebody has hired musicians and spent a lot on production, we typically pay a little more. If it is just MIDI tracks or a one-person shop, the scale is a little less. Generally, we pay anywhere between $200–$350 per track. So with a 12-song CD, that can put over four-grand in your pocket. However, we've paid as little as $100 because the composer just turned in MIDI files that we had to re-record with real instruments.

Now some composers may balk at such a low figure, but I must remind them that the cost of music has gone down significantly. Everybody wants a deal; music buyers are asking for more and more and paying less and less for music. This trickles down to the composer, obviously.

Don't forget about the back end, though, which I'll talk about in greater detail in a moment. Here at Fresh Music our composers keep 100% of the writer's share. You keep your copyright and just license it to us. You essentially sign a contract that maintains your copyright, indemnifies us against infringement claims, and assigns us the exclusive right to sell and market your music. We essentially act as the publisher and keep the publisher's share.

Now some libraries pay higher amounts, say $5,000 for a CD, but they expect you to carry more burden. They may ask for many revisions and have you turn in the edits. Here at Fresh Music we do the 60-second, 30-second, and stinger cuts ourselves. So, elsewhere you may make more money, but there is more work involved.

Another way to look at this is this way: A professional composer may write three songs in a day. That can be a $1,000 day, right there. If it takes you a month to compose one song, then obviously you will be making less comparatively. Having the chops and the skills to write well and fast and understand what a client wants can make this somewhat more lucrative for certain people.

Of course, no composer should look at composing for a music library as his only source of income. It does make for a decent supplemental income though, if you are willing to do what's necessary, can write in a lot of different styles, and keep at it.

What royalties do composer's receive?

When songs are performed in public, composers and publishers earn performance royalties. The money earned is split 50-50 between the writer and the publisher. These royalties are collected and administered by performing rights organizations (PROs): ASCAP, BMI, and SESAC. The money earned varies by use, with music played on broadcast TV being the most lucrative. If NBC uses your music, your check can be substantial. The TV and radio broadcasters must file cue sheets that detail the music they played and pay the licensing fees. The PROs determine and collect those fees and then disperse the funds to writers and publishers based on the cue sheets.

At Fresh Music, we register the songs for our composers and fight for your money, mainly because when you get a check, we get a check. Recently, a composer called and was surprised by the check he'd received from his PRO. I congratulated him, knowing that Fresh Music would get the same check a few days later!

Part of my job is working with the PROs to make sure our composers are getting the money they deserve. The PROs, in turn, are very aggressive about cue sheet compliance and especially going after foreign rights when music plays overseas.

This royalty stream is not inconsequential. It is, although, rather unpredictable. We call it "mailbox money" because one quarter the check could be $3,000, and the next only $3. You just never know how or where your music might get used. My feeling is it can't hurt to have it out there with the potential to earn money. That's better than being hidden on a hard drive with no prospects of ever earning any cash.

Anything else you'd like to add?

If you are a composer looking to write for music libraries, do your homework first. Figure out if this is what you really want to do. It is a lot harder than it might first appear. You have to understand that there are professionals in this niche who work very hard to compose, produce, and deliver quality tracks. These people are your competition.

Also, know how the library operates. Carefully look at what they have already and, more importantly, what they *don't* have that you can do. When you make your approach, don't overwhelm them with needless junk. Don't waste your or our time. Send a short letter, a clearly labeled CD—don't forget to print your phone number and email address on the CD—and then wait. If we like what you did and can use it, we'll be in touch.

However, if we don't use your stuff this time around, don't get discouraged. There are many factors that could result in an initial negative, for instance, bad timing. Don't give up. Listen to what we tell you, go back to the drawing board, and try submitting again.

You have to realize that every time I put a CD in the player or click a link, I'm hoping I'm going to hear the next big thing. I want to scream YEAH! It doesn't happen a lot, unfortunately, but when it does, I'm very happy as I quickly reach for the phone to call the composer.

CHAPTER 15

Final Words

"'Why not' is a slogan for an interesting life."—Mason Cooley

Congratulations! You made it!! You now possess a better understanding of the soundtrack and jingle business and what it takes to succeed. How far to take it is completely up to you. This won't be an easy journey, but few worthwhile pursuits in life come without at least some challenges and obstacles. Yet, I know that you can do this. You have a distinct advantage because you chose this valuable resource to help you along the way. Remember these key elements, too.

▶ Truly desire success and be willing to do whatever it takes to make it happen.

▶ Be willing to balance opportunity with some calculated risks.

▶ Bring passion and enthusiasm to your music.

▶ Respect your clients and be grateful and appreciative of their support.

▶ Have a clear vision and dream for both your music business career and life.

▶ Research, learn, understand, and exploit the knowledge you discover.

▶ Adapt and wear many hats when needed.

▶ Promote. Promote. Promote.

▶ Take control of every aspect of your commercial music business.

▶ Persevere.

▶ Share your wonderful musical gift with the world. I'll be listening.

▶ Have fun!

Ponder this: "Life isn't measured by the breaths we take, but by the moments that take our breath away."

One thing I've learned all these years is that security is fleeting. Learn to depend on yourself and prepare to make your own way and live your own life. Your best friend and ally is knowledge. When you know what to do, you can do anything. Everything. And as you realize your goals, you *will* have the security you crave. There will be even greater benefits, too, that pay richer dividends than money alone. Making your own way in life means you will gain the fruits of your labor and the autonomy, self-esteem, love, and all those other things—big and small—that make life so special and rewarding. And you will do all this through your music. *That*, my friend, is what this is all about, right?

Let there be no end to your quest to succeed. Never stop promoting, never stop developing your skills, never stop building and enhancing your reputation, never stop experiencing more with your life and growing as a person, never stop if problems surmount, never stop trying to do and be more, and even if you've achieved some success, never stop doing your best. I feel that David Carradine said it best, "The ultimate quest has no ending, and that fact is what gives the quest its ultimate value."

So, get started right *now*. Take a small step today, and each and every day after that, toward the life and professional music career you want to lead. You should assemble a workable studio, a great sounding demo, a huge list of possible music buyers, and a few paying clients. What's next? Continue to operate your commercial music business effectively and efficiently. That means keeping your demo updated, promoting continuously and ruthlessly, and staying in touch regularly with all your prospects and clients. If you write great music, charge fairly for it, give more than anyone ever expects, and learn to exploit superior promotional skills and opportunities, then you will be the success you envision. So? What are you going to do first?

Usually, when you buy a book, that's all there is to it. I disagree with that notion. Just because you've finished reading doesn't mean the relationship we started on page 1 need end. Let's keep the door open for further conversations. If you have any problems, need some sound advice, or maybe just a little encouragement, please contact me. You see, I want you to keep in touch. Let me know of your successes, any problems you come across, all *your* tricks of the trade, and most of all, *your* milestones so I can share your celebration. Drop by my Web site at www.jeffreypfisher.com or send an email to jpf@jeffreypfisher.com and let's talk.

Thank you for your support; I sincerely appreciate it. And let me wish you continued success with all *your* endeavors.

Jeffrey P. Fisher
August 2005

Index